THE WINES
OF SPAIN

Based on an original idea of
VALENTIN MORAGAS ROGER (†)

THE WINES
OF SPAIN

Authors: JOSE DEL CASTILLO
DAVID R. HALLETT

With the collaboration of:

Spanish version	English version
ASUNCION JAEN BOTELLA	DR. ANICETO CHARRO ARIAS
ANGEL GAMBOA Y SANCHEZ-BARCAIZTEGUI	ANA CHARRO DE HALLETT
J. A. RAMIREZ-ESCUDERO VALDES	STEWART J. GARDINER

Foreword by C. E. WHITFIELD
(Chairman of The Wine Development Board)

Proyección
Editorial s.a.

APARTADO 215
BILBAO - SPAIN
1972

Drawings and Paintings:

Valentín Moragas
Nicolás Jönas
José A. Rodríguez Miranda
Fernando Amiano
José M. Castejón
Gisela Rähm

Photographs:

Ministry of Information and Tourism
«La Semana Vitivinícola» (Weekly wine magazine)
Guillén Franco, J. A.
Arbex, J.
Más, A.
«Paisajes Españoles»
Foyé, E.
Foat
Ruiz, J. M.
«Estudios Kert»

Printers:

ELEXPURU HERMANOS, S. A.
San Martín, 153. ZAMUDIO-BILBAO (Spain)

Printed in Spain - D. L. BI 1.978/1972.
ISBN 84 - 7201 - 002 - 3

A SPECIAL WORD FOR OUR ENGLISH READERS

THE WINES OF SPAIN *is the fruit of three years work. In the first place, there was the preparation and writing of the Spanish edition which was so badly needed to fill the gap on the subject of wines within the Peninsula itself; secondly, there was the task of adapting, re-arranging and translating the material for the English reader whose previous knowledge of Spanish wines has been somewhat clouded and far from complete especially as many of the books about wine frequently come through indirect or foreign sources.*

This highly prized book (Declarado de Interés Turístico Nacional) *on* THE WINES OF SPAIN *has been rendered into its present version by* DAVID R. HALLETT, *writer and intellectual, whose expertise and knowledge concerning the wines and gastronomy of Iberia goes without saying. He has worked in conjunction with a great team of connoiseurs and specialists and this present book, which you, reader, have in your hands, is the most complete that has been published to date on the subject.*

GABRIEL GARCÍA-VALENZUELA GUIMÓN.
MANAGING DIRECTOR.

GRAPES AND WINE

(Photo Ernest Foyé.)

Acknowledgements

Our sincerest thanks to the following organisations and magazines which have collaborated in producing THE WINES OF SPAIN.

—The Ministry of Information and Tourism in Spain.

—The Regulating Councils of the «*Denominaciones de Origen*».

—The British Wine Development Board.

—«*La Semana Vitivinícola*» (A weekly wine magazine).

—The Agricultural Publications Department of the «*Banco de Bilbao*».

FOREWORD

Since, from the earliest days of man, civilisation has followed the vine, it is logical that the cultivation of the vine and the production of wine are completely understood in a civilisation with more than three thousand years of recorded history.

José del Castillo and David Hallett have captured in this book the nuance, the charm, and the delight of the wines of Spain.

In a pleasant easy style, the authors tell of the great variety of grapes that thrive in the many different terrains and adjust to the climate, whether it be the hot summer or cold winter of the high plateau of New Castile, or the soft temperate calm of the coastal fringe.

Long in history, the wine growers of Spain do not dwell in the past. Their laws of «Denomination of Origin» are as modern and complete as any laws in the wine world. With more «amateurs» mastering the art of tasting and fine wines gaining an ever increasing and appreciative audience it is sound commercial sense that the winegrower should vigorously protect his heritage.

Wine offers a tranquillity that binds societies of men together and **«is a constant reminder that God loves us and wants to see us happy».** THE WINES OF SPAIN *will be read and enjoyed both by the student and the expert and each will owe a debt of gratitude to the authors.*

CHARLES WHITFIELD

Chairman, Wine Development Board,
LONDON, SEPTEMBER, 1972.

This version of the Wines of Spain is based on the fruits of the work of Señor José del Castillo and his team of experts whose book LOS VINOS DE ESPAÑA has been recently published and acclaimed as one of the most significant books about Spanish wines to date.

A word of special thanks must be given to Doctor Charro Arias of the Department of Bromotology at the University of Santiago de Compostela who offered many suggestions which have improved on the original version immeasurably.

Finally, THE WINES OF SPAIN would not have been possible without the unstinting efforts of my wife who all along has given so much in gathering and preparing the material for this present English version.

D. R. H.

PREFACE

There is something intriguing and even mysterious about the world of wine for its history is long and as old as the Bible and its theme as eternal as the laws of nature are permanent.

Spanish wines are for the most part unknown outside of Spain except of course for the Fine Sherry, Montilla and Moriles, and the Rioja wines of international fame. Lack of publicity have made them so. Bearing this in mind, it is the intention of this book to give the reader an idea of the vast number of districts where other great wines are made and to introduce him to the fascinating and arduous wine route or *Andadura del Vino* as it is called stretching from the Golfo de Rosas in the Mediterranean to the Cantabrian shores of the Bay of Biscay.

This wine route roams through some of most picturesque and grandiose country in the Peninsula . Wherever you go, the vineyards blend perfectly with their setting: the Alto Panadés overlooking the Mediterranean coastland; the opulent hillsides of the Rioja valley along the banks of the river ~~Duero~~ Ebro; the terraced slopes of Galicia, bathed by the soft spring rains and blown by the Atlantic breezes; the sheltered and sequestered valleys of the Los Picos de Europa in the northern provinces where a bottle of *corriente* wine can be had for next to nothing.

Wine, good wine cheers and heartens. It also strengthens and unifies. In reading THE WINES OF SPAIN, it is hoped that lovers and connoisseurs of wine everywhere will discover for themselves the great and rare qualities of what one imperial lady referred to as *estos famosos vinos de España*.

DAVID R. HALLETT.

To write a good wine book is no easy matter. Even taking into account expert knowledge on the subject and a passion for wine, it requires, on the other hand, a fluent pen and considerable writing skill and ability to include numerous data without wearying the reader.

José del Castillo has admirably accomplised this task. A prolific and enquiring journalist, he has spent his life in close proximity to the vine even helping in the wine harvest in his early youth. In his column in the Barcelona newspaper as an authority on gastronomic themes, he has demonstrated a no mean expertise. Journalist of «*Solidaridad Nacional*» and «*El Noticiero Universal*», radio commentator on the Spanish network, correspondent of various foreign newsagencies, he was sent as special correspondent to the Instituto de Cultura Hispánica and the Barcelona City Council in the famous España-America Exhibition in 1952. He gained «*Ciudad de Barcelona*» award in 1955. He knows Spain and the South American continent like the back of his hand.

David R. Hallett has a very broad background indeed. Born in England in 1933, he later went to Canada where he finished his studies, graduating from the University of British Columbia in Vancouver in 1956. He has lived in France and has travelled widely on the Continent. He knows the Burgundian and Alsatian wine growing regions particularly well and the Chateau vineyards in the south.

For the past few years, he has resided in the north of Spain, where he has made countless visits to the Rioja and Castilian vineyards and bodegas as well as the Sherry wine-cellars of international fame. Apart from these above mentioned regions, he is a great connoiseur and authority on Galicia in the northwest, his beloved and adopted country where the *Ribero, Condado, Rosal* and *Albariño* wines are made.

To lovers of good wine
wherever they be...

WINES OF SPAIN
(Painting by Nicolas Jönas.)

THE WINES OF SPAIN

Part One

THE VINTAGE

Oh dawn, fair maid,
For I am going to the vintage.
I shall return bleeding
Like a warrior captain.
Dawn is the time when the
grape cluster spills its sweet blood.
... Now the young maidens barefoot
Tread the «sangría» of the winepress,
Now along the river bank the mules are heard...

These lines were written by the Spanish poet and diplomat Agustín de Foxa after his return from a professional mission just before he died. His eyes, open to all horizons, were very familiar with the tropics and mists of northern Europe but there always remained deep within his memory the vintage time; the clusters of grapes ripening in the golden sun; their intensely coloured skins of topaz, gold and ruby; the Autumn chores among the golden leaves.

The vintage is a happy and merry time throughout the Peninsular bringing generations of people together. Fathers and sons, wives and maids, even grandchildren, everyone in the wine growing areas takes part in some way or another in this delightful labour.

The vintage whose history goes back many centuries, is renewed with the coming of Autumn, the life giving cycle and time of hope. The music of humorous voices can be heard on the hillsides, and plains and down in the valleys. The voices have a cadence of their own and the dance rhythms recall the pagan rituals of long ago when the wine god Bacchus influenced the destinies of man. Slowly the cane baskets are filled up, while the merriment and laughter continues. The simplicity of the rural life spreads its vitality all around as the peasant folk go about their ancestral labours. In every region, district and village from the Atlantic shores of Galicia to the Mediterranean waters of the Costa Brava, along the Rioja valley near the Cantabrian coast reaching south to Andalucia the vintage is on. The provident harvest promises to fulfil the illusions of everyone.

The feasts are many during the months of August and September and are held in the name of the local patron saints. Most of these feasts are of

a touristic nature and for this reason are called **Fiestas de Interés Turístico.**
On these occasions there is always a fiesta queen seated on a flower adorned
chariot followed by processions of beautifully dressed children. Then there
are the academic ceremonies and gastronomic contests.

THE VINTAGE CALENDAR AND FEASTS

The wine feast of Albariño, held on the 20th August, is typical. Then there
is the feast of San Ginés, in Jerez de la Frontera. In the Rioja, Logroño,
Valdepeñas, La Mancha, and Catalonia, the feast takes on great pageantry
for there is a magnificent display of the culinary arts, especially in San
Sandurní de Noya where
the queen of Spanish
sparkling wines is pro-
duced.

THE VINTAGE TIME

When thinking of the
vintage, the many quo-
tations from the classical
poets Virgil and Horace
immediately come to
mind. Throughout the
countryside the labour
begins. The harvest pros-
pers with the warm sun
and high temperatures of
summer. There will be no
bread or wine, however,
if it rains at the feast of
San Juan, as the saying
goes. This does not mean
there will be no wine at
all but rather it will be
of an inferior quality. It
is easily seen therefore
how the vintage can vary from region to region and even from valley to
valley.

In Galicia, the vintage takes place in the middle of September if the
summer has been sufficiently warm. This is possible as the Spring comes early
there and although the Galician wine is never very strong, the growers prefer
to gather the harvest at this time fearing the early rainfalls and high winds
that come with the Autumn. Only in Orense does the wine harvest come
late and is gathered around early October.

In the Duero valley the vintage takes place still later, around the middle
of October. In the Ebro and Rioja valleys, the harvest falls just after the
12th October, the feast of Pilar. If the year has been particularly cold it is
left until the early part of November. The renowned *Tempranilla* grape of
Haro in the Rioja is picked at the beginning of October.

The date of the vintage is fixed 15 days beforehand by the *Hermandad de Labradores* in accordance with the *Consejo Municipal* (Municipal Council) and the vineyard owner. The vineyards are attended to only once and done vine by vine, stock by stock. The work is done quickly as the rains sometimes come earlier than expected ruining the harvest and those involved in the wine business. But in some parts, the ripe grapes are selected to make either the *vinos nobles o finos* produced by leaving the ripened grapes exposed to the sun for a short time. The ripe grape is a guarantee for the making and preparation of wine. The ripest grape clusters are those nearest the wine shoots or stocks and those which receive the most sun, facing east and south. After, the grapes late in maturing are cut. These are located at the ends of the vine stocks and face north and west. In both cutting operations, the harvesters use the *oncete*—a kind of primitive knife curved at the point. Elsewhere a penknife or ordinary scissors are used.

The baskets used for carrying the grapes vary according to the place. They go under the names of *capazos* (hampers), *cuévanos, cestos, porteadoras,*

sarnachos, and in Galicia they call them *culleiros*. All of these are of a different shape and material and are usually made of tough grass, cane, reeds or light wood.

In the plainland and flatter areas, transportation is easy as the lorries have direct access to the vineyard. The manner of loading depends to a certain extent on the kind of wine to be made. In the case of the *vinos de pasto*, or ordinary wines, the grapes are heaped into a vehicle whose platform is lined with a waterproof canvass. The labourers who bring the baskets in from the field are called *sacadores*.

In the very important vitivinicular districts, family friends and extra hands from the villages are not enough to cope with the vintage and **cuadrillas** are engaged from nearby villages where the vintage has already been completed. The cuadrilla always has its *mayoral*, a veteran who knows how to manage his workers and at the same time look after their interests. They are people of breeding, strong will and have in the past provided great leaders and soldiers, especially in the Carlist War and the Wars of Independence.

The hired *cuadrilla* are very common in Castile, Andalucia and Aragon, where the wealthy landowners and large estates abound. In Galicia, on the other hand, where the land is divided up into strips known as *minifundio*, the vintage can be easily handled by the family and a few relations. In the Duero valley, people from nearby and around help in the labour as they are needed. Tradition and custom tend at all times to govern dealings between landlord and grape-picker.

THE WINE WAY

From the Golfo de Rosas to the Bay of Biscay

The wine route is as long as it is old, and it is difficult to stop talking about vineyards and wine making when you once start. Pliny the Elder said of wine that it was the «blood of the earth».

Let us now look at this fascinating wine route in relation to the Peninsular taken as a whole where there are more than 6,250 municipal wine producing areas which in 1970 had a total of 117,820 wine industries.

When speaking of wine, the internationally known brands come to mind such as: *Jerez, Rioja, Málaga, Alella*. The more commonly known table wines, for example the *vino verde* or green wine, the new wines, the wines found in the rural country cellars or *bodegas*, wine skins, taverns, bars and wholesale merchant houses are quite ignored. Like the vineyards themselves, the *bodegas* and the country inns are to be found everywhere along the wine route.

Wine tasting is best enjoyed by making a gastronomical tour of the lands where it is produced, visiting the cool *bodegas* and their wine presses. In this manner, the difference between the wines of the dry arid lands of the south, those produced along the fertile valleys and river beds, the terraced vineyards in the hilly areas or «Dalates», and the sloping terraces typical of Galicia and the Priorato regions, can be better understood.

It is a pleasure to take it leisurely along the littoral from the Golfo de Rosas to the Bay of Biscay, where the vineyard country is with us nearly all the way:

In Gerona, there are the vineyards of Ampurdan and the Selva; on the Costa Brava, the Llansa and the fine wines of Perelada; in the Maresme, the ivory Alella red and white wines; in Barcelona, the red, white, and rose wines of the Panadés, the very strong Tarragona wines and the deep red wines of Ulldacona and Montsiá.

Crossing the Ebro Delta in the province of Castellón, the vineyards of the San Mateo districts come into view where the famous Benicarlo claret is made. This wine, they say, could bring the dead to life.

Further south, in Valencia, there are the golden wines of Murviedro, well known in the 15th century; the red wines of Pla and the white wines of Cheste, Chiva, Turia, Albaida and the *rosados of* Utiel.

In Alicante, the Denia, Benisa, and Calpe red wines have a great reputation and also the famous Monovar and Matolo wines of Elche.

In Murcia, the *tintos* of Retamosa abound and in Almería, the dry Iberia of constant blue skies, the Fiñana is made.

Along the Granada coast, there are the *blancos* and *claretes of* Motril and the Alpujarras wines and arriving in the Costa del Sol, the delicious Pedro Ximenez and sweet, golden coloured Rome wines.

In Cádiz, there are to be found some of the oldest and most distinguished wines in the world —the sherry wines or *vinos de jerez*. There, many of the vineyards overlook the great ports of Cádiz, Puerto Real, Puerto de Santa María, Chiclana, Sanlúcar, Rota, to the sea beyond.

Crossing the mouth of the Guadalquivir river, the Costa de la Luz appears and we are in the province of Huelva. Here are found the wines of Alanís, founded in the 16th century, and the pale wines of Moguer which Columbus liked so much and took with him on his voyage to the New Wortld.

Leaving behind the southern coast of Andalucía and heading northward to Galicia, the traveller enters the green, moist country of *lloviznas* or soft rains, the *gaita* (a sort of bagpipe) and «*muñeira*» (Galician folk dance), the country of the Celts and the *vino verde* (green wine). The wines of Leiro in Ribadavia, Tostadillo and Rosal wines are all light and refreshing.

In Asturias, the wines are much scarcer. The *vino verde* is made as it is in Galicia and although the Albarín and Carrasquín wines do not satisfy the Asturian demand, they can always be supplemented by what Pliny called «apple wine», and this is found practically anywhere along the north coast of this province.

In Santander, the *Narruca Alba* and *Blanco Francés* grapes give only a limited production of fairly light wine. The same can be said of the Basque

A BARREL OF SHERRY WINE
(Courtesy of La Semana Vitivinícola.)

provinces of Vizcaya and Guipúzcoa where with a lot of work and trouble the local wine growers manage to get a minimal wine harvest from the black grapes of *Dos Orillas* and *Zura Rubia*. The «*chacolí*», a fresh green wine, made for the most part in Baquio and Guetaria of the Vascongadas, is a very popular local wine.

In the north of Spain, they have the reputation of knowing how to drink *como Dios manda* or «how God ordains». Their cellars have wines coming from all over the country and Bilbao in Vizcaya has a particularly wide variety and stock of Spanish wines which are exported to the United Kingdom.

From the Cape of Creus to the Bidasoa river, the wine country is always present and if its cradle is along the Mediterranean coast, it still flourishes in other parts where the wines are just as renowned. Anywhere along the Spanish coast, the hotels and restaurants, are a reminder of the importance of gastronomy (i.e. wine and food) in the lives or the people.

EATING GRAPES

The soil conditions, climate and vine variety are the factors that allow for fresh table grapes to be eaten from June to December. In fact, it is possible to have fresh table grapes all year round provided the climate has been good. The first grape harvest begins in Andalucia with the *Palomino* grape, closely followed by the *Garrido fino, Cañecazo, Leirán, Beba, Muscatel Uva del Rey, Mantuo and Chanes*.

In Levante, the earliest grapes are the *Gateta, Franseset, Verdill, Muscatel* gordo, *Valencia, Rosati, Planta nova, Tardán, Aledo de Navidad* and last of all, the *Uva Morada*.

Among the more common types of eating grapes are included: the *Albillo, Verdejo, Vidriells, Picadillos, Malvasías, Turruteses, Cañorroyos, Texadura, Alba, Cateta, Mencía, Pinuelos, Azaria, Alarige, Ebenes, Morates*, as well as the *Rojal, Amoravía, Marisancha, Botón de Gallo, Teta de Vaca, Ferrales, Oliveta, Ragol, Lanjarón, Ziuti, Muscatel*, etc.

THE VINES   The vine grows stronger and prospers when the roots and vine stocks
have to work hard in order to survive. In Corella (Navarre), a Muscatel
wine is produced of the *Rayo de Sol* type that even in the 19th century
won first prizes in many contests. The same happened with the select Rancio
Dulce wine made from the *Garnacha* grape.

Each region has its own special grape variety for making its select wines,
and each kind of grape gives a special flavour to the wine.

In the Rioja, the *Tempranilla, Gracián* and *Mazuela,* grapes are used
to make the branded red wines and a proportional blending of the *Viura*
and *Malvasía* musts for the select white wines.

In Jerez, the *Pedro Ximénez* and *Palomino* grapes provide the bases of
all its carefully prepared wines. In Málaga, it is the *Pedro Ximénez.*

In the province of Valladolid, the white wines are obtained from the
Verdejo variety mixed with the *Jerez* grape. From this the Verdejo de Rueda
is made, a wine of traditional fame.

More will be said about the different vines and their respective regions
later.

CASTRA VINARIA

THE BULL'S HIDE

Estrabo, in this writings about Spain, said: *Its contours seen from west to east look like the hide of a bull whose front part corresponds with the east and whose breadth corresponds with the part stretching from north to south.*

This simile is very well known and gives a vivid picture of the physical contours of this land.

The first visitors to come to Spain many centuries ago were the Phoenicians and Greeks. These sailors, borne on the crests of the waves, their sails filled and their oars bent, journeyed along the eastern sea routes, and introduced the first vines. From this time on, there is a live testimony of the beginnings of vine cultivation and from legendary Tartesos, the silver anchored boats belonging to King Argantonio carried the wines of Cádiz eastward.

When Pliny called Spain «Castra Vinaria», vine cultivation had been going on for centuries.

SPANISH WINE ITS HISTORY

Spanish wine has a very long history, which goes back in time before the coming of the Romans. One has only to visit the museums and look at the modals, coins, sculptures, pottery, and mosaics to appreciate this. The Tartesians, in the sixth century, were acquainted with Spanish wines and the grape cluster was used as a symbol of abundance on their coins. Lebrija, an Andalucian village, has been referred to as the country of the Satyres.

The grape named by Pliny *Cocolabis* made a heavy foamy wine of high alcoholic content. The «*Vinum Gaditanum*», so the inscription reads on an amphora of 31 B. C., was certainly a wine from Jerez. The Laure wine, both sweet and rich, also of Andalucian origin, was esteemed one of the best in the world.

Estrabo, Plinio, Columela, all of them allude to the vines of Spain and the «parras» from Palermo, brought from Italy, to improve the primitive, coarse Iberian wine. They speak about the «layetanos» and «tarraconense» wines of Catalonia. Even beer which was called «Careaú» was already known to the Iberians.

In Rome, on Mount Testaccio, fragments of Spanish wine pitchers dating from the year 140 B. C. can still be found everywhere.

The Moslems when they tried the sweet sherry and aromatic Montilla broke their religious laws. King Alhaquem II wanted to stamp out vine

growing altogether but his councillors persuaded him not to, fearing that the wine drinkers accustomed to sweet wines would resort to wines made from fruit, much stronger and more addictive than those made from grapes.

It was the Moslems who discovered the *soleo* or sunning of the grapes to make sweet wine, and the making of the *Zebibi*, a raisin wine, made in Sevilla. And when the Christians reconquered the lands from the Moors, they continued to cultivate the vineyards and make wine, keeping the wine presses and replanting the original vine stocks. There is evidence of these wines in the Arab song books.

Saint Isidoro of Sevilla in the 7th century praises the Spanish wines and in his work on **Etimologies,** he has written down the twenty three different kinds that at the time were cultivated in the Peninsular.

When the Christians, who freed the town of Seville from Arab domination settled, they began to select vines from distinct areas and experiment with them to get the best wines. It is not surprising that the *mudéjares*—Arabs living under Christian rulers—were good growers.

In the poem of El Cid (1245) Per Abbat ends by saying «Give us wine». Gonzalo de Berceo in his life of Santo Domingo de Silos begs that the poets be given a glass of wine as their reward. The Arcipreste de Hita in the «*Libro de Buen Amor*» sings of the excellencies of wine but chastises the bad quality of some of the *serrano* or sierra wines.

Spanish Legislation has always been careful to protect and foster this national wealth giving certain «**fueros**» (privileges) to those in the wine trade. In the «**Fuero Real**», also known as the «**Libro de los Consejos de Castilla**» it was ruled «No one must sell wine for more than the fixed price of the master. Neither must two wines be mixed together, nor put chalk nor salt and whoever breaks the law pays sixty *sueldos* (money issued at that time) and forfit half for the King and half for the populace».

The great majority of the laws governing wine were inherited from the Arabs. Gabriel Alonso Herrero published an agricultural treatise in 1513 which contains a scientific classification of Spanish wines and their fifteen distinct characteristics and varieties.

In the «**Novísima Recopilación**», where it speaks of «*Abastos y Regatones*» *de la Corte*» (Provisions of Haggling in the Parliament), it is forbidden to buy and sell wine in and within five leagues of Madrid. In 1795, the conditions under which wine could be sold in public houses were drawn up.

Valcarcel in his «**Agricultura General**» cites 116 distinct types of vine particularly suitable for the Spanish climate. Cecilio de Luna wrote about the Pedro Ximénez vine of Málaga and listed 33 grape varieties in this province. Finally in 1814 Don Simon de Roxas Clemente, the initiator of modern viticulture, classified more than 500 vine varieties in Spain of which 120 were found in the ancient kingdom of Granada and Andalucía.

WINE VARIETIES

Spain, because of her variety of soil, warm summers, and ideal climate can produce every kind of wine. There are four main categories: **vinos generosos** *secos*, **vinos generosos** *dulces*, **vinos corrientes** and **espumosos**.

The **vinos generosos** *secos* are select dry wines only produced in Spain. Among these, the Sherry or *Jerez*, the *Montilla*, *The Oloroso* de Jerez, the *Moriles* and the *Manzanilla*, are unexcelled and genuinely Spanish.

The **vinos generosos** *dulces* or select sweet wines, come mainly from *Málaga*, *Tarragona*, *Valencia*, *Alicante*, *Castellón*, *Priorato*, *Sitges* and *Cariñena*.

The **vinos corrientes** are the red and white wines, made in the popular way using any kind of grapes.

The **espumosos** are commonly known as sparkling wines.

THE «DENOMINACION DE ORIGEN»

The «**Denominación de Origen**» is the THE CONTROLLED NAME OF THE AREA OF ORIGEN. It is the name that is given to the wine from the beginning. It is the soil, terrain, the growing, making and blending processes. All these above factors are best explained by the term «geographic determinism».

Concerning this geographic determinism, three factors are involved:

1. The production area.
2. The preparation and *crianza* or maturing of wine involving a series of techniques employed to preserve and maintain the distinct and real essence of the wine.
3. The typification which protects the reputation of the wine according to its peculiar characteristics of bouquet, name, brand, colour, aroma and taste.

THE ADVANTAGES OF THE «DENOMINACION DE ORIGEN»

According to the regulations of the Minister of Agriculture, the «D. de O.» protects the wine grower by forbidding the transfer of grapes from one area to another and so causing a flux in the market prices. It supports the winemaker, freeing him from outside competition and promotes and stimulates growing in the area.

HISTORY OF THE «DENOMINACIONES DE ORIGEN» IN SPAIN

The «D. de O.» was started in France to protect the French Cognacs and Champagnes in the foreign market. Spain was forced to do the same and

defend her own wines mainly in Jerez and Málaga because on the international market there was a good deal of falsification of the brand names.

This gave place to an international agreement in Madrid. It was established then that the wines could not use the names of countries or regions other than their own or real place of origin. In this way, the «D. de O.» was incorporated into the Spanish wine laws.

Some of the names appearing on the first list of the «D. de O.» have disappeared recently. They are the following: Toro, Rueda, Martell, Noblejas and Extremadura.

Below is a list of the names and addresses of the present «Denominaciones de Origen» in Spain.

Alella y Panadés:

President: Don José María Vidal-Barraquer Marfá.
Amalia, 27 (Estación de Viticultura y Enología).
Apartado de Correos 43.
Teléfono 892 00 50.
Villafranca del Panadés (Barcelona).
Calvo Sotelo, 11. Alella (Barcelona).

Alicante:

President: Don Fernando Rovira Carbonell.
Teniente Alvarez Soto, 1. Alicante.

Almansa, Mancha, Manchuela y Méntrida:

President: Don Eduardo Iriarte Brugos.
Ronda de Santa María, 21.
Teléfono 21 25 39. Ciudad Real.

Cariñena:

President: Don Carlos Escrivano Isava.
General Sanjurjo, 10, 4.º-A.
Teléfono 23 45 69.
Zaragoza.

Cheste, Utiel-Requena and *Valencia:*

President: Don Eduardo Aristoy Peris.
Gran Vía Marqués del Turia, 78.
Teléfono 27 29 95.
Valencia-5.

Huelva:

President: Don Salvador Trevijano Molina.
Gran Vía, 5.
Teléfono 19 21.
Huelva.

Jerez-Xérez-Sherry and *Manzanilla-Sanlúcar de Barrameda:*

President: Don Antonio Barbadillo y García Velasco.
Avenida Alvaro Domecq.
Apartado de Correos, 324.
Jerez.

Jumilla:

President: Don José Luis García García.
González Adalid, 4.
Teléfono 21 27 09.
Murcia.

Málaga:

President: Don Miguel Díaz Caffarena.
Jefatura Agronómica.
Teléfono 21 81 22.
Málaga.

Montilla and *Moriles:*

>President: Don Manuel Santolalla Lacalle.
>Avenida del Generalísimo, 24.
>Teléfono 22 54 84.
>Córdoba.

Navarra:

>President: Don Francisco Traver.
>Avenida Carlos III, 36.
>Teléfono 23 00 34.
>Pamplona.

Priorato:

>President: Don Ramón Vidal Barraquer-Marfá.
>Paseo Sunyer. Estación Enológica.
>Teléfono 37 16.
>Reus.

Ribero and *Valdeorras:*

>President: Don Luis Vega Escandón.
>Capitán Eloy, 17.
>Teléfono 10 19.
>Orense.

Rioja:

>President: Don Eugenio Narvaiza Arregui.
>Avenida de Pío XII. Edificio C. N. S.
>Logroño.

Tarragona:

>President: Don José Antonio Ruiz Birlanga.
>Real, 28.
>Teléfono 20 45 08.
>Tarragona.

Valdepeñas:

>President: Don Eduardo Iriarte Burgos.
>Cervantes, 17.
>Teléfono 31 18 04.
>Valdepeñas (Ciudad Real).

EL DESCANSO

«DESCANSO»

(From the painting by Gisela Rahm.)

THE WAY TO DRINK

«It is good to know that glasses
Serve us for drinking
It's a bad thing that we don't know
What it is to be thirsty.»

ANTONIO MACHADO.

WINE TASTING

Good wine brightens the eyes, cleans the mouth and gives health.

The appreciation of good wine begins, as with love, with **the eyes.** After looking at the wine against the light to examine its colour that ranges from a delicate white and pale amber to a deep red with a slightly purple tint, the first requirement has been performed in the ritual of wine tasting.

The **smelling** of the wine is the second requirement for the smell can never betray the sensitive olfate glands which pick up the «bouquet»: its fragance, perfume, exquisite «crianza», nobility, «solera» and vintage. Whether it be smooth, coarse or acid, it is in smelling the wine that its real qualities are discovered.

Difficult though it may seem, the desire alone is enough to initiate oneself in this delightful art of the connoisseur for apart from the mystery there is the pleasure of savouring a good glass of wine.

Let us see how he does it. He takes the glass with the index finger and thumb in the right hand raising in to eye level. The glass is then lowered down to the nose so as to test its aroma. This procedure consisting of a gentle gesture is a ritual that has gone on for generations and centuries.

It reminds one of scenes contemplated in the museums of Europe where on vases and earthenware vessels are depicted happy gatherings, solemn feasts and country outings of, for example, Frans Hals, Tenier and Van Dyck.

At any gathering or festive occasion, there are always people who through their «savoir faire» are ready to teach us if we would but listen.

The glass is rotated lightly between the fingers to see the scarcely visible shades of colour. A wine that is pleasing to the eyes is pleasing to the taste. The *tinto* of a deep red ruby and garnet colour and the white pale and light wines of a very fine transparency and golden clarity are always tempting us to try them.

The glass is poised slightly on the lips and the head is inclined slightly forward; the greater the composure, the greater the elegance. Only a little wine is imbibed which is washed around in the mouth carefully without puffing out the cheeks. In this way, the mucous glands are throughly soaked. With the tip of the tongue the wine is then passed to the roof of the palate and faenum. These two part of the mouth are the most sensitive. It is better to open the lips a little so that the oxygen makes contact with the wine releasing any gases.

Many reputed gourmets say that taste is nothing more than the sensation or impression received by the palate.

A third measure of a glass is enough to savour the aroma of the wine. **It is never drunk quickly** but slowly. To drink is to taste and savour. The effect of drinking is reflected in the face—the eyes light up, the face mellows, the expression is happier, words come easily and the conversation flows.

Learning and knowing how to drink is a lifelong affair. It is an eloquent reflection of one's education. It is the proof and evidence of a refined life style.

Baudelaire in one of his *petits poémes en prose* identifies wine with poetry and virtue. He says it helps in two simple ways: firstly to keep the head erect and secondly, to fight against the passing of time.

With the lips bearly touching the glass, the wine is sipped and drawn into the palate and savoured with a calm and reflective state of soul. The *catador* or professional wine taster needs only to try one glass and he immediately knows the class, quality, texture, and the slightest shade of colour.

The select wines are normally drunk out of delicate cut glassware. It is the stately shape of the glass that commands respect and a special consideration for the wine and its exquisite aroma. This is particularly so where *Jerez* and *Manzanilla* wines are concerned. For each kind of wine, there is a special type of glass. However, the common or ordinary wines are served in very simple plain glasses and vary according to the region. For example, there is the granadine pot, the «*chiquito*» of the Basque country and in Galicia a shallow china cup; very strange to see are the glasses named *cuerno de oro* (horn of a bull). Of course, the ritual of wine drinking can only be done with the best wines.

THE GLASS

To be able to taste wine first you must have the wine and second the glass.

The ideal glass is the clear, cristal, transparent glass. The coloured cut glasses although rather novel have the disadvantage in that the wine cannot be seen clearly and for this reason a good gourmet never uses them. Perhaps the ideal glasses are to be found in Andalucía. In the *catavinos* (sherry glasses) the stem is moved around gently in order to contemplate the liquid against the light while the fragrance of the wine rises to the upper part of the glass mixing with the oxygen of the air outside.

The *caña*, a slender cane shaped glass, is used for the Manzanilla. Its name is derived from the cane used to make the *venencias*—a long stick used for sampling sherry. The golden rule for serving wine is to leave a third of the glass unfilled. The glasses used for serving white wine are generally smaller than those used for red. The elliptical shaped glasses are suitable for serving the select and high quality wines.

As just mentioned, in Galicia a wide white cup called a *cunca* is used which is suitable for the «*copeo*», or drinking of a glass of wine.

In the Vascongadas (Basque country), Navarre and the Rioja, the «*chiquito*» a robust short stubby glass is used. Similar to the «*chiquito*» is the *maceta granadina*. And so each region has its own way of drinking by way of the «*copeo*», «*chateo*» and «*chiquiteo*».

SPOUT DRINKING

Porrón or drinking from the spout is very common too. First there is the flask shaped Levante or Catalonian kind. The Castilian looks like a cruet with a very thin neck and pronounced arc.

A popular saying goes: «Wine drunk from the spout best quenches the thirst».

There are specialists in *porrón* drinking who are able to make amusing comments while they do so or pour the wine on their forehead letting it run down the nose and into their mouth without losing a drop. This can be seen done in a Spanish London restaurant where the host has made his reputation before an admiring and cosmopolitan public.

APOLOGIA DE LA BOTA

(PART II. Don Quixote. Chapter XIII)

None better than Cervantes could write the «Apología de la Bota». The dialogue of Sancho and the Knight of the Wood has left us for always, the grace and skill of the good wine tasters.

«By my faith, brother», replied he of the Wood, «I have no stomach for your wild pears, nor your sweet thistles, nor your mountain roots: let our masters have them, with their opinions and laws of chivalry, and let them eat what they commend. I carry cold meats, and this bottle hanging at my saddle, happen what will; and such a reverence I have for it, and so much I love it that few minutes pass but I give it a thousand kisses and hugs». And so saying, he put it into Sancho's hand who, grasping and setting it to his mouth, stood gazing at the stars for a quarter of an hour: and having done drinking, he let his head fall on one side.

... «But tell me, sir, by the life of him you love best, is not this wine from Ciudad Real?»

«You have a distinguished palate», answered the Knight of the Wood «it is of no other growth, and besides has some years over its head.»

THE IDEAL COMPANIONS
(Photo J. M. Ruiz.)

«Trust me for that» said Sancho, «depend upon it, I always hit right and guess the kind».

«But it is not strange, Senor Squire, that I should have so great and natural an instinct in the business of knowing wines, that let me but, I hit upon the country, the kind, the flavour and how long it will keep, how many changes it will undergo, with all other circumstances that pertain to wine.»

From *Don Quijote de la Mancha.*
(Chapter XIII, Part Two.)

. . . .

The soft and tanned leather skin or **Bota** as it is called, whether in one's hand or hanging from the shoulder is a lot easier to handle than the *cantimplora* (metal flask) or the bottle. It is ideal for trips into the country and hunting. It can be carried to work outside in the fields or down in the mines. Its curious shape is often seen in paintings and tapistries. AT THE GREAT FEASTS OF SAN FERMIN AND THE BULLFIGHTS IT IS THE CONSTANT COMPANION.

The wineskin is lined with resin ~~fish~~ inside to keep the wine fresh. The favourite souvenir of the tourist, it is even better appreciated when filled with good *tinto* wine.

The following two refrains are worth nothing:

1. Never venture outside without a wineskin and when you do, don't forget to fill it up.

2. Every wineskin smacks of the wine it is filled with.

The first companion of Sancho Panza as well as the Medieval Knight, its curious shape is often seen in any Art Gallery where the paintings of Goya are on display.

The wineskin was quick to cross the seas in the Caravels that discovered the New World. A faithful and indispensable friend, it has always been present at any great historic happening. Portable, it can be hung anywhere and never loses its shape. It can never be broken. The making of this popular souvenir is bound up with craftsmanship as old as time itself.

Related to the wineskin is the *pellejo*, a much larger skin, still used to carry wines usually on the back of a mule.

There is a special art in drinking from the *Bota*. It is placed comfortably at belt level and squeezed and the upward jet is drunk down with the greatest of pleasures. The usual way, however, is to drink it holding it up to the mouth.

The *bota* and the guitar are perhaps the two things which are most typical and symbolic of Spanish life.

THE PUMPKIN   Of lesser importance than the wineskin and the *porrón* is the pumpkin. This is used for excursions into the country and is just as popular as the *bota* in many parts.

BREAD AND WINE HELP
YOU ALONG THE WAY

Gastronomy

Food and eating have never been spoken about so much as in our time. The newspapers, women's magazines and cookery books keep the modern housewife in touch with one of the most delightful of arts. Whenever gastronomy is spoken of, a whole series of concepts, rituals and rules are inevitably involved.

Washington Irving said that the Spanish peasant knew how to eat with a «sobriety and manner difficult to equal in other countries».

AT THE TABLE AND
PLAYING GAMES

A Spanish proverb says: «*At the table and playing games the gentleman is discerned*». And dining at the table assumes centuries of tradition and customs where true civilisation is revealed. Together with the cuisinary arts goes the drinking, meaning the wine that goes with every menu.

It is a mistaken belief to think that the gastronome is a fat middle aged man with a red face and quite given over to excessive eating and drinking. There is nothing more erroneous, as **the gourmet** is generally a man who is **very selective** and not carried away by others when choosing the menu. **He knows how to choose** his food without show or conceit and as his taste dictates.

The gourmet makes the pleasures of the table something shared. He only eats alone when there is no other choice.

The gastronome knows where to find the best places to eat which are not the most expensive. He knows intuitively how to choose the menu in a restaurant or hotel, and the safest and most seasoned dishes. In the same way, he selects his wines taking into account the lesser known local brands.

FROM THE
RESTAURANT TO
THE TAVERN

The gourmet not only frequents first class hotels and restaurants but often likes to visit a rustic establishment whose reputation depends on its typical dishes and good wines fresh from the bodegas. It is not unusual just

before lunch to see him looking round for a tavern, bar or restaurant famous for its food.

There are always opportunities of finding new places to eat whether it be for a party or rendez-vous and there are nearly always typical dishes on the menu with good wines to go with them. Being a visitor in a strange town is a good excuse for eating in a good class restaurant and the name together with the food and wine menu is a clear indication of its category. Often, however, those establishments which boast the most do not come up to expectations. When visiting a restaurant for a first time, it's better to consult the head waiter and ask his advice concerning the quality of wines. Afterwards, if the food and wine have been good it is quite customary to tell one's friends.

WINE AT THE TABLE

Wine is the protagonist at any table. In fact, in France the meal is created around the selection of wines. It is the wine that sets the tone, brings people together, sustains the conversation, and quickly forms friendships and strengthens old ties.

For this reason, the place of wine at the table is a privileged one and the guarantee of the proof and quality of wine is shown by the label on the bottle. How the wines are to be served depends on the occasion, atmosphere and the kind of meal.

WINE AND COOKING

Spanish cooking, eminently Latin, uses olive oil as its base. Olive oil is the natural companion of wine and, like it, varies according to type.

The history of Spanish cooking is one of the oldest in Europe and millions of visitors come to Spain each year to try it out. That wine is in the same category as Spanish cooking there is no doubt.

A WINE—CELLAR SEEN IN PERSPECTIVE
(Photo Paisajes Españoles.)

There is a wide selection of wines for every taste and caprice coming from Castilla la Vieja, La Mancha, Jumilla, Cariñena, Ampurdán, and the Priorato. These wines are listed in most restaurants and taverns, as well as the local bodegas.

The good supply of *valientes* wines, referred to as the **machos** (virile strong wines) is proof of their renown, worthiness and good reputation. They are to be drunk, however, with moderation, especially in the case of visitors from abroad who are unused to them and easily tempted to exceed the bounds of moderation.

GASTRONOMICAL
GUIDE

The gastronomical guide shows four main zones, each with their own peculiar characteristics. In the north, the food is seasoned with *salsas* or sauces similar to the French. In «Castilla» and central Spain, the roast dishes are the most popular and in the South and Andalucía, the fried dishes are paragon. It is in the east that the rice dishes mostly abound called *paellas* although of course the «paella» is very popular throughout the whole of the Peninsula .

In the same manner, wines are found in areas which more or less coincide with the gastronomical limits or boundaries. In the north, the *vinos verdes* are so called because the grapes are picked earlier and consequently have a slighty sour taste. Within this range fall the *chacolí* Basque wine, and the Galician and Rioja wines.

In Old and New Castile or the two «Castillas», the vineyards are either found along the hills and banks of the rivers, such as the Tajo, or in flat open country. For this reason, they are divided into the hillside and plainland wines.

Towards the south, the wines have a perfume reminiscent of the dancers of Cádiz and are rightly called «*vinos perfumados*».

In the Levante area, the vineyards have a very long history indeed, dating back to the Phoenician and Greek periods. These lands blown by the light off shore breezes produce some of the most delicate and highly praised wines of all.

Finally there are the noble and illustrious Navarese and Aragonese wines from the banks of River Ebro. These wines are accompanied by such select dishes as the *chilindrón*.

Spanish cooking has sometimes been called classical and at other times baroque. The classical influence is easily explained by the rather severe and serious character of the Castilians themselves. The baroque in cooking is nowhere better exemplified than in the «paella» in its many varieties ranging from the Alicante and Elche, the «caldero», the «abanda» and of course, the classical paella of Valencia. More than 70 different **paella** dishes are known and an equivalent number of wines to go with them. The same can be said about the «pote gallego» and the «escudella» and «carn d'olla» in Catalonia.

FOOD IS FIRST OF
ALL SEEN

The first impression of a restaurant is a visible one. The feeling of friendliness is something that is experienced directly by the visitors who eat there for the first time. The category of restaurant is shown very clearly in the manners and gestures of its patrons, the care in service and the class of «chef». The good cooking is indicated by the number and quality of the clientele. The guests sense at once the human «rapport» and atmosphere.

It is common in modern restaurants to have an open kitchen where the meats, fish, vegetables and cheeses are displayed to the public.

For every occasion and circumstance, wine is essential at the table. The brands, blends, speak eloquently for themselves as do the barrels, the clay spout vessels or porrones, and the jugs used for the coarser, rustic «tinto» wines.

SELECTING WINE

With regard to the bottled wines, the wine lists always have a selection of the most famous bodegas, vintage and blends, kinds and brands so as not to disappoint the good gastronome who may be also an expert wine taster.

In the event of there not being a certain wine listed, then the wine waiter should be consulted. It is not enough for a wine to be well known, nor is it a question of price in making the selection. On many occasions, a good *corriente* wine will solve the problem when wondering about the right wine for the right dish.

The quality of the wine is always shown on the label. It tells us the wine cellar, blend, year of vintage and the guarantee requirements as laid down by the DENOMINACION DE ORIGEN.

Nothing new is said in affirming that one of the most enduring of Spanish realities is her wine. Ortega y Gasset defined it in his elegant and philosophic manner as a **Cosmic Problem.** It is not for nothing that Spain is a wine country and the rustic wines are the base of any menu.

KNOWING WINES

The **catador** (wine taster) of the bodega with his special technical knowledge of blending is a race apart. He is king and master. He knows the quality of each blend and vintage. A word from him is final. The wine when it is defined by him becomes an irrefutable truth.

AUTUMN. BACCHUS RAISES HIS GLASS.
(From the painting by Maella. Prado Museum.

WINE AND THE TABLE

Manner of serving wine

The wine must always be ready long before it is served. This is one of the basic rules respected by hosts and head waiters alike. In private homes, this is not so common, however, even when there is a wine cellar at hand to invite and toast one's friends.

Although in Spain there are a great variety of wines, the tendency is to select an available wine to go with the food. In France the reverse is true. The food is chosen to go with the wine in fact the whole menu revolves around the wine that has been ordered.

In Spain, then, the wine stock is checked as required always taking the food into account first of all. If only one kind of wine is drunk, it is chosen to go with the main dish and it is better to have a wine of little body and low alcoholic content. If a bottled wine is not in stock, a wine of the year will do or an old solera wine found somewhere in the bodega.

It is a good idea to look at the wine to see if it has become cloudy. This often happens to the *tintos*, even though the essential factors of aroma and taste remain unaffected.

It is also a good idea to have a thermometer at hand which in Winter should not drop below 6 degrees and in Summer not exceed 15 degrees. The *bodega* should be a dry place whose temperature is constant throughout the year.

CLARIFICATION OF WINE

Where the world of wine is concerned, time is most important and nothing can be rushed regarding its preparation. Wine is a gentleman and consequently needs special attention. The decanting is done carefully before the meal.

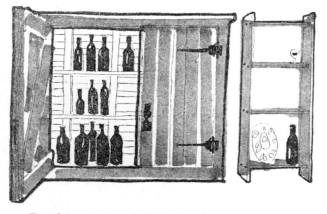

The jug is washed with warm water, rinsed and allowed to dry. Once the jug is dry, the wine is transferred by means of a funnel making sure it is not shaken. As soon as some particles float on the funnel itself, the transfer is considered as over, and the wine will appear to have come back to life again.

Bottles are kept in a horizontal position for two reasons. Firstly, so that the leas are not disturbed when pouring and secondly so that the cork doesn't lose contact with the wine and in this way preventing the air from entering.

THE CORK

The discovery of the cork was a revolution indeed. It was the monk of Champagne **Dom Perignon** who invented the cork as a bottle seal. Before that, the stoppers were made of leather, burlap or wood wrapped in a rag soaked in oil. The drawback was in the fermentation. In the Spring, the gases generated caused the stoppers to fly off. This doesn't mean the cork is completely safe as excessive humidity can damage it.

UNCORKING THE BOTTLE

When serving the coarser «corriente» wines, the ideal is to use a primitive earthenware jug.

There is something of a ritual about the uncorking of a bottle. The bottle with its seal is displayed in a cane basket before the eyes of the host and his guests. This is followed by the uncorking which must be done carefully so as not to splinter the cork. It is protocol to look at the state of the cork and then smell it as the aroma reflects the condition of the wine.

The wine waiter, just in case there is any doubt, pours just enough wine to taste and then tries it. Once he is assured of the good state of the wine he pours a little into the host's glass who in turn tastes it.

The bottle is always wrapped in a serviette leaving the label visible to the guests.

THE WINE-WAITER
OR «COPERO»

The special skill of the «sommelier» or **copero** in serving wine can be only achieved after long experience. The «sommelier» or *sumiller* continues in the tradition of the *copero*.

In the «Libro de Cocina» (16th century) of Roberto de Nola, the first cookery book published in Spain, the author says this about the job of the *copero:*

«The *copero* must be a man of very clean and noble condition, neither incontinent nor ingratiating but quiet and discrete, because at a given moment, laughter and talking may cause embarrassment. He must bring the glasses with grace».

SERVING WINE

The above author says about the serving of wine:

«The glass **or** vessel must be taken in the right hand, in the best possible grace and style, the hand being higher than the level of the nose».

The natural grace of the *copero* is absolutely essential at solemn functions, official banquets and moments of great social character.

Nowadays, the *coperos* are very few and are only found in high class restaurants. Nevertheless, the ritual of the exquisite and elegant style of serving wine whether as host in one's own home or outside must never be lost.

We have said earlier that when only one wine is taken during a meal, the wine must go with the main dish. The *vino de pasto*, or *corriente* wine, goes very well with the unpretentious and simpler dishes.

However, when frequenting establishments of select atmosphere and tone, a rigorous selection of wines, as they are listed on the wine list, must be respected.

There may be two kinds of wine *blanco* or *tinto* (white and red). For any one meal, three wines are enough, one *blanco* and two *tintos*. As a rule, the *blanco* and *rosado* wines are taken with the hors d'oevres and fish dishes and the red wines with the main course and cheeses. The white wines are also taken with plain food without much seasoning.

WHITE WINES FIRST

The *blancos* are always taken with the **seafood** and the *tintos* with **red meats** and highly seasoned food. It follows then that the lighter precede the stronger wines and the cool wines before those at room temperature.

WHITE WINES IN
THE SPRING AND
SUMMER-RED WINES
IN THE WINTER

The white wines because of their make up and nature are preferred in the summertime as they are served fresh and go very well with cold food. The *tintos*, on the contrary, are served in the wintertime.

SELECTING WINES

Ideally the wine should be about 5 years old. If it has 2 or 3 years in the barrel and 8 to 10 in the bottle so much the better.

Old vintage bottles, preserving very old wines are found in restaurants and bodegas and they need only to be opened to discover their delicious aroma and «solera». Old grocer shops as well are often an emporium of long lost vintage bottles.

THE GLASSWARE

The glass must be fairly large and never more than half filled. The reason for choosing fairly large glasses is that they offer a greater surface area for evaporation than the smaller ones.

«Large, smooth, and transparent glasses, where the wine sparkles like a jewel; such are the glasses of a good wine drinker», said Julio Camba, an extraordinary gourmet and wine taster, in his book «The House of Luculo and the Art of Eating». And he continued in his soft, humorous way:

«The fashion of cut and polychromated glass originated in Germany, in a bad harvest year and has prospered ever since. However good wine rests on its own laurels».

The French, good connoisseurs of wine, have outlawed the small glasses that extinguish the bouquet and have also outlawed the thick crystal glasses, as they prevent the intimate contact between the wine and the lips. The *tinto* glasses are normally bigger than the ones used for the *blancos*.

The connoisseurs are of the opinion that the best type is the *balón* or balloon shaped glass even for champagne. The classical shaped «champagne» glass is no longer used because of the excessive surface area which allowed the bouquet to evaporate. For this reason, the «flauta» or flute shaped high and narrow glass is now in use as is the so called «tulipán», which is preferred by the experts in the art of good drinking.

TABLE OF WINE TEMPERATURES	Wines	Temperature
	Tinto (red)	18º - 20º (centigrade)
	Rosado (rose)	8º - 10º
	Blanco seco (white dry)	6º - 8º
	Blanco semidulce (white semi sweet)	4º - 6º
	Espumoso (sparkling)	3º - 5º
	Fino (select)	15º - 18º
	Oloroso and Amontillado	20º
	Vermouth, amargos and espumosos dulces (bitter and sweet sparkling wines)	0º

TEMPERATURE OF FRENCH WINES		
	Vinos blancos dulces (white sweet)	6º - 8º
	Champagnes	8º - 10º
	Blancos Secos (dry white)	10º - 12º
	Beaujolais and red wine from La Loire	12º - 14º
	Red Burgundy wines	16º
	Red Bordeaux wines	18º (minimum)

The *tintos* are served at room temperature—warm but not exceeding 15º—«Chambre» as the French say. The bottle should never be warmed by leaving it in hot water, nor put over a radiator. The best thing is to leave it in the room where it is to be drunk.

The following is a brief guide:

The white dry wines—fresh
The white semi—sweet—very fresh
The select fine—cold.
The olorosos and amontillados—room temperature.
The sparkling wines and champagnes—very cold.
Brandies—room temperature.

The aroma and the taste of wine increases with the rise in temperature. If the wine is lukewarm on the palate it becomes unpleasant to drink and its good qualities are neutralised. It is possible to heat wines only in countries where the temperature in winter falls considerably. For example in Germany and northern France, it is not unusual to have warm wine served up in a large jug and how delicious it is.

The white table wines of little tannic acid and body always taste well if served fresh but never cold. The cold numbs and renders the tongue insensitive to the good virtues of wine.

The champagnes and sparkling wines are served cold so that they retain all of the carbonic gases. For this reason a sweet sting is felt in the mouth.

The cognacs can be heated over the naked flame as in the high class restaurants or better still warmed in the palm of the hand. The balloon shape of the glass is ideal for doing this. The cognac tastes better when the ether and other impure gases have been expelled and the aroma, master of the free space in the glass, is more refined.

LIGHT RED TABLE WINES, ROSE AND CLARET WINES

These include light or medium bodied wines of little strength, varying between 10° to 12°. They are generally served with light game dishes, meat, rice, vegetables and cheeses.

Hot snacks, pies, sandwiches, fried food and «foie-gras».

Hot dishes except roasts, veal, beef, pork, and ~~fowl~~. fowl.

«Pasta» and various egg dishes, «tortilla» (Spanish omelette) and light rice dishes.

They go well with cod, conger eel, hake, and sardines.

RED DRY TABLE WINES OF BODY AND ALCOHOLIC STRENGTH

From 12° and upwards. They are served with **paellas** (where the meat is included) and other rice dishes like curry.

Roast meat dishes in general, steaks, meat fillets, chateaubriand, tournedos, entrecotes, pork chops, kidneys, liver, roast or fried bacon, sausage meats.

With game including: partridge, pigeon, pheasant, wild duck, *azulones* and *lavancos*.

Typically Spanish hot dishes like the **Fabada Asturiana,** and the **Olla Podrida.**

WHITE TABLE WINES-MEDIUM AND DRY

They are served with a few hot meat dishes but above all with fish: bream, hake, salmonettes, salmon, sole, trout and shellfish.

Other dishes include: chicken in white wine or champagne, pigs foot or trotter, veal, sweet breads, partridge, frogs legs, ham and tomato, mussels, and shellfish in general, *angulas* Bilbao style and the typical **pisto manchego.**

STRONG WHITE WINES

Up to 20°.

For cold dishes: stuffed turkey, partridge, pheasant, boar's head, cold ham, cold roast beef, and veal.

With these above dishes the following aromatic white wines can be served as an alternative Jerez or Málaga, Montilla, Moriles, Valdepeñas, Rioja Blanca, Alella, Tarragona, Sauternes and French Graves as well as light red wines.

SEMI-SWEET WHITE AND MILD WINES

Ideal with egg dishes either scrambled, hard boiled and **tortilla.** (Spanish omelette.)

Fish dishes such as fried *calamares*, **zarzuela de pescados,** shellfish, cod «*pil pil*» style, fillets, of sole or turbo, and any boiled fish.

DRY WHITE WINES «JEREZ» STYLE

Shellfish and oysters.

AN ABUNDANT HARVEST
(Photo Paisajes Españoles.)

WINE REFRAINS

A) From HERNAN NUÑEZ

«Quien es amigo del vino, enemigo es de sí mismo».
He who is wine's friend is enemy of himself.

«Quien pan y vino compra, menester ha bolsa».
He who buys bread and wine needs money in his purse.

«Pan a hartura y vino a mesura».
Eat bread to content and drink wine with measure.

«Pan de trigo, leña de encina y vino de parra, sustentan la casa».
Wheatbread, oakwood and wine from the grapevine sustain the home.

«Pan y vino andan camino, que no mozo garrido».
Bread and wine are good for the road but not a graceful youth.

«Quien come y bien bebe, hace lo que debe».
He who eats and drinks well, does as he should.

«El que mucho vino cena, poco pan almuerza».
He who has supper with much wine, lunches with little bread.

«A buen comer tres veces beber».
To eat well is to drink plenty.

«No vayas sin bota camino, y cuando fueras, no la lleves sin vino».
Don't venture forth without a wineskin and if you should make sure it's full.

«A torrezno de tocino, trago de vino».
With a rasher of bacon, a drink of wine.

«Condición de buen amigo, condición de buen vino».
As a good friend, so is good wine.

«Colérico sanguíneo, borracho fino».
A sanguinery choleric is a shrewd drunkard.

«Después de muerto, ni viña ni huerto».
After death there is neither vineyard nor fruit garden.

«El pez y el cochino, la vida en agua, la muerte en vino».
Fish and pork, life in water and death in wine.

«El buen vino, la aventura trae consigo».
Good wine brings good luck.

«Lo que no va en vino, va en lágrimas y suspiros».
What you don't spend on wine, goes on tears and sighs.

«Mayo come trigo, agosto bebe vino».
In May eat corn, in August drink wine.

B) From DON FRANCISCO RODRIGUEZ MARIN

These refrains are attributed to Don Francisco Rodríguez Marín and furnish a fairly complete collection.

«Cuando el amo está mohino, o le falta pan, o le sobra vino».
When the master is peevish, it is either because he hasn't bread or he has
    had too much wine.

«De las uvas sale el vino, y del vino los desatinos».
From the grapes comes the wine, and from the wine folly and madness.

«De Santo que bebe y come, no fiées, mujeres».
Women, don't trust saints who eat and drink.

«Después de mucho beber, pedir consejos para no caer».
After a lot of drinking, seek advice so as not to fall.

«Dijo el mosquito a la rana: Más vale una gota de mi vino que toda tu agua».
Said the mosquito to the frog: a drop of my wine is worth all of your water.

«Dinero de maldición, el que va a la botica y no al bodegón».
Cursed is the money that is spent on medicine and not on wine.

«Donde el vino suena, no hay cosa secreta».
Where there is wine, there are no secrets.

«Ea, ea, que el que bien lo bebe, bien lo mea».
He who drinks a lot of wine passes a lot of water.

«El buen vinagre, del buen vino sale».
Good vinegar comes from good wine.

«El buen vino, darlo a catar, es darlo a comprar».
«El buen vino, dos gustos da: uno a la nariz y otro al paladar».
Good wine once tasted is then bought.
Good wine gives two pleasures: one to the nose and the other to the palate.

«El buen vino, el pregón llevar consigo».
Good wine speaks for itself.

«El francés bien canta, despúes de remojar la garganta».
The Frenchman sings well after wetting his whistle.

«El buen vino saca al hombre de tino».
Good wine confounds man.

«El secreto y el vino son mortales enemigos: cuando el vino entra, el secreto
se sale afuera».
Secrets and wine are mortal enemies for when wine enters, the secrets are out.

«El vaso cuando está lleno, suena menos».
The glass rings less when it is filled.

«El vino y la mujer, el juicio hacen perder».
Wine and women are the cause of madness.

«El vino y la verdad, sin aguar».
You can't dilute wine and truth.

«En agosto, en las uvas se hace el mosto».
The grape must is made in August.

«En beber y comer, tiento has de tener».
You must be careful in eating and drinking.

«En el vino y en las mujeres, mil pésames y mil placeres».
Regarding wine and women, a thousand sorrows and a thousand pleasures.

«Hijos y vino, buenos amigos».
The familiy and wine make for good friends.

«Hombre beodo, ni cumple palabra ni guarda secreto».
A drunken man, keeps neither secrets nor his word.

«Hombre envinado, hombre desaliñado».
A man steeped in wine, is a man in disarray.

«La comida del mezquino, poca carne y ningún vino».
The mean man's meal has little meat and no wine.

«Las mujeres y el vino, hacen perder el tino».
Women and wine will drive you insane.

«La verdad y el vino son buenos amigos».
Truth and wine are good friends.

«La viña en flor no necesita al viñador ni a su señor».
The blooming vineyard needs neither vine tender nor lord.

«Agua por San Juan, quita vino y no da pan».
Rain at the feast of Saint John spoils the wine and bread harvest.

«Más abriga el jarro que el zamarro».
Better the jug of wine than the sheepskin.

«Más predica un azumbre de vino que diez padres capuchinos».
Four measures of wine livens the soul more than ten capuchin monks.

«Mesa sin vino, no doy por ella un comino».
I wouldn't give a rush for a table without wine.

«Moro fino, come tocino y bebe vino».
The shrewd moor eats bacon and drinks wine

«Mucho te quiero pero no vengas por uvas a mi majuelo».
I love you very much but don't come asking for grapes in my vineyard.

«Ni olla sin tocino ni alegría sin vino».
There is no stewpot without meat neither good spirits without wine.

«No hay tales amigos como mi pan y mi vino».
There are no such friends as bread and wine.

«Y bebe o vete».
Either drink or go away.

«Uvas con queso, saben a beso».
Grapes with cheese taste of kisses.

«Pollo nuevo y vino añejo hacen mozo al hombre viejo».
Young chicken and old wine make the old young again.

«Por la mujer y por el vino, herra el hombre su camino».
Wine and women are the cause of man's erring along life's way.

«Quien buen vino tiene, gusta dos placeres: lo huele y lo bebe».
He who has good wine has two pleasures—smelling and drinking it.

«Quien no gusta del vino, tiene otros peores vicios».
He who doesn't like wine has other vices far worse.

«Quien vino no tiene, agua bebe».
He who has't wine drinks water.

«Tabernero diligente, de quince arrobas hace veinte.
The industrious innkeeper, gets twenty measures out of fifteen.

«Tras buen taco, buen trago».
When you've finished cursing, have a drink.

«Tu vino, tu mujer y tu caballo, para ti solo el gozallos».
Your wine, wife and horse are for you alone to enjoy.

«A los borrachos y a los niños, les protege el Angel».
Drunkards and children are protected by the Angels.

«Bueno es el vino, si el vino es bueno: pero... si el agua es de la fuente pura
y cristalina... mejor es el vino que el agua».
Good is the wine, if the wine is good; but if the water is from a pure crys-
taline source, still the wine is better than the water.

«El vino demasiado, ni guarda secreto ni cumple palabra».
Neither secrets nor words are kept with too much wine.

«Uvas con queso y pan, no hay en el mundo tal manjar».
There is no such food in all the world as grapes with bread and cheese.

«Uvas, sol y aire, y serás rico como nadie».
Grapes air and sun and you will be richer than anyone.

«Viejo que buen vino bebe, tarde muere».
The old man drinking good wine lives to a ripe old age.

«El vino es la leche de los viejos».
Wine is the milk of the old folk.

«Vino de Alaejos (Valladolid), cerca de mí y no lejos».
Wine from Alaejos, I would rather you were near me than far away.

«Vino y mujeres dan más pesares que placeres».
Wine and women give more sorrow than pleasure.

«Viñador, bueno es que sepas que las cepas dan las uvas, y no las uvas las
cepas».
Wine grower, it is well that you know the grape vine produces the grapes
and not the grapes the grapevine.

«Vinador mezquino, dales vino a los que te hacen el vino».
Wine grower, give wine to those that have made the wine for you.

«Yantar sin vino, convite canino».
Food without wine is a dog's meal.

«Siempre que me véis con el agua al cuello, vino quiero».
As long as you see me up to my neck with problems, it's wine I want.

«Donde hay buen vino y la tabernera es guapa, allí se me caiga la capa».
Wherever there is good wine and the tavern maid is pretty, there I will
hang up my coat.

«Donde hay mucho vino, hay poco tino».
Where there is plenty of wine, there is little prudence.

«El pez ha de nadar tres veces: en agua, vino y en aceite».
The fish has to swim three times: in water, in wine and in oil.

«Bebe vino cada día, pero nunca en demasía».
Drink wine each day but never incontinently.

«Bienes lejanos, viña sin amo».
Far away possessions are like a vineyard without a lord.

«Belleza de buen olor, no ha menester pregón».
Beauty of bouquet needs no praising.

«Buen vino tras buen caldo, no tengo bastante boca para alabarlo».
A good wine after supper, I haven't words to praise it.

«Cada cosa en su tiempo y uvas en habiendo».
Each thing in its season and grapes when they are about.

«Comer sin vino, comer mezquino».
To eat without wine is to eat meagrely.

«Comida sin vino no vale un comino».
A meal without wine is not worth a rush.

«Con pan, vino y queso, no hay camino tieso».
With bread, cheese and wine the going is much easier.

WINE ITINERARIES

The touristic routes whether taking in the great monuments of the past, the castles, romanesque churches and basilicas or the windmills of La Mancha, are all very different and some unexplored. The same can be said where the wine routes are concerned and below is a list of them.

THE ALAVA ROUTE

The Alava and Riojana route begins in Vitoria, the capital of the region. It then passes through the towns and villages of Laguardia, Logroño, Navarrete, Fuenmayor, Cenicero, Elciego, Villabuena, Abales, San Vicente de la Sonsierra, Labastida, and Haro.

THE JEREZ ROUTE

The Jerez route starts at Jerez de la Frontera and continues on to Sanlúcar de Barrameda, Chipiona, Rota and Puerto de Santa María.

THE CORDOBA ROUTE

Begins at the capital of the province and passes through Montilla, Aguilar de la Frontera, Moriles, Lucena, Cabra and Dona Mencía.

THE CIUDAD REAL OR LA MANCHA ROUTE

This route follows the same route of Don Quixote into Daimiel, Ciudad Real, Infantes, Argamasilla de Alba, Valdepeñas, Tomelloso and Pedro Muñoz.

«SOLERA» WINES

Courtesy of La Semana Vitivinícola Española.)

THE MURCIA ROUTE

Begins at Jumilla and Yecla and goes through the villages of Bullas and Ricote.

THE PALENCIA ROUTE

In preparation.

THE PONTEVEDRA ROUTE

There are three of them:

a. The *Albariño* route begins at Vigo or Pontevedra and passes through Mosteiro, Ribadumia and Meis, then into the village of Cambados and through Sanjenjo.
b. *El Rosal* route starts from Vigo or Pontevedra and goes through the Miñor valley, Bayona, La Guardia, El Rosal, Tomillo, Tuy and Porriño.
c. The *Condado* route starts at Condado and goes through Puenteareas, Mondariz, Villasobroso and Salvatierra de Miño.

THE TERUEL ROUTE

It starts at San Martín del Río and passes through Báguena, Burbáguena, Calamocha, Monreal del Campo, Muniesa, Mas de las Matas, La Ginebrosa, Fuentespalda, Valderrobres, and Cretas.

THE VALENCIA ROUTE

a. Through the Albaida valley. It begins in Valencia and continues through Játiva, Puebla del Duc, Cuatrotonda and Gandía.
b. Through Cheste, Chiva Turs and Carlet.
c. Through Liria, Villar del Arzobispo, Chelva Pedralva and Casinos.
d. It starts at Valencia, and passes through Cheste, Requena, Utiel, returning by the same route or through Pantano del Busco, Villar del Arzobispo, Casinos and Liria.

THE VALLADOLID ROUTE

a. The *claret route* passes through Fuensaldaña, Mucientes and Cigales.
b. The *white wine route* takes in Serrada, La Seca, Rueda and Nava del Rey.
c. The *red wine route* includes Tudela del Duero, Sardón and Peñafiel. Along this route are found the very well known bodegas of *Vega Sicilia*.

THE RIOJA ROUTE

In the Rioja, two routes have been traced from east and west of Logroño. The first leaves the west of the capital and passes through Laguardia, Elciego, San Vicente de la Sonsierra, Haro, Cenicero, Navarrete and Fuenmayor.

The eastern route starts in Logroño and goes through Alcanadre, Autol, Aldeanueva de Ebro, Alfaro, Calahorra and San Adrián.

Along the mentioned routes, it is common to call in on the bodegas of illustrious rank and try the old vintage wines.

THE WINE
AND THE VINEYARD

Part Two.

ANDALUCIA: WINE AND SUN

Oh noble nectar of Jerez,
Who can resist your white praise,
You who give inspiration to the weak, joy to the sad,
To the sick, health and strength to the old.

GASPAR NUÑEZ DE ARCE.

XERES-JEREZ-
SHERRY

The name alone is like a banner. This incomparable wine is one of the few whose reputation has extended beyond local frontiers to become internationally known, indeed, universal. It is the soil, climate, location and environment generally that have made the sherry wines unique and inimitable. The district of Jerez has come to have so many associations that any personal theories and philosophies concerning Andalucía are bound to fall short of the mark. There has not been a traveller or historian interested in local customs and Spanish civilisation who has not endeavoured to express an original view of Jerez. José María Pemán tells us that Andalucía is rather like an enormous and illustrious family whose second surnames because of the ties and interrelationships have varied infinitely. Manuel de Falla gives us, best of all, a most convincing interpretation of the real depth and style of life of this intriguing land.

The wine, the bull, and **the horse** form A TRILOGY which best symbolise the *way of life* of these people whose fame has spread throughout the world. Jerez de la Frontera epitomises and is the quintessence of Baja Andalucía (Lower Andalucía). Its purest expression, however, is to be found in the cultivation and making of wine.

JEREZ

Sherry-yes, but which one? *Fino, Oloroso, Raya, Amontillado?* Like the *«Cante Hondo»*, not one of these will give precedence to the other and like the *flamenco*, there are very few people who really know and can appreciate these great wines.

There are a series of factors such as the composition of the soil, veil of the yeasts, and *«la Flor»* which go into the making of this immortal wine.

Jerez-Sherry making begins where the triangle of Jerez de la Frontera, Puerto de Santa María and Sanlúcar de Barrameda forms, and also includes the districts of Chiclana, Puerto Real, Rota and Trebujena. Here the noble *Palomino, Palomino fino,* and *Pedro Ximénez* vines are grown as well as the *Albillo, Mantua de Sanlúcar, Mollar, Moscatel, Calena* and *Peruna*.

The landmarks of the famous triangle form the **Zona del Jerez Superior.**

Let us have a look at the kinds of wine to be found. The *fino* or select sherry of 15º to 17º is pale dry and light. Its aroma is delicate. With the passing of time, it is converted into an *amontillado* having a bitter almond flavour and golden colour. Its full body and age give it a hazelnut flavour The *oloroso* is stronger, varying between 18º to 20º, less pungent but more aromatic. With time, its colour, like the *amontillado*, becomes golden. It is very much like the *Palo Cortado,* being a happy medium between the *amontillado* and the *oloroso*. However, it is not so fine and aromatic having more body and colour and about the same alcoholic content.

Finally there is the *manzanilla* wine which is much softer and feminine.

THE JEREZ DISTRICT

The official producing sherry area includes the province of Cádiz, which for a long time has cultivated vineyards whose grapes are used in the making of this wine. Within this area, the finest production is found in Jerez de la Frontera, Puerto de Santa María and Sanlúcar de Barrameda where the soil is largely of the *albariza* type.

THE SOIL AND THE VINEYARD

The types of soil most characteristic of the district of Jerez are:

1. *Albariza*—hard and marly ground having a high proportion of limestone.
2. *Barros*—dark and heavy earth.
3. *Arenas*—sandy ground.

As a general rule, the tougher it is for a plant to survive the better will be the quality of the wine even though it is less. Quality and quantity are invariably at odds with each other especially in the case of wine. Of the three kinds of soil listed above, that of least apparent fertility i. e. the «albariza», produces the «Jerez Fino» or fine sherry.

THE VINEYARD DISTRICTS

AREA	DISTRICT	CLASE OF WINE
Jerez	Anina	*Finos*
	Balbaina	*Finos*
	Los Tercios	
	Macharnudo	*Amontillado*
	Carrascal	*Olorosos*
Sanlucar	Miraflores	*Manzanilla*
	Torrebreda	
Chipiona & Rota	Madronales	*Muscateles and sweet wines*
	Tehigo	*Vino de color*

The vineyards recognised by the authorities, respecting the production of **Jerez** are the *Palomino, Pedro Ximénez, Perruno, Fino, Albillo, Cano Cazo, Garrido Fino, Mantúo, Pilas and Rey.* In the soils of «*albariza*» the commonest vine used in making the **fino** is the *Palomino.* The vine cultivated to make the best **sweet wine** is the *Pedro Ximénez.* It should not be forgotten that in the 19th century Spain was attacked by the «phylloxera» pest and very few grapevines survived. The present day stocks are all native but

with the difference that they have been grafted with American vines that are inmune to the desease.

THE DIFFERENT
CLASSES OF WINE

It is the very sherry blenders themselves with the seal of Domecq on their bottles who can best tell us about their wines. It is a story worth knowing and only the people from Jerez really know how to tell it.

The sherry wines are divided into two main families: *Finos* and *Olorosos.* These vary according to their age and quality. Every brand is fundamentally *seco* and if a sweet wine is required, it is obtained by adding wine alcohol. This addition of alcohol is called ~~el cabeceo.~~ 'encabezado.

The *finos* are dry and light. They are of a palid gold colour, delicate and fresh on the palate. The *amontillados* are old *finos* but with more body and class. They have an amber colour and a smooth dry smell, while the *olorosos* have more body and are generally stronger, heavier and darker in colour before the *cabeceo.* The medium sweet *medio dulce* or mild *abocados* are *olorosos* mixed with sweet wines which are so popular with the northern Europeans. The *cream* sherries are a blend of medium sweet and mild wines with the Pedro Ximénez giving it a smooth velvet quality.

BLENDING AND
OTHER PARTICULARS

As has been said already, the district of Jerez has a very special soil and ideal conditions of climate for the making of wine: a lot of rain in winter and the springtime and continous warm weather and radiant sun in the summer. Nearly all of the vintages are good in quantity as well as quality.

THE FERMENTATION

«After several hours in the bodegas the ferments (yeasts) and the fuzz on the grapeskins starts off the first fermentation. It is at the time of the first fermentation lasting 3 to 4 days that nearly all the sugar is turned into alcohol. Then the slow and second fermentation takes place, which goes on until December or January. At this stage, the opaque fermented juices have become clear and converted into wine.

THE
«FLOR DE JEREZ»

Suddenly the new wine produces the «*Flor de Jerez*» or Sherry Flower, a unique phenomenon characteristic of the *finos*. The «*flor*» is a white film of yeasts cells that cover the surface of the wine in Spring and Autumn of each year. The «*flor*» absorbs the oxygen from the atmosphere, protects the wine from the microbes in the vinegar and gives the *finos* their unique character.

CLASSIFICATION OF
WINES

In the first three months of the year, the new wine is classified and this requieres skill and mastery. The steward of the bodega dips the *venencia* a long cane with a silver cup shaped spoon at the end, into the barrel taking care not to disturb the surface and takes out a sample of the new wine. This is then classified according to its aroma and each barrel is marked with chalk.

THE «CABECEO»

After the wines have been classified they are **fortified** or *encabezados*. To the *olorosos*, for example, wine alcohol is added to bring them up to 16° or 17°; the *finos* to 15°. A degree higher would kill the «*flor*». Most wines are fortified and their alcoholic content boosted up for export purposes.

THE «CRIADERAS»
OR NURSERY
«SOLERAS»

Each barrel ages separately in yearly vintages called «anadas», which are the wines that make up the «criadera» or «nursery solera». Here, the Sherry settles, becomes old and smooth, and within a year or two, when it is mature enough, is transferred to the «solera».

THE SOLERA

As the oldest Sherry has the peculiarity of absorbing completely the younger wine, the Sherry makers blend them in the «soleras» which are found in rows or tiers in the «bodegas». The Sherry, when it has aged and is ready for drinking, is then taken from the bottom row. Only a third from each butt is taken out and this quantity is filled with wine from the second row that is not so old. These barrels, in turn, are mixed and blended with these

RÍO GUADALQUIVIR

TREBUJENA

SANLÚCAR DE BARRAMEDA

Miraflores

Macharnudo

Chipiona

Torrebreba

Añina

Carrascal

Madroñales

Balbaina

JEREZ DE LA FRONTERA

Tehigo

Rota

Los Tercios

PUERTO DE SANTA MARÍA

RÍO GUADALETE

CÁDIZ

PUERTO REAL

SAN FERNANDO

Nicolás Jonas. 1970

CHICLANA DE LA FRONTERA

ZONAS DE PRODUCCIÓN
JEREZ~XÉRÈX~SHERRY
NARANJA = *Albarizas*
AMARILLO = *Barros y Arenas*

JEREZ-XEREX-SHERRY
(Drawing by Nicolas Jonas.)

CLASSIFICATION OF SHERRY WINES

FINOS

Manzanillas finas
- Colour: Very pale yellow.
- Taste: Very subtle and slightly bitter.
- Smell: Very delicate.

Manzanillas pasadas
- Colour: Topaz.
- Taste: Succulently subtle and bitter. It has an olive flavour.
- Smell: Very smooth and strong.

Finos (Palmas)
- Colour: Topaz.
- Taste: Very dry. Almond flavour.
- Smell: Smooth and pungent.

Amontillados
- Colour: Ambar-Topaz colour.
- Taste: Very dry. Almond-Hazelnut flavour.
- Smell: Very biting and incisive.

OLOROSOS

Rayas
- Colour: Dark gold.
- Taste: Tasty but common.
- Smell: Intense.

Olorosos
- Colour: Dark gold.
- Taste: Substantial and nutty.
- Smell: Intense but not very strong.

Palos cortados
- Colour: Amber.
- Taste: Substantial and dry.
- Smell: Intense and sharp.

DULCES

Pedro Ximénez
- Colour: Mahogany.
- Taste: Very sweet.
- Smell: Raisin fruit.

Muscatel
- Colour: Gold to mahogany, according to age.
- Taste: Sweet.
- Smell: Unusual.

of the third row. The highest row or tier is then filled with the «criadera».
Through this process, the «solera» Sherry maintains its constant high quality.

**«PAGOS» OF THE
SHERRY WINES**

The Sherry *pagos* (~~wine-growing areas~~ *crus*) can be divided into three groups:
The first is found on the last flank of the town where the land in the
main is of sand or clay. The most important of these *pagos* is Montealegre.

The second includes other *pagos* also near Jerez itself, but stretching
to the southwest. Here the soil is of a superior quality for here abound the
albarizas, and *bujeos*.

Finally, the third and most important group in extension and quality,
consists of the *pagos* called the *afuera* which stretch in an unbroken line from
the northeast to the southwest. These are the best *pagos* in the area: —*Carrascal, Macharnudo, Añina,* and *Balbaina,* which have an average land
area of some 1300 «*aranzadas*» for each *pago*. This last group makes up the
greater part of the **Jerez Superior** area.

**THE AREAS OF
JEREZ SUPERIOR**

Below is an alphabetic list of all the «pagos» with land specifications drawn
up by Pemartín (¹), with the following letters to indicate the types of soil.

A, *albariza;* B, *barros;* b, *bujeos;* L, *lustrillos;* these which are marked R,
denote the land used for other crops, and the U, the lands absorbed through
urban expansion.

*Abiertas de Caulina, a (r); Albadalejo, a (R); Alcántara, A; Almoca-
dén, A; Amarquillo, b; Anaferas, A; Arboledilla, a (R); Balbaina, A; Barbadillo, a (R); Barriel, a (R); Bohas, B; Bonaina, A* and *b; Bonete, A;
Buena Vista, a (R); Buruguena, A; Cabeza de la Aceña, a (R); Cabreste-
ra, a (R); Calderera, A; Canaleja, a* and *B; Candelero, A; Cantarranas, A*
and *B; Cañada del Carrillo, A* and *B; Capirete, A; Calahorra, A; Carrascal, A;
Catalana, a (R); Cerfate, A; Cerro del Mármol, A; Cerro del Pelado, A; Cerro
de Obregón, A; Cerro de Orbaneja, A; Cerro de Páez, B; Cerro de Santiago, A;
Cibullo, A; Clavería, A; Colores, b; Corchuelo, L; Cortadero, A* and *b; Cruz
de las Calalleras, B (U); Cruz del Husillo, A; Cuadrados, A; Cuadrod, A* and *b;
Cuartillo, A* and *L; Cuatro Norias, B; Culebra, B; Charcón, B; Desampara-
dos, a (U); Doña Juana, A; Doña Rosa, B; Ducha, A* and *b; Espartina, A*
and *B; Flamenco, a (R); Fuente de la Teja, a (R); Galera, B; Gallega, A;
Garrido, a (R); Geraldino, a (R); Gigalbín, A* and *B; Gibalcón, A; Granja, B;
Jarreta, B; Laguna del Jabonero, B* and *a (u); Lárgalo, B* and *a; Las Tablas, A;
Lazo, B; León, A; Llano del Moral, B* and *a; Llano de San Blas, b; Machar-
nudo, A; Majada Alta, A; Mancebía, b (U); Manjón, B* and *a; Manzanillos, A;
Mariañez, A; Maricuerda, A; Marihernández, A; Montana, A; Martizano, A;
Matacardillo, B; Membrillar, B* and *a; Miraflores, B* and *a (U); Monte-
alegre, B* and *a; Noriega, b; Palmosa, b; Panesa, A; Pantanar, B* and *a;*

(¹)   Author of the important book *Diccionario del Vino de Jerez.*

Parpalana, A; Parrilla, L and B; Pedro Díaz, B and a; Pedro Vela, B and a; Perlirón, B and a; Pelona, B and a; Peonías, A; Peral del Cangrejo, B and a (U); Percebá, B and a (R); Picadueñas, B and A (U); Pie del Rey, B; Piedra de Mirabal, B and a; Pinar, B and a; Plantalina, L and b; Pocillos, B and a; Pozo de la Astera, A and b; Pozo de Ramos, B and a; Puerto Escondido, L; Quemadero, b; Quinta, b (U); Ramona, A and b; Roboatún, B and a (U); Ruiz Díaz, a and b; Salinillas, A; San Antonio, a (U); San José, B and a; San Julián, A; Santa Fe, B and a (U); Serrana, B and a (U); Sida, A; Sierra de San Cristóbal (L); Solete, B and a; Tabajeta, A and b; Tizón, A and b; Tocina, A and b; Torre de Cera, A; Torrox, A and b; Ullate, L; Valcargado, L and b; Valdepajuela, A and b; Valle de San Benito, B and a (U); Vallesequillo, B ans a (U); Vega del Moscatel, b and a; Vegas de Elvira, B and a (U); Vicos, A and b; Zarzuela, A and b.

THE «PAGOS» OF SANLUCAR DE BARRAMEDA

The *pagos* of the district of Sanlúcar de Barrameda, whose average land area is less than that of the district of Jerez, spread out and surround the city from the northeast to the west and there are some isolated «pagos» to the southeast and to the south. The inland «pagos» are *albariza* and those near the sea and along the coast are of «*arenas*». The former are included in the area of Jerez Superior, and the latter suitable for the blending of *manzanillas*.

Below is a list of the *pagos* of Sanlúcar de Barrameda:

Alegría, A; Algaida, A; Algarroba, A; Amarguillo, A; Amores, B; Arboledilla, A; Armijo, A; Atalaya, A; Barrameda, B; Bohorca, A; Cabeza de Vaca, B; Cabezudo, A; Callejuela, A; Cañada Garrotal, A; Capuchinos, B; Carnero, A; Casa del Moral, A; Casilla del Fiscal, A; Cementerio, B; Collanta, A; Coronado, A; Cortijillo, B; Cuadradillo, A; Cuesta Blanca, A; Custodia, a; Charruado Pardo, A; Dehesilla, B; El Rocío, A; El Señor, a; Elvorilla, A; Frediani, A; Galerilla, B; Galvana, A; Gallarda, B; Hato de la Carne, B; Hazo del Pozo, A; Hornillo, A; Huevo Blanco, B; Jara, a; La Cañada, A; La Heredera, A; Las Cuevas, B; Las Vegas, B; Látigo, A; Madre del Agua, a; Maestre, A; Maestrillo, A; Mahína, A; Majadilla, B; Majuelo Martínez, A; Marimacho, A; Marquesita, A; Martín Angel, A; Mazacote, a; Mediadora, A; Minas, a; Miradamas, B; Miraflores, A; Monte Olivere, A; Munive, A; Norieta, B; Palmosa, A; Papa Levante, B; Pastrana, A; Pinar del Duque, a; Pozo Nuevo, a; Punta del Aguila, a; Relojera, A; Remata Caudales, A; Rinconada Cantero, B; Rompeserones, B; Salto del Grillo, B; Sambordón, A; San Jerónimo, A; Sanlúcar el Viejo, B; Santa Brígida, B; Santa Tecla, B; Santillana, A; Santo Dios, B; Serrana, B; Tiznado, A; Vetade de la Serrana, B.

THE «PAGOS» OF EL PUERTO DE SANTA MARIA

In this region of Puerto de Santa María there are also *pagos* of *albariza* included in the area of **Jerez Superior,** and other sand or *arena pagos* along the coast. They are:

Almajar, a; Balbaina, A; Berbén, a; Cantarranas, a; El Aguila, a; Fuenterrabía, a; Garañina, A; Juncal de Villarana, a; Los Tercios, A; Mochicle, a.

OTHER «PAGOS»   In the Puerto Real there are two *pagos: El Marquesado of albariza* and *arenas*, and *Los Arquillos* of arenas exclusively.

In Chipiona, there are some *pagos* of *albariza* and some of *barro* soil. Here, in this area, a few vines of *Palomino Fine* variety survived the phylloxera disease and solved the problem of the American grafts.

The following is a list of *pagos* indicating the soil type of each:

Cercada de la Regla, B; Cerro de Colón, A; Copina, B; Chipionilla, B; El Benito, A; El Faginado, B; Espantamero, B; Esparragosa, B; Falón, B; Galera, B; Granadillo, B; La Lechera, B; La Loma, B; Los Rizos, B; Miranda, B; Monte Oruco, B; Montijo, a; Niño de Oro, a; Alivar, A; Pago Llano, B; Platera, A; Quince Pinos, B; Rincón Malillo, B; Santo Domingo, B; Talona, B; Toril Mamelo, B; Valdeconejo, a; Valdivielso, B; Ventisquero, a; Vicaría, a.

The three pagos in the district of *Rota* have *albariza* soil and they are: *Barragán, Ledesma,* and *Torre Breva.*

In *Trebujena* there are also some excellent *pagos* of *albariza* and *barro: Alcántara, A; Arroyo de las Palomas, B; Dehesa, A; La Carrera, A; La Catalana, B; La Noria, B; La Rosa, B; Mirabalete, B; Redondón, A.*

In *Chiclana de la Frontera*, all three classes of soil are found: *Carrascal, a; Claverán, B; El Pleito, a; Las Canteruelas, B; Pago del Humo, B; Pinar de María, B; Ramiro Gil, B; Rosalejo, A.*

And in the district of *Lébrija*, whose southern part reaches the wine producing area of Jerez there are two *pagos* of *albariza: Las Pedreras* and *Cerro Cordero,* and one of *arena, Pago Dulce.*

EXPORTERS AND VINTAGERS IN JEREZ DE LA FRONTERA

Alejandro Gordón.
Antonio Muñoz Muñoz.
Antonio Parra Guerrero.
A. R. Valdespino, S. A.
Barón de Algar & Cía.
Bertola, S. A.
Bobadilla & Cía.
Bodegas de S. Guerrero Benítez.
Bodegas Marqués del Mérito, S. A.
Cayetano del Pino y Cía., S. L.
Croft Jerez, S. A.
Emilio Lustau, S. A.

Federico de la Calle.
Fernando Carrasco Sagastizábal.
Fernando García Delgado, Sucesor.
Francisco Espinosa de los Monteros.
Garvey, S. A., Bodegas de San Patricio.
González Biass & Cía., S. L.
Herederos del Marqués del Real Tesoro, S. A.
Hijos de Agustín Blázquez, S. A.
Hijos de Fernando Fernández-Gao & González.
Javier Vergara Gordón.
José Bustamante, S. L.
José de Soto, S. A.
José Pemartín & Cía., S. A.
José Romero P. Gil.
J. Ruiz & Cía.
Luis Pérez Lobato.
Mackenzie & Co. Ltd.
Manuel Antonio de la Riva, S. A.
Florido Hermanos.
Heredeos de Argüeso, S. A.
Hijos de A. Pérez Mejía.
Hijos de Jiménez Varela, S. L.
Hijos de Rainera Pérez Marín, S. A.
Manuel de Argüeso, S. A.
Manuel García Monge, S. A.
Pedro Romero, S. A.
Viuda de Esteban, Bozzano.
C. A. Y. D. S. A.

EXPORTERS AND VINTAGERS IN CADIZ

Lacave & Cía.
Miguel M. Gómez.
Manuel Guerrero & Cía.
Manuel Misa, Sucesor.
M. Gil Galán, S. A.
M. Gil Luque.
Miguel Cala Ramírez.
Palomino & Vergara, S. A.
Pedro Domecq, S. A.
Rafael O'Neales.
Rafael Ortega Palencia.
R. C. Ivison.
Sánchez Romate Hermanos, S. A.
Sandeman Hermanos & Cía., S. R. C.

Tomás Rivero & Hermanos, S. L.
Tomás & Francisco Afab Caballero.
Williams & Humbert, Ltd.
Wisdom & Warter, Ltd.
Zoilo Ruiz Mateos, S. A.

EXPORTERS AND VINTAGERS IN PUERTO DE SANTA MARIA

Bodegas A. Sancho, S. A.
Carlos & Javier de Terry, S. L.
Cuvillo & Cía.
Duff Gordon & Cía.
Fernando A. de Terry, S. R. C.
Hijos de Jiménez Varela, S. L.
John Williams Burdon.
José de la Cuesta, Sucesor.
Luis Caballero, S. A.
Osborne & Cía., S. A.

EXPORTERS AND VINTAGERS IN SANLUCAR DE BARRAMEDA

Antonio Barbadillo, S. A.
Bodegas de los Infantes de Orleáns Borbón, S. A. E.
Carlos Otaolaurruchi, S. R. C.

EXPORTATION FIGURES
AND OTHER STATISTICS OF THE SHERRY WINES

Sherry wine exports reached a record figure of 699,737.8 hectolitres in 1969. In the past decade, the Sherry wines sales abroad have doubled, since in 1960 only 332,076 hectolitres were exported. Morever, 1969 has not been a good year for exports as there has been only a marginal increase of 3.31 % over the 1968 figure, the lowest growth rate figure of the 60's.

Great Britain is still the biggest customer and imports 409,112.3 hecto-litres which makes up 58.46 % of the total exportation. Nevertheless, her purchases in 1969 were less than those of 1968.

Holland comes second importing 148,329 hectolitres; third, Denmark with 30,900 and finally Germany with 20,303.

The draw back to the Sherry wine sales, is the fact that only 8.20 % of the exports, that is to say, 7,393.4 hectolitres, are bottled, while the remaining 91.80 %, which represents 642,344.3 hectolitres, is sold in bulk to be bottled abroad later. This explains why there is so much reexportation in certain countries, particularly in the case of Great Britain which sells vast amounts to the United States.

SHERRY «THE
AMEFICAN WAY»

The Americans have discovered a new method of making Sherry wine in seven days. Dr. James A. Cook, head of the Department of Oenology at the University of California, says that they can produce a Sherry that can compete with any European kind at their current market prices.

Dr. Cook is a non drinker, however, and this fact explains everything. The comments of Doctor Cook are interesting where he says: «With a ty-pical American impatience we have accelerated a process which in An-dalucía would take 15 to 20 years to complete. The Spanish method con-sists of allowing the wine to mellow gradually and naturally. We have achieved the same results in only 7 days shaking the ferments up vigo-rously».

If this were really true, and the wine industry were to prosper along American lines, as Dr. Cook says it would, the 45 million vines from the *pagos* of *Macharnudo, Balbaina, and Añina,* as well as the surrounding areas that reach beyond Trebujena would have a very precarious future indeed and so would the many vineyards that grow along the left bank of the Guadalquivir: The *Palomino, Castellana Mantúa,* which thrive as nowhere else and in no other ground to produce the real Sherry. For example, the *Albero* sherry is the fruit of the *albariza* soils which have a very special composition of chalk and limestone.

Good stock, give me good stock *«Dámelo de raza»* as the saying goes. It is the good stock or solera that counts the most in the long slow blending process. The topaz colour and almond taste, slightly buttered, smooth and delicate flavour is characteristic of the FINE sherry.

The AMONTILLADO, lightly almond coloured and having a fruity flavour, is a select and palid wine. Its high alcoholic content is not at first very apparent since it is a very carefully prepared wine. While the OLOROSO has a wider range of colour varying from burnt topaz, orange and scarlet. Being harder and drier, it leaves on the tip of the tongue and palate a sweet after-flavour. Its very name «Oloroso» meaning scented reveals its fragrant aroma.

* * *

Why in the University of Davis have they made only one sherry wine? They could well increase their production to include the whole range of Andalucian wines for example the wines of *Condado de Niebla* extending to Moguer, which make a young golden wine drunk by most of the people of Baja Andalucía and in Sevilla where it is particularly popular.

It is a pity our American friends have forgotten about the MONTILLA and MORILES wines to the south of Córdoba, including *Aguilar de la Frontera, Lucena, Cabra, Doña Mencía,* and *Puente Genil.*

How is it they haven't discovered the special *Pedro Ximénez* grape? It is said that the first Pedro Ximénez vine to take root in the south of Spain was brought by a soldier campaigning with Charles V near the Rhine in Flanders.

There is another kind of the *Pedro Ximénez* wine made from raisins normally taken with the dessert.

It is very clear then why the Californian enologists have confined themselves to one type of wine, the renowned «Sherry» of international fame. Otherwise the amount of cobalt and radioactivity needed to produce these other wines so quickly would be inmense.

PEDRO XIMENEZ GRAPES
AND A FINE SHERRY WINE

(Photo Guillén Franco.)

HUELVA
AD THE WINES OF CONDADO

«The Shoreland of the Three Caravels»

Wine, sentiments, guitars, and poetry.
Are the songs of my land
Songs...
Who sings of songs sings of Andalucia...

MANUEL MACHADO.

EL CONDADO

With a little intuition and imagination it is not difficult to understand why the Trebujena vines grow along the very river banks of the Guadalquivir where right beside them the fierce wild bulls graze, and marshland and vineyard blend together.

From Almonte, where the **cofradías** of the «*Blanca Paloma*» or the ‹*Virgen del Rocío*» gather together on certain feast days, sea upon sea of grape vines come into view: *Bollullos del Condado, La Palma del Condado, Niebla, San Juan del Puerto, Rociana, Villalba del Alcor* and other municipalities such as: *Chucena, Hinojos, Lucena, del Puerto, Villarrasa,* coming down into *Moguer* and *Palos de la Frontera.*

The vines are reflected in the waters of the Río Tinto, opposite the beautiful bridge of Punta Umbría. Not far off lies the town of *Manzanilla* and *La Palma.*

The Guadalquivir unites rather than divides the bordering provinces of *Cádiz* and *Huelva.* In the latter province, apart from the ordinary wines of 11° to 13°, the select and solera wines are made of 15° to 16° and later reach 18° to 20°:

These wines have always enjoyed a great reputation and continue to do so despite their little publicity. Advertising them is still really unnecessary as their prestige alone is enough to sell their new and solera vintages. A large quantity of the *Condado* wines are left to age in bottles and are labled accordingly. Their ageing due to the ideal conditions of climate and soil, gives them certain characteristics not unlike the Sherries.

The real truth of the matter, however, lies in the traditional «savoir faire» or **gracia** in obtaining the base which later on with the ageing process will go into the making of the FINOS, MANZANILLAS and AMONTILLADOS and give colour to the other wines. This is a Spanish custom known as making the «*arropes*». A concentrated and fermented must is held to the naked flame until it becomes almost like caramel and is then added to the dark bodied wine, and this in turn is used to age and ~~cover~~ other wines.

                                      to colour

THE
DENOMINACION
DE ORIGEN
«HUELVA»

The DENOMINACION DE ORIGEN-HUELVA includes the lands of the old *Condado de Niebla*, found along the banks of the Guadalquivir and the Río Tinto touching Moguer and Monasterio de La Rábida and the districts of Niebla and Palma del Condado.

The vineyard area is 56,938 acres, of which 1,688 are used for the growing of eating grapes. The last vintage taken in 1968 was calculated at 650,000 hectolitres.

The wine producing area comprises the following municipal districts: *La Palma del Condado, Villalba del Alcor, Manzanilla, Chucena, Hinojos, Lucena del Puerto, Almonte, Bolullos, Par del Condado, Villarasa, Bonares, Moguer, San Juan del Puerto, Trigueros, Beas, Niebla, Palos de la Frontera* and *Rociana del Condado*.

WINE NURSERIES

La Palma del Condado, Rociana del Condado, Almonte, San Juan del Puerto and Villalba del Alcor, are the only areas where the wine is matured.

GRAPE VARIETIES

The grape varieties used in the making of these wines are the so called *Palomino or Listán, Mantúa, Garrido Fino, Pedro Luis* and *Pedro Ximénez*.

The characteristics of the wines under the «*Denominación de Origen*»-*Huelva* are as follows:

CLASS OF WINE	COLOUR	ALCOHOLIC CONTENT	DEGREE BAUMÉ
Ordinary wines	Very pale	11º - 14º	
«*Finos*» and «*Palmas*»	Pale, straw	14º - 16º	
«*Amontillado*»	Gold	15º - 17º	
«*Rayas*»	Amber	17º - 20º	
«*Soleras*»	Palid, amber	16º - 20º	

CLASS OF WINE	COLOUR	ALCOHOLIC CONTENT	DEGREE BAUMÉ
«Olorosos dulces»	Amber	15º - 20º	2º - 6º
«Olorosos secos»	Amber	16º - 20º	
«Dulces» and «Mistelas»	Gold	15º - 20º	5º - 12º
Dark Coloured wines	Dark	8º - 18º	8º - 14º
Concentrated	Dark	—	32º - 40º

The ordinary wines vary from 11º to 14º and are recognised by their pale colour.

The strong wines of very dark colour vary from 8º to 18º and the very strong, dark concentrated wines go to make up an extraordinary reserve used for «coupage» or blending. The *Bollullos* and *Palma del Condado* wines have always been in demand, especially for customers abroad.

Speaking of the old vintage wine of Huelva, there are many writers who quote the fifth Chapter of the Gospel Saint Luke: *«None who drank the old vintage wine wanted to drink the new, because it is said: the old is better».*

Many of these wines, coming from *albariza* soils and valuable as maturing and vintage wines, are stored away in the oak barrels of the Sherry soleras, until they are bottled for consumption in the markets abroad.

PRODUCERS & EXPORTERS INCLUDED IN THE «DENOMINACION DE ORIGEN—HUELVA»

Viuda e Hijos de Fco. Galán.	San Bartolomé, 8. Villalba del Alcor.
Casa Lazo, S. A.	San Juan del Puerto.
Bodegas Pichardo, S. A.	C. M. Morales, 5. La Palma del Condado.
Bodegas Ramos.	General Mola, 68. Bollullos del Condado.
Don Celedonio Ferrero Conca.	Teniente Molina, 19. Rociana del Condado.
Hijos de Francisco Vallejo, S. L.	M. Astry, 2. Bollullos del Condado.
Bodegas Valdera.	General Mola, 53. Bollullos del Condado.
Don Juan Oliveros Perea.	Avenida Coronación, 28.
Sucesores de A. Genovés.	Almonte, 8. Bollullos del Condado.
Bodegas Daza.	Calvo Sotelo, 20. Chucena.
Don Juan Camacho Camacho.	P. Vacas, 33. Bollullos del Condado.
Bodegas Clemente.	José Antonio, 16. Bollullos del Condado.
Don Miguel Salas Acosta.	Bollullos del Condado.
Don Fco. Camacho Camacho.	P. Vacas, 14. Bollullos del Condado.
Hijos de Julián Espinosa, S. R. C.	Apartado 3. La Palma del Condado.
Bodegas Salas.	Huelva, 28. La Palma del Condado.
José y Miguel Martín Alvarez.	Almaras, 40. Bollullos del Condado.
Don Alonso Valdayo Terriza.	M. Astray, 31. Bollullos del Condado.
Bodegas Iglesias.	R. Carranza, 29. Bollullos del Condado.
Bodegas Oro, S. L.	General Mola. Bollullos del Condado.
Bodegas Caparrós.	R. Carranza. Bollullos del Condado.
Don José Calve Cadaval.	P. Larios, 10. Bollullos del Condado.
Don Manuel Perea Díaz.	C. de Niebla, 1. Bollullos del Condado.

Don Antonio Villarán Ramos.   San Vicente, 25. Bollullos del Condado.
E. Flores Macías & Cía.   Cánovas, 5. Moguer.
Don José Saucí Díaz.   R. Carranza, 35. Bollullos del Condado.
Don Francisco Andrade Zarza.   Avenida de Portugal. Bollullos del Condado.
Bodegas Espina.   Santa Ana, 1. Bollullos del Condado.
Bodegas «Santa Fe».   Almaraz, 40. Bollullos del Condado.
Don Diego Calvo Mantis.   R. Carranza, 37. Bollullos del Condado.

VINTAGE TIME. THE FIRST MUSTS
(Photo Guillén Franco.)

MONTILLA - MORILES

«Give wine to the embittered spirits»

The Sierra de Cabra is rightly called the «*Andalucian Balcony*» for the land falls sharply away in a symphony of rocks and colours like the crests of waves in a stormy sea and finally is confounded with the rugged wild country of the Alpujarras and the Sierra Morena.

To the northeast stretches some 100 miles of plainland perhaps inviting the visitor to set foot in the open plainland of Córdoba or go up into the Sierra de Jaén, Alcaudete, Martos to the very expanses of the Meseta or Table land itself. To the east lies Granada and the snows of Sierra Nevada and on the distant horizon the peaks of Mulhacén and Veleta are just visible.

All around or «*a la redonda*» as the local people say the *vega* unfolds in all its diversity of sierras and foothills, farm and woodland, olive orchards and vineyards, gardens and villages. There is Rute, for example, strong and stout and as hard as its alcohol; the white grapes of the flat open country of Moriles and Montilla and the heavy scent from the bodegas; the thick hedges enclosing the lovely «alamedas» of Puente Genil.

It is quite unnecessary to make a list of the favourite wines in the area as the MON-TILLA and MORILES are to be found nearly everywhere. One glass is enough to prove its class and to appreciate its grace and virtue. Like the *Sherry* and *Rioja* wines they are stocked in any good restaurant that prides itself as such. In England particularly, they enjoy a reputation unparalleled elsewhere, and in fact, are just as easy to come by as a good whisky and are drunk with very much the same ritual at certain hours during the day.

The *Pedro Ximénez* vine, from which this wine is made, has always been the main stock in the Spanish Embassies.

The wine production of Córdoba is very high and its wines are strong fragrant and select.

They have a slightly bitter taste and more body than the sherry. In so saying, there is nothing more agreeable than having a glass at any time of the day and on any occasion. In *Alcolea*, found very near the capital, as in *Hornachuelos* and *Palma del Río*, the *Montilla* and *Moriles* wines are taken at meal times, and with light snacks.

From Córdoba southward, all of the districts make excellent wines. *Cabra, Lucena, Doña Mencía, Montarque, Puente Genil, Priego and Rute* need only to be tried to prove it. *Rute*, moreover, makes a very fine «**aguardiente**».

Under the name of *Montilla* and *Moriles*, whose pale and topaz wines are fragrant as they are select and bitter, it would be only right and fitting to include in our tour the wines of *Montarque, Puente Genil* and *Rute*, which also makes the famous «**anises**».

The quality of these wines is attributed by both wine blenders and writers to the vines which were brought from the Rhine and Moselle valleys in the Middle Ages. The Galicians tell of how the vine stocks were carried along the banks of the Sil river by the Cluny monks on their pilgrimage to Santiago de Compostela. As in Andalucía and the case of Montilla, Berkenmayer says that a certain Pedro, son of Simón of German origin, introduced the *Pedro Ximénez* variety. In any event, as Cunqueiro says half seriously and half humourously, «*the first and greatest traveller of this planet is wine*».

The total of 45,000 acres of vineyard is shared among the following municipalities of *Aguilar de la Frontera, Baena, Cabra, Castro del Río, Espejo, Fernán Núñez, La Rambla, Doña Mencía, Lucena, Montalbán, Montemayor, Monzurque, Nueva Carteya* and *Puente Genil*, a territory of romance where the Spanish Reconquest is concerned.

THE WINE
NURSERIES

The following is a list of the wine nurseries in the region: *Montilla, Los Moriles, Aguilar de la Frontera, Lucena, Cabra, Doña Mencía, Puente Genil and Córdoba.*

GRAPE VARIETIES

The grapes that make the select wines of Montilla and Moriles are the *Pedro Ximénez* but in smaller quantities the varieties of *Layren, Baladí, Baladí-Verdejo* and the *Muscatel* are also used.

To improve the quality, the vine is pruned as much as possible «*a la ciega*» or «*caquera*». It is grown in unirrigated land and when it is fully ripe has a pale waxen colour. When it is over ripe it takes on a pink shade. It is then necessary to cut them otherwise the grapes tend to shrivel and form raisins. The grapes make very strong wines of 15° or more.

MORILES and MONTILLA are considered to be the most important «*pagos*» or vine growing districts as they have some of the very best soils. They are followed by the *Capellanía* and *Lagarito* of lesser alcoholic strength and often referred to as «*los vinos chicos*». Finally there are the districts of *Benavides, La Tercia, El Bombo, El Naranjo* and the *Moriles Altos* in *Albero*.

THE MYSTERY OF
THE MATURING
PROCESS

According to the wine merchants, the secret of the good quality of the wine is accounted for by the earthenware vessels made by the «Cordobés» Juan de la Hoz, and the mystery of the *albariza* and silicous soils that give to the vine roots that distinctly bitter flavour as peculiar as it is unique.

The fermentation process in this part is not unlike that of Jerez. The large quantities of sugar cause the temperature rise. This lasts for about a month after which time the clarification takes place. When the wine is completely transparent it is either sold on the market or transferred to the oak butts, where it acquires the necessary age for bottling. Like all Sherry wines, the *Moriles* and *Montilla* produce the *«flower»* that covers the surface in the spring and autumn.

After six years, it then has *solera*. At this point the ~~maturing~~ *ageing* process really begins and its palid delicate tone becomes golden, ranging in a scale of shades from light to dark. With time it becomes exquisite in aroma and bouquet until after many years of ~~blending~~ *maturing* and ~~maturing~~ *ageing* it becomes a nectar of the gods.

In accordance with the old and traditional methods of maturing wine, no additives are needed in the bottling of these wines. In *Moriles* and *Aguilar de la Frontera,* an egg white is beaten up and allowed to stand for 15 days to complete the clarification process.

In ancient Rome, these wines enjoyed great popularity and prestige. Columela, in his second book of «Re Rustica», praised them. They arrived in the Eternal City in amphoras with the inscription engraved on them. These were the predecessors of the actual brands found all over Europe today. It is almost certain that they were served on more than one occasion to celebrate the victories of Caesar on his triumphal return from the wars and to reconcile Anthony and Cleopatra in their more difficult moments.

KINDS OF WINE AND
THEIR STRENGTH

The alcoholic strength of these select wines goes from 15º to 16º. The old *finos* are a little more, 16º to 17º, being slightly more volatile and acid in flavour. The *olorosos* and the *olorosos viejos* range from between 18º to 21º.

The Regulating Council of the *Denominación de Origen* protects the following brands: —*Fino, Palmas, Finos Olorosos, Palos Cortados, Olorosos, Rayas, Pedro Ximénez, Muscatel, vinos de color, dulces* and *Mistelas.*

In order that a wine of the above named can be introduced on the market, it must fulfil the following conditions:

	ALCOHOLIC DEGREE	BAUMÉ DEGREE
Bottled.	16º	—
Other type of container	15º	—
Sweet mild, agreeable	17º	2
Sweet	16º	8
Pedro Ximénez	16º	12
Muscatel	16º	6

So as not to use up the solera reserves and to guarantee the quality of the wine, the exporters are not allowed to take more than 60 % of the total volume of solera wine used in the maturing process.

PRODUCTION

The production in 1968 was of the volume of 500,000 hectolitres of dry wines and 50,000 hectolitres of sweet wines and the exports reached 3,305,000 litres.

BODEGAS UNDER THE «DENOMINACION DE ORIGEN» MONTILLA AND MORILES

Bodegas Moriana: Calvo Sotelo, 109. Aguilar de la Frontera.
José Murillo Payar: Cabra.
Antonio Alargón Constant: Mayor Santa Marina, 14. Córdoba.
Viuda e Hijos de Domingo Campos: Coronel Consejo, 32. Córdoba.
Carbonell & Cía.: Angel Saavedra, 15. Córdoba.
Rafael Cruz Conde, S. A.: Calle de la Bodega. Córdoba.
Montes & Cía., S. A.: Carlos Romero, 17. Córdoba.
Moreno, S. A.: Fuente de la Salud, 5. Córdoba.
Pérez Barquero, S. A.: Doce de Octubre, 6. Córdoba.
Juan del Pozo Baena: Reloj, 1. Córdoba.
Alfonso Ramiro Rodríguez: Camino de Rabanales, 4. Córdoba.
Viuda e Hijos de F. P. Salinas: Alfonso XII. Córdoba.
Manuel Sánchez Aroca: Sevilla, 5. Córdoba.
Cristóbal Moreno Navas: Doña Mencía.
Laureano Aguilar: Pajarillas, 46. Lucena.
Aragón y Cía., S. A.: Ancha, 29-33. Lucena.
José Mora Jiménez: Curados, 7. Lucena.
Mora Romero: San Pedro, 42. Lucena.
José Morón Cabrera: Plaza de Barrera, 53. Lucena.
Torres Burgos, S. A.: Ronda de San Francisco. Lucena.
Pedro Víbora del Pino: Avenida de José Solís, 4. Lucena.
Alvear, S. A.: María Auxiliadora, 1. Montilla.
Bellido & Carrasco, S. R. C.: Dámaso Delgado, 17. Montilla.
José Cobos, S. A.: Horno, 47. Montilla.
Compañía Vinícola del Sur: Burgueños, 1. Montilla.
Antonio Espejo: Marqués de Vega Armijo, 26. Montilla.
Tomás García: Llano de Palacio, 1. Montilla.
Gracia Hermanos, S. A.: José María Alvear, 54. Montilla.
Montialbero, S. A.: Dámaso Delgado, 29. Montilla.
Montulia, S. A.: Beato Juan de Avila, 3. Montilla.
Navarro y del Pino: Arcipreste Fernández Carrasco, s/n. Montilla.
Navarro, S. A.: Navarra, 1. Montilla.
Luis Ortiz Ruiz: Márquez, 1. Montilla.
Carmen Pérez García: Teniente Torres del Real, 3. Montilla.
J. Jaime Ruz: Avenida de las Mercedes, s/n. Montilla.

POURING WINE FROM A «VENENCIA»
(Photo Guillén Franco.)

Miguel Velasco Chacón: Burgueños, 1. Montilla.
José Chacón Pineda: Conde de Vallellano, 10. Moriles.
Hermanos Fernández Varó: Plaza de Abustos, 1 y 3. Moriles.
Viuda de Emilio Machuca: Coronel Cascajo, s/n. Moriles.
Campos, S. A.: Industria, 3. Puente Genil.
Delgado Hermanos: Solís Laguna, 2. Puente Genil.
Hijos de Enrique Reina: José Echegaray, 6. Puente Genil.

LIST OF EXPORT COMPANIES		
Alvear, S. A.	María Auxiliadora, 1	Montilla
Aragón y Cía., S. A.	Ancha, 31	Lucena
Carbonell y Cía., S. A.	Angel de Saavedra, 15	Córdoba
J. J. Cobos, S. A.	Horno, 47	Montilla
Cía. Vinícola del Sur, S. A.	Burgueños, 5	Montilla
Rafael Cruz Conde, S. A.	Bodega, s/n.	Córdoba
Gracia Hermanos, S. A.	José María Alvear, 54	Montilla
Montialbero, S. A.	Dámaso Delgado, 29	Montilla
Montisol, S. A.	Llano Palacio, 4	Montilla
Montulia, S. A.	Beato Juan de Avila, 3	Montilla
Moreno, S. A.	Puente de la Salud	Córdoba
Bodegas Navarro, S. A.	Navarra, 1	Montilla
Luis Ortiz Ruiz	Márques, 1	Montilla
Pérez Barquero, S. A.	Doce de Octubre, 6	Córdoba
Miguel Velasco Chacón, S. A.	Burqueños, 3	Montilla
Vinsol, S. A.	José María Alvear, 54	Montilla

The exportation of Montilla-Moriles wines in 1969 was as follow:

Bottled	Litres
Germany	32,206
United States	7,894
France	4,777
Belgium	3,906
Italy	3,024
Morroco	2,060
Venezuela	2,025
Switzerland	1,261
Denmark	1,000
Great Britain	853
Andorra	530
Ireland	500
Austria	250
Peru	207
Sweden	45
Canada	12
Total	60,550

Bulk	Litres
Holland	5,288,432
Great Britain	94,807
Total	5,383,239

MALAGA «CANTAORA»

> *«Málaga is famous for her wine and spirits*
> *For her pretty ladies*
> *And courageous men».*
>
> ANONYMOUS.

MALAGA

Beautiful Málaga has her wine and the wine has her name as does her song the «Malagueña». Manuel Machado aptly called her *Málaga Cantaora*. Her personality is nowhere better revealed than through her wine and song.

The great number of luxurious hotels, the attraction of such places as Torremolinos, Fuengirola, and Marbella, and not forgetting the modern «valkyrias», those blue-eyed young maidens with fair hair who are forever searching and seduced by the legend and myth of the dark latin people, are all well known.

Throughout Málaga, vineyards are to be seen everywhere. They have a total surface area of 59,500 acres, found mainly in the districts of Archidona, Coin and Vélez-Málaga. The wines protected by the «Denominación de Origen» are those made by the traditional methods and produced in the capital of the province.

The classical maturing process and knowledge of wine generally is inbred in the race. The select **Lachrima Christi** and other kinds such as the **dulces, semi-dulces, sancochos** and the **secos** are obtained from the *Pedro Ximénez, Lairén, Morisco, Jaén blanco, Jaén tinto, Jaén doradillo, Ragol, Imperial,* and *Rome* grapes.

As a general rule, the two most renowned grapes of Málaga are the *Pedro Ximénez* and the *Muscatel*. These two alone are enough to produce wines of great quality and exquisite sweetness that range in colour from red, gold, pale yellow, amber, dark gold, to almost dark black.

The work of the writer priest Cecilio García de la Leña deserves to be mentioned here. His book **La Muy Ilustre y Antigua Hermandad de Viñeros de Málaga** contains a list of the immense variety of vines in Málaga from which come the wine making and eating grapes. They are: —*Pedro Ximénez, Jaén Blanco, Almuñécar, Larga, Moscatelón, Muscatel, Flamenco, Moscatel Morisco, Vigiriego, Don Bueno, Tintas, Cabriel, Casiles, Albillas, Teta de Vaca, Jaén Doradillo, Jaén Prieto, Mantúas, Marbelli, Alicante, Mollar,*

TREADING GRAPES IN ANDALUCIA
(Photo Guillén Franco.)

Sevillana, Morisco Ubies, Corazón de Cabbrio, Quebranta Tirajas, Perrunas, Uva de Loja, Lanjarón, Santa Paula, Fray Gusano, Teta de Negra, Torongies, Layranes, Verdejas and *Corinto.*

HISTORY OF THE WINES OF MALAGA

These wines were made famous by an Andalucian of Illustrious birth. He was the philosopher and historian Columella (A. D. 44). In his fourth book of «*Re Rústica*» and the third book of «*Agricultura*», he speaks of the vines growing on the hillsides and classifies them accordingly either as eating or wine making grapes, depending on their quality and the soil conditions of each. Horace felt too, a passion for the terraced vineyards as well as Pliny, Democritus and Virgil, who sang and praised their beauty. In his Second Book of the Georgics he grants them a place of rank and elegance which inspired some of the best pastoral poetry to be written. The Arab writers refer to the sweet wine of Málaga and the *Zebibí*, a raisin wine of great reputation in Moorish Andalucía.

The history of Pedro Ximénez is mentioned in the «*Cosmografía de Merula*», published in Amsterdam in 1636. Moreover, there are other historians who have proved that the Greeks carried on the cultivation of this grape previously introduced by the Phoenicians. The Láchrima Christi that is distilled drop by drop without squeezing the grape was called by the Greeks «*Petropos*» or «*Mosto Virgen*». Ruy González de Clavijo in his records describes how during the reign of Enrique III highly prized samples of these «**vinos generosos**» were carried aboard a «Carraca» and taken to the Great Tamarlane, himself. In 1214 a wine competition was held in France where it was proclaimed that «If the Pope of wines came from Cyprus, then the Cardinal of wines was from Málaga. It is related that Catherine the Great always had at her table the sweet wines of Málaga which she referred to as «*estos famosos vinos de España*».

WINE MATURING
AREAS

All the wines produced in the *bodegas* of the municipal area within the province and made in the traditional way are considered as Málaga wines.

CLASSES AND
COLOURS OF THE
MALAGA WINES

After being picked, cleaned and the rotten grapes sorted from the good ones, they are left in the sun for fifteen days. Neither the grapes nor their musts ever leave their area of origin as this would spoil their delicate falvour. It is from these very pure wines prepared entirely through natural processes that the famous alter wines are prepared.

The *Muscatel* grapes, apart from their use in the making of the light Muscatel and transparent Muscatel, are the ones that go into making the exceptional raisins of Málaga.

The great diversity and variety of wines includes the *Láchrima Christi, the Pajarete* and *Rome*, which are often mixed with the **vino tinto** to get one of the finest varieties held in particularly high regard by the Nordics. The colour is «*rojo-obispo*» or incarnadine.

The *semi-sweet wines* are made by adding a proportion of *tinto* wine to the must of the *Pedro Ximénez* grape and a perfectly balanced wine of 16° is obtained that can hold its own with the *Port* and *Cyprus* wines.

Below is a table showing the class, colour, and alcoholic content of the Málaga wines.

		Alcohol	Extract	COLOUR
Málaga dulce color (sweet)		14°-23°	20°-50°	Very dark brown to almost black.
Málaga blanco dulce (sweet)	Gold.	15°-18°	20°-40°	Golden yellow.
	Dark.	15°-18°	20°-35°	Dark amber.
Málaga semidulce (semi-sweet)	White.	14°-23°	20°-35°	Golden yellow.
	Red.	16°-20°	20°-35°	Red.
Málaga Lachrima	Gold.	14°-23°	20°-35°	Old Gold.
	Dark.	14°-23°	20°-40°	Dark amber.
Málaga Lachrima Christi	Gold.	15°-18°	20°-40°	Old gold.
	Dark.	15°-18°	20°-45°	Dark amber.
Pedro Ximénez		16°-20°	20°-50°	Very dark with reddish glints.
Málaga Moscatel		15°-20°	20°-40°	Golden yellow to dark amber.
Málaga Rome	Red.	15°-20°	20°-35°	Red.
	White.	15°-20°	20°-35°	Golden.
Málaga blanco seco (dry)		13,5°-23°	14°-30°	Pale yellow to amber.
Tintillo de Málaga		15°-16°	20°-45°	Red.
Málaga Pajareta		15°-20°	20°-35°	Amber to dark amber.

BODEGAS LISTED
UNDER THE
DENOMINACION
«MALAGA»

Barceló Blanco, S. A.: Llano del Mariscal, 6. Málaga.

Barceló Carles, S. A.: Malpica, 3. Málaga.

Barón del Rivero: Plaza de Salamanca. Málaga.

Bodegas Malagueñas: Salitre, 34. Málaga.

C. Rein y S.: Salitre, 34. Málaga.

Carlos, J. Krauel: Esquilache, 12-16. Málaga.

Carlos Navarrete: Llano del Mariscal, 6. Málaga.

Compañía Mata, S. A.: Purificación, 1. Málaga.

E. Crooke: Don Juan Díaz, 2. Málaga.

Félix García Gómez: Huerta del Conde, 6. Málaga.

Flores y Pimentel, S. L.: Plaza de Toros Vieja, 5. Málaga.

Gros, H., S. en C.: Esquilache, 12-16. Málaga.

Guillermo Rein: Salitre, 34. Málaga.

Hijo de Quirico López: Purificación, 1. Málaga.

Hijos de Salvador Pérez Martín: Calvo, 15. Málaga.

Hijos de Antonio Barceló, S. A.: Malpica, 3. Málaga.

Hijos de M. A. Heredia: Don Juan Díaz, 2. Málaga.

José Garijo Ruiz: Avenida del Generalísimo Franco, 12. Málaga.

José María Flores e Hijo, S. en C.: Plaza de Toros Vieja, 5. Málaga.

José Suárez Villalba: Juan Sebastián Elcano, 5. Málaga.

Juan Mory y Cía.: Calvo, 4. Málaga.

La Vinícola Andaluza: Calvo, 4. Málaga.

Larios, S. A.: Don Juan Díaz, 2. Málaga.

López Hermanos, S. A.: Salamanca, 1. Málaga.

Luis Barceló, S. A.: Llano del Mariscal, 6. Málaga.

M. Egea y Cía.: Purificación, 1. Málaga.

Pérez Texeira, S. A.: Calvo, 15. Málaga.

Rafael Díez Gómez: Juan Sebastián Elcano, 125. Málaga.

Ricardo Barceló: Malpica, 3. Málaga.

Manuel Pacheco Morón: P. de la Harina, 4. Málaga.

Casa Romero, S. L.: Tizo, 3-7. Málaga.

J. González, Castro: Salamanca, 1. Málaga.

Dalmau Hermanos y Cía.: Salamanca, 1. Málaga.

Bodegas Abadía: Don Juan Díaz, 2. Málaga.

Guillermo Klein: Don Juan Díaz, 2. Málaga.

Scholtz Hermanos: Don Cristián, 9. Málaga.

Souviron Hermanos: Calvo, 15. Málaga.

T. Rein y Cía.: Salamanca, 1. Málaga.

Bodegas La Aurora: Don Juan Díez, 2. Málaga.

Federico Leal: Calvo, 15. Málaga.

Flores Hermanos, S. A.: Plaza de Toros Vieja, 5. Málaga.

Bodegas La Victoria: Malpica, 3. Málaga.

Vicusol, S. A.: Esquilache, 12-16. Málaga.

Bodegas Kranel: Esquilache, 12-16. Málaga.

Hacienda Vinícola Fiammuva: Calvo, 4. Málaga.

PRODUCERS & EXPORTERS IN MALAGA

Hijos de A. Barceló, S. A.
Malpica, 1.
Luis Barceló, S. A.
Llano Mariscal, 6.
Flores Hermanos, S. A.
Plaza de Toros Vieja, 5.
Félix García Gómez
Huerta, 1.
José Garijo Ruiz
Peinado, 5.
Carlos J. Krauel
Calvo, 15.
Larios, S. A.
Don Juan Díaz, 2.
López Hermanos, S. A.
Salamanca, 1.
Compañía Mata, S. A.
Purificación, 1.

Juan Mory & Cía., S. A.
Calvo, 4 .
Pérez Texeira, S. A.
Calvo, 15.
Guillermo Rein Segura
Polígono Industrial.
Casa Romero, S. L.
Tirso, 7.
Scholtz Hermanos, S. A.
Don Cristián, 11.
Hijos de José Suárez Villalba
Juan Sebastián Elcano, 141.
Vinícola Andalucía, S. A.
Calvo, 4.
Manuel Pacheco Morón
P.º de la Harina.

LEVANTE

«La Flauta de Pan» - The Flute of Pan

*Wine gives brightness to the countryside, exhalts the heart,
lights up the eyes and invites us to dance. Wine is a wise
fertile god. Dionysious, Bacchus, are
a perpetual reminder of the festive spirit that crosses the
live dense forests like a warm wind.*

JOSE ORTEGA Y GASSET.

ALICANTE

Alicante, the prosperous province of the Costa Blanca, is the sunshine land so well described by **Azorín** and **Miró** in their writings. It is one of the driest places in Spain, having an average winter temperature of between 8º and 20º centigrade which provides the necessary hours of sunlight for the full ripening of her grapes.

Alicante's wine growing areas are perfectly defined. The first of them is the continental or inland part of the province, which include the *«municipios»* of *Villena, Campo de Mirra, Benajema, Baneres, Biar, Salinas, Onil, Ibi, Sax, Castalla, Elda, Petrel, Tibi, Agost, Alicante, Monforte del Cid, Monóvar, Novelda, Pinoso, Aspe, La Romana, La Algieña, Hondón de las Nieves, and Hondón de los Frailes.*

The second area takes in the mountainous territory of the promontory of *Monge* that eventually slopes down to the sea merging with the capes of *San Antonio* and *La Nao*. This region is called *«La Marina»*, a mountainous maritime area very popular with the tourists.

It includes the following municipalities or *«municipios: Denia, Javea, Orba, Vall de Leguart, Tormos, Murla, Parcent, Benichembla, Alcalalí, Castell de Castells, Llibar, Jalón, Senija, Sagra, Benidoleig, Setla, Mirarosa, Miraflor, Vergel, Benimelí, Ondara, Sanet, Negrals, Benitachell, Calpe, Benisa, Teulada, Gata de Grgos,* and *Pedreguer.*

VINICULAR GROWTH

Alicante has always been in the lead where wine making is concerned and throughout the province there is no lack of bodegas. In the post war period of 1914 this province sent a lot of its wines to France so that the latter could meet her export demands and it was at this time that a great number of French vintners and exporters established themselves and ever since have maintained business relations with the Central European and Nordic countries.

The mild climate and nature of the grapes themselves account for the great popularity of the Alicante wines. The following grapes are used: *Muscatel, Malvasia, Garnacha, Novelda, Aspe, Agost, San Vicente del Raspeig, Monforte del Cid, Elche, Albatera, Crevillente,* and *Orihuela.* The most prominent among the above mentioned is the «Muscatel» variety which has a particularly fine «bouquet».

Under the **«dulces»** or sweet wines, there are the *blancos, tintos, claretes,* and *mistelas* as well as an aperitive wine perfumed with the aromatic herbs of the district and made in very much the same way as the Vermouth. i. e. with old solera wines. Their alcoholic content is from 12º to 18º.

The *tintos* are **valientes** and range from 12º to 16º. They have an intense bright red colour and are very rich in dry extract, having a fixed and little volatile acidity. Its excellent properties and flavour make it a wine that can be taken directly or used in the blending process with other wines. The red table wines made in the proximities of Castalla, Biar, and Agost have a bright colour and range from 12º to 14º.

There is one more outstanding wine that is the *Fondillon*. It is a «tinto» obtained from selected grapes of a delightful aroma. It is a pity that the production of this natural wine of 15º to 16º is so limited because it is in great demand.

The ordinary *blancos* of 10º to 16º are very easy to mature and age.

The *rosados* and *claretes* are *finos* and very rich in dry extract. They make very good table wines as the grapes are of excellent quality and include: *Monastrell, Bobal, Aforcallá, Garnachal, Tintonera, and Moscatel Romano.*

GRAPE HARVESTING
(Photo Paisajes Españoles.)

After two years of maturing they have all the good qualities of the old vintage wines. As the climate is very dry, the growing of eating grapes is a particularly good business.

CO-OPERATIVES IN ALICANTE		
Cooperativa Agrícola San Ramón	Agost
Cooperativa Bodega La Divina Aurora	Benejama
Coop. Agrícola Virgen de la Cueva Santa	Beniarrés
Coop. La Purísima Xiqueta y San Isidro Labrador	Benisa
Coop. Sindical del Vino Nuestra Señora del Carmen	Cañada
Bodega Cooperativa	Castalla
Hermandad Sindical de Labradores y Ganaderos	Gata de Gorgos
Coop. Agrícola Nuestra Señora de la Luz	Gayanes
Hermandad de Labradores	Hondón de las Nieves
Hermandad Sindical de Labradores	Hondón de los Frailes
Caja Rural Cooperativa Agrícola	Ibi
Coop. Agrícola Jesús Nazareno	Javea
Bodega Cooperativa de la Romana	La Romana
Hermandad de Labradores	La Romana
Bodega Cooperativa	Mañán
Bodega Cooperativa Santa Catalina	Monóvar
Coop. Vitivinícola Virgen de la Salud	Onil
Cooperativa Viticultores de San Isidro	Petrel
Bodega Cooperativa	Pinoso
Coop. Vinícola San Blas	Sax
Coop. Agrícola de Labradores y Ganaderos	Tárbena
Bodega Cooperativa	Villena
Bodega Cooperativa Nuestra Señora de las Virtudes	Villena
Hermandad Sindical de Labradores y Ganaderos	Villena

A LIST OF THE BODEGAS RECORDED IN THE REGISTER OF THE DENOMINACION DE ORIGEN «ALICANTE»

José Amorós Quilés	Monóvar
Antonio Tomás Conce	Villena
Francisco Agulló y Cía.	Elche
José de Barrio, Sub.	Alicante
Sebastián Fernández González	Alicante
Bodega Cooperativa	Monóvar
Exportadora de Vinos, S. A.	Monóvar
Bodegas Schenk	Alicante
Ricardo Madrid	Alicante
Federico Madrid	Alicante
Hijos de Luis García Poveda	Villena
Salvador Poveda Luz	Villena
Juan García Hurtado	Villena
Primitivo Quilés	Monóvar
Martín Hernández Menor	Villena

The many and diverse routes through the ancient kingdom of Valencia coincide perfectly with the present day wine route. It is rather like looking at an oil canvass upon which are painted the reds, pinks, whites, light and dark ambers. The good climate and terrain account for the wide variety of grape produce which come under three **Denominaciones de Origen**: UTIEL-REQUENA, CHESTE and VALENCIA.

Under the «DENOMINACION DE ORIGEN»-VALENCIA, the favourite *cuarte* on the very borders of the capital is a claret of good alcoholic content; the *mistela* of amber colour in Sagunto; the *Campo de Liria* of 18°; the wines of *Carlet, Ayora,* and *Onteniente;* the *espumosos* of the *Puebla del Duc* and the *rosados* of *Albaida*. In general, all of these wines are in the 11° to 17° and the **rancios** and **generosos** in the 15° to 23° range.

In the district of REQUENA-UTIEL, where the province of Valencia meets Castile bordering Cuenca and Albacete, the wines are notably thicker and more intensely coloured. However they are weaker and have a light coarseness typical of mountain wine. The *tintos, rosados* and *claretes* are generally heavy and cannot be excluded from our list here.

In the central region is the «DENOMINACION DE ORIGEN»-CHESTE. The «blancos» are plentiful and go from 12° to 18°. Turia is also in the same area and makes excellent table wines of the same strength and properties.

GRAPE VARIETIES

The following grapes are used in the winemaking: *Bobal, Garnacha, Crujidera, Pedro Ximénez, Planta Fina, Merseguera, Macabeo, Planta Nova, Malvasía, Monastrell, Tintorera, Valdepeñera, Tortosí, Aledo, Alcayata, Gayata, Cencibel, San Jerónimo, Planta de Pedralba, Gateta*. The eating grapes are *Moscatel, Rosetti, Cardinal, Franceset, Planta Nova, Valencí Blanco, Aledo* and others.

The cultivated surface is 276,150 acres, having a density of 800 vines per acre.

TYPE	Alcoholic content	Dry extract reduced to grams/litre	Total sulph. acidity grams/lit.	COLOUR
Utiel-Requena				
Tinto	10-13°	20-32	3-5	«Tinto»
Rosado	10-13°	15-25	3-5	«Rosado»
Clarete	10-13°	12-25	3-5	«Clarete»

TYPE	Alcoholic content	Dry extract reduced to grams/litre	Total sulph. acidity grams/lit.	COLOUR
Cheste				
Dry white table wine	11-15°	15-25	2-4	White and gold
Semi-sweet white	12-16°	15-35	2-4	White and gold
Sweet white	12-18°	20-40	2-4	White and gold
Valencia				
Malvasía	13-18°	20-40	2-4	Very dark to golden
Puerto	13-23ᶜ	15-40	2-4	Golden to red
Pedro Ximénez	12-16°	15-40	2-4	Dark with reddish glints
Moscatel sweet	12-18°	15-35	2-4	Dark amber to golden yellow
Dry Moscatel	12-17°	15-25	2-4	Amber to pale yellow
Dry Generoso	15-23°	15-25	2-4	Golden
Sweet Rancio	13-23°	15-45	2-4	Golden
Dry Rancio	13-23°	15-25	2-4	Golden
Red Valencia	12-17°	20-35	3-5	Dark red
«Fino», selected table wine	11-14°	15-25	3-5	White or red

A LIST OF NAMES OF EXPORTERS WRITTEN INTO THE DENOMINACION DE ORIGEN «VALENCIA»

C. Augusto Egli, S. L. — Maderas, 21. Valencia

Bodegas Schenk, S. A. — Camino Hondo del Grao, 78. Valencia

Chrubino Valsanguiacomo, S. A. — Vicente Brull, 4. Valencia

Ferd. Steiner, S. A. — Francisco Cubells, 42. Valencia

Vicente Gandía Pla, S. A. — Maderas, 13. Valencia

A. y J. Garrigos, S. L. — Consuelo, 13. Apartado 6093. Valencia

José Hernández Iranzo — Méndez Núñez, 27. Valencia

Hijos de Pons Hermanos — Avda. del Puerto, 199-201. Valencia

Ramón Mestre Serra — Vía Layetana, 30. Barcelona-3

J. Antonio Mompo, S. A. — Arquitecto Alfaro, 31. Valencia

Francisco Selma Cerrillo — Camino Hondo del Grao, 71. Valencia

Teschendorff & Cía. — Peña, 25. Valencia

La Vinícola Ibérica, S. A. — (Exportadores de Vinos). Tarragona

Antonio Pérez Calvo — San Antonio-Requena. Valencia

Sociedad Anónima Nuevas Industrias Vinícolas de Occidente, «Sanivo» — Serranos, 48. Valencia

BODEGAS AND COOPERATIVAS IN VALENCIA

Cooperativa Vinícola y Caja Rural Santa
    Bárbara   Casinos. Valencia
Bodega Cooperativa Cheste Vinícola   Cheste. Valencia
Bodega Cooperativa Pedralba Vinícola   Pedralba. Valencia
Cooperativa del Campo Valenciana «Co-
    viñas»   Requena. Valencia
Cooperativa Vinícola Requenense   Requena. Valencia
Bodega Cooperativa y Caja Rural Nues-
    tra Señora de la Paz   Villar del Arzobispo. Valencia

CASTELLON DE LA
PLANA

Castellón de la Plana, otherwise known as the Costa del Azahar because of its orange groves, stretches along the Mediterranean coast from Valencia northward to Tarragona bordered by Teruel along its western boundary. The wine producing areas correspond with the geographic zones: The Coast and the Bajo Maestrazgo, a rugged mountain area.

The coast includes the districts of Benicasim, Oropesa, Torreblanca and Alcalá de Chisvert. All of these districts produce *claretes* and *blancos* of 12 to 14º, while in the districts of *Benicarló, Vinaroz, San Mateo, La Jana, San Jorge and Triguera, tintos, claretes* and *blancos* of between 12.5 to 14º are in good supply.

The Benicarló wine enjoys great prestige in South America where it is shipped in large quantities. It is a strong full bodied wine and sometimes goes under the name of Carlon, a phonetic corruption of Benicarló.

The Bajo Maestrazgo region includes the following districts: *Cuevas de Vinroma, Torre de Endomenech, Villanueva de Alcolea, Benlloch, Vall d'Alba, Cabanes, Villafames, Puebla Tonesa,* and *Useras.* These ordinary *tintos* are stronger than those of other regions. The vineyard surface area is 49,250 acres, with a density of 1,100 vines per acre.

VILLAFRANCA DEL PANADES
(Photo Paisajes Españoles.)

THE VINTAGE
(Water colour by Fernando Amiano.)

THE GRAPEVINE AND THE SEA

La Dolça Catalunya - Sweet Catalonia

THE WINES
OF CATALONIA

Catalonia has a privileged place in the making and maturing of wines that goes back some 2000 years. This says a lot in itself and it is possible to trace the origin of her wines back to Greco-Roman times. But even in Medieval times in the archives and chronicles of the monasteries of the Kingdom of Aragón, there is ample proof of their super abundance.

The names TARRAGONA, PRIORATO, PANADES, and ALELLA, all of them protected under their respective *Denominación de Origen*, are wines whose reputation has become world wide for they have really established themselves on the international markets. The remaining areas, although less known, also produce wines of prestige which are used for «coupage» and the making of vintage wines.

TARRAGONA

Tarragona holds a pre-eminent place within the Castra Vinaria ranking fifth place in vineyard surface area and third in the making of *mosto*, an unfermented grape juice.

The Romans, who knew their wines well, made the «Tarraconense» province one of the most privileged territories in the Empire.

The province has five well defined wine growing regions: —*El Campo de Tarragona, El Priorato, La Tierra Alta, La Ribera del Ebro* and *La Conca de Barbará.*

El Campo de Tarragona stretches from the coast of *Monroy* to *Torredambarra.* Its capital is *Reus* and includes the judicial districts lying within the area, a part of *Valls* and some villages of the *Mont-Blanch* district. It has a surface area of 85,000 acres. Its wines have an alcoholic content of 11 to 18º and go from a pale to dark red having a slightly blue tint. To make the «tintos» the following class of grape is used: —*Cariñena, Garnacha Negra Ull de Llevre, Sumoll* and *Morenillo,* and for the *blancos:* —*Macabeo, Malvasía, Moscatel, Picapoll blanco, Pansal, Garnacha blanca, Cartuxa* and *Vinyate.*

THE PRIORATO AREA

The Priorato area is outstanding for the «*valentia*» (strong and robust character) of its wines. They are so popular that, according to the finding of the historian José Pla, they are the highest in alcoholic content around the terrestrial globe.

With the Sierra del Montsant in the distance, the PRIORATO is an impressive panorama of terraced vineyards along the river Ciurana that nourishes the highly prized red slate soils.

The six villages that comprise the judicial district of *Priorato:* —*Gratallops, Porrera, La Vilella, Alta, Torroja, Poboleda* and *La Morera*, stretch along the river Ciurana.

The district, convulsed by a volcanic eruption, has not been seriously studied. So thick are the wines that they can be almost masticated and are particularly suitable for making vintage and old wines.

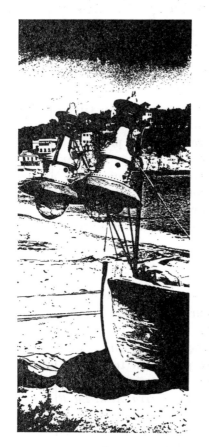

According to some very exhaustive studies that have been recently carried out, it is the red siluric slate which gives these wines their alcoholic strength and thick body. The quality of the soil combined with the blowing of the Mistral, a northwest Alpine wind, known in the region as the «seré», is particularly favourable for a good grape harvest. The hard and coarse winds make the new wine *mostos* especially strong.

The growing of grapes and winemaking provide the only means of livelihood in the area. For the tourist and visitors, however, the real attraction is the old Benedictine and Carthusian monastery of Scala Dei.

Apart from the above mentioned sites and towns, there is the *Bajo Priorato* along the Ciurana river and the towns of the *Tierra Alta* whose capital is *Gandesa*. The capital of the Bajo Priorato is Falset which is also the capital of the entire district.

The quality and variety of the wine is good. The *tintos* which have a very bright and live colour tend to stale with time. The ordinary *corrientes* start at 19º and some reach 24º.

The transparency and limpidity of the *blancos* are pair with the agreeable «bouquet», having a special aroma and raspberry taste. The *dulces* are thick and strong of 14º to 22º.

The area in which the Priorato wines are made and matured includes *Tarragona, Pallaresos, La Secuita, Vallmoll* and *Valls* in the east; *Alcover, Albió, Aleixar* and *Alforja* in the north; *Montroig, Villanova* de *Escornalbou, Argentera,* and *Padrell* in the west.

The **rancios** or old wines are left to age for at least 3 years.

The grapes that go into the making of the Priorato *tintos* are the *Cariñena, Garnacha negra* and the *Garnacha negra peluda*. The Priorato *blancos* are made from the *Macabeo* and *Pedro Ximénez*.

«LA TIERRA ALTA»   LA TIERRA ALTA is a broken and rugged
land of contrast and altitudes. The grape vines
and olive trees grow side by side to produce
some excellent wines and olive oils respectively. This region is what was formerly called
the «Castellanía» and during the reign of King
Berenguer IV became part of Catalonia. Its
capital is *Gandesa* and includes the districts of
*Arnés, Batea, Bot, Corbera de Ebro, Faterella,
Casaras, Gandesa, Horta de San Juan, Pobla
de Masaluca, Prat de Compte, Pinell de Bray,*
and *Villalba de los Arcos.*

The *blancos* and *tintos* of the TIERRA ALTA are **valientes** and the *mistelas*
and *dulces* are of very good quality.

THE «CONÇA DEL   The Conça de Barbara is located high up on the top of a hill overlooking
BARBARA»   an arena like lanscape.

The region consists of the following districts: —*Solivella, Rocafort de
Queralt, Montbrió de la Marca. Sarreal, Pira, Vimbodi, Espluga, de Francolí,
Cabra del Campo, Figuerola, Plá de Santa María, Vallclara, Rojals* and *Vilabert.*

«La Conça del Barbará» makes very pleasant and stimulating *tintos* and
blancos of a special «bouquet» and alcoholic content of 10º to 14º. This wine
is in great demand and highly prized by the connoisseurs.

The *Ulldecona* area around the *Sierra de Montsia,* very near the Ebro
Delta, includes the districts of *Ulldecona, Mas de Barberans, Godall, La Galera,
Fraginals* and *Santa Bárbara.* These wines range from 11º tp 13º.

In general, the Tarragona wines have always been in great demand in
the Nordic countries and Central Europe as well as South America.

CHARACTERISTICS OF THE WINES PROTECTED BY THE «DENOMINACION DE ORIGEN» «PRIORATO»

Wine	Density	Alcoholic Content	Fixed Acid Dry Extract		Colour
			Reduced	Tartar. Acid	
Red dry Priorato	Less than 1000	13.75-18	22-35	3.5-7	Red.
Red sweet Priorato	1007 to 1027	13 -19	22-35	3.5-7	Red.
Red «licoroso».	1028 to 1059	13 -20	22-32	3.0-6	Red, red-brown
Dry white Priorato	Less than 1000	13.75-18	15-28	3.0-6	Amber, golden
Sweet white Priorato	1007 to 1027	13 -19	15-28	3.0-6	Amber, golden
White «licoroso».	1028 to 1059	13 -20	15-25	2.5-5,5	Golden.
Dry «rancio» Priorato.	Less than 1000	16 -21	15-35	2.5-6	Old gold.
Sweet «rancio» Priorato	1007 to 1036	15 -20	15-35	2.5-6	Old gold.
Mistela Priorato	1059 to 1075	13.75-18	—	2.0-6	—

BODEGAS UNDER THE «DENOMINACION DE ORIGEN» «PRIORATO»

Amigó Hnos. y Cía.: Gaudí, 28. Reus.
Bodegas Salvat, S. A.: Avenida de los Mártires. Reus.
Cochs, S. A.: San Celestino, 15. Reus.
E. Izaguirre, S. A. Reus.
Amadeo Ferrate: F. Soler, 6. Reus.
Ramón Mestre Serra: Plaza Morius, 1. Reus.
S. A. F. Miró Sanz. Reus.
Francisco Simó y Cía.: Cam. Riudams, 16. Reus.
Pablo Casas y Vidiella. Reus.
Viuda de Luis Quer, S. L.: Avenida de Calvo Sotelo, 12. Reus.
Vinos Ricart. Reus.
Emilio Miró Salvat: Arrabal Jesús, 3. Reus.
Hijos de Marcelino Rofes: San Miguel, 2. Reus.
De Muller, S. A.: Real, 27. Tarragona.
René Barbier y Cía., Sdad. Vinícola: J. A. Clavé, 1. Tarragona.
José Oliver, S. A.: Castaños, 6. Tarragona.
La Vinícola Ibérica, S. A.: Torres Jordi, s/n. Tarragona.
Juan Mory y Cía., S. A.: León, 44. Tarragona.
J. M. Pamies Torres: Smith, 59 bis. Tarragona.
Ferd. Steiner, S. A. Tarragona.
La Tarraco Vinícola, S. A.: Real, 23. Tarragona.
J. López Bertrán y Cía.: Nueva San Fructuoso, 23. Tarragona.
Dalmau Hnos. y Cía.: Real, 9. Tarragona.
Bodegas Montblanch, S. A. Tarragona.
Bodegas Tapias, S. A.: Mar, 17. Tarragona.
S. A. La Vid. La Secuita.

LIST OF EXPORT VINTAGERS UNDER THE «DENOMINACION DE ORIGEN» «TARRAGONA»

Amadeo Ferraye	C. F. Soler, 6	Reus
Amigó Hnos. y Cía.	Gaudí, 28	Reus
Bodegas Salvat, S. A.	Avenida de los Mártires	Reus
Bodegas Tapias, S. A.	Mar, 17-18	Tarragona
Cochs, S. A.	San Celestino, 15	Reus
Dalmau Hnos. y Cía., Suc.	Real, 9	Tarragona
De Muller, S. A.	Real, 27	Tarragona
Dubonnet Española, S. A.	Castaños, 6	Tarragona
Emilio Miró Salvat	Avenida Generalísimo, 55	Reus
Francisco Simó & Cía.	Riudoms, 16	Reus
José López Bertrán y Cía.	Nueva San Fructuoso, 23	Tarragona
José María Pamies	Vapor, 13	Tarragona
José Oliver, S. A.	Castaños, 6	Tarragona

QUENCHING THE THIRST
(Photo F. I. S. A.)

Juan Mory & Cía.	León, 44-46	Tarragona
Juan Solé Bargallo	Masricart, 82	La Canonja
La Tarraco Vinícola, S. L.	Real, 23	Tarragona
La Vinícola Ibérica, S. A.	Torres Jordi, 3	Tarragona
Ramón Mestre Serra	Plaza Morlius, 1	Reus
René Barbier, S. A.	A. Clavé, 1	Tarragona
S. A. F. Miró Sans	San Lorenzo, 15	Reus
Vinos y Vermuts Rofes, S. A.	San Miguel, 2	Reus
Vinícola Reusense, S. A.	Espronceda, s/n.	Reus
Vinos Padró, S. L.	Avenida Generalísimo, 56	Brafim
Vinos Ricart, S. A.	Calvo Sotelo, 41	Reus
Viuda Luis Quer, S. L.	Calvo Sotelo, 17	Reus

BARCELONA

Barcelona is a very prominent wine producing region which can be divided into the following important areas: EL PANADES and ALELLA and the lesser known *El Vallés, La Segarra and Bagés.*

EL PANADES, stretches along the Mediterranean coast and takes in the surroundings of the monastery of Monserrat. It is divided into the *Bajo Panadés, Panadés Central* and *Alto Panadés.*

The following municipal districts form the PANADES: —*Aiguamurcia, Albiñana, Avinyonet, Banyeros, Bellvehí, Cabreras de Igualada, Calafell, Castellet, Gornal, Castellví de la Marca, Creixell, Cubellas, Cunit, Fontrubí, Gelida, La Bisbal del Panadés, Les Cabaynes, La Granada, La Llacuna, Llorens, del Panadés, Mediona, Montmell, Olivella, Olesa de Bonesvalls, Olérdola, Pachs, Plá del Panadés, Pontons, Puigdalba, Roda de Bará, San Cugat de Sasgarrigues, San Jaume del Domenys, San Martí de Sarroca, San Pere de Ribes, San Pedro de Riudetvitlles, San Sadurní de Noya, San Quintín de Mediona, San Vicente de Calders, Santa Fe de Panadés, Santa Margarida y Monjos, Santa Oliva, Sitges, Subirats, Torrelavid, Torelles de Foix, Vendress, Vilafranca del Panadés, Villanueva y Geltrú* and *Vilovi.*

«EL BAJO PANADES»

Produces *tintos* of dark colour and strong alcoholic content made mainly from the *Sumoll* and the *Malvasía* vines.

«EL ALTO PANADES»

The vineyards of *El Alto Panadés* are situated at 700 metres altitude which makes them some of the highest in Spain. The *Parellada* and *Montonech* grapevines are used which produce an exquisite white wine of low alcoholic degree.

Almost all the soil of the *Panadés* is of the ideal *albariza* type.

«EL PANADES CENTRAL»

It is precisely in this area that **the internationally famous sparkling wines are made with its centre in San Sadurní de Noya.**

The alcoholic content of the different kinds of Panadés wines is as follows:

Panadés seco 13º to 18º
Blanco San Cugat 11º to 14º
Blanco Supermaduro 13º to 18º
Rosado Panadés 9º to 14º
Clarete Panadés 9º to 14º
Tinto Panadés 11º to 16º
(Red tinto «Bajo Panadés)

The *Panadés seco* is a good table wine and ideal to drink with the typical Catalan dishes, roasts and dishes prepared in the French style with plenty of sauce.

In accord with the strictest demands on table wines, the grapevines of the *Xarelo* and *Macabeo* of the *Panadés Central* are used which make the white diamantine wines of 11° to 13°. These are particularly suitable with fish, white meat, fowl, ham, lamb chops and shellfish dishes.

The *Alto Panadés*, a highly productive area, provides the palid wines of low alcoholic content made from the *Parellada* vines. They have a fresh fruity flavour, a slightly acid taste similar to the Rhine wines and *vinos verdes* and an exquisite «bouquet».

Finally in this region, there are the world famous sparkling wines got from the *Xarello* and *Macabeo* vines. Apart from the capital, San Sadurní

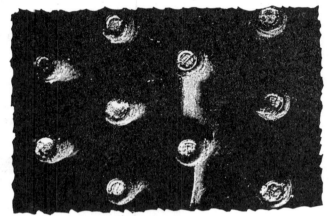

de Noya and its great bodegas of Codorniu (Codorniu, 1551 and Raventós 1872) the sparkling wines are also made in *San Esteban de Sas Roviras, Plá del Panadés, La Bleda, La Granada* and *Pach.*

THE «ALELLA» WINES

El Maresme, a region protected from the trans mountain winds, has always been distinguished for its grapevines and the making of the prestigious *Alella* wines. According to historians, the Alella grapevines are of Asiatic origin and were brought to the Iberian Peninsula by the Greeks and Phoenicians, who established themselves in the Golfo de Rosas. The analogy between these Catalan and Greek wines which have come from Near Orient is a curious one for it is said that the Roman Emperors always compared the Alella with the wines from Lesbos and Lacedemonia. Yet another coincidence is the origin of the Moselle and Rhine wines brought to Europe from the Holy Land at the time of the Crusades.

The town of Alella is located in the folds of the Figurals mountains and also cultivates carnation fields to supply the Central European markets. A region of soft undulating country which gradually slopes down to the sea, it has the following places under its «DENOMINACION DE ORIGEN» —*Masnou, Teya, Tiana, Martorellas Vallromanas, San Pedro de Premiá, San Ginés de Vilasar, Cabrils* and *Premiá del Mar.*

The most important white wines are: —*Pansa Blanca, Pansa Roja, Garnacha blanca, Garnacha rosédo, Picapoll, Macabeo, Malvasía;* the *tintos* include *Smoll, Garnacha negra* and *Tempranilla.*

The *Alella* wine is of a soft texture, fresh and becomes aromatic after three years of vintage. After five years it converts into a *generoso seco* or *dulce*, and in fifteen years reaches its peak. It can continue to mature and foster its great virtues well beyond the age of forty.

The table wines whether *blancos* or *rosados* do not exceed 10º and the *tintos* 12º; the «generosos» of 14º range from a cherry to golden colour.

«EL VALLES»

Among the most representative wine producing towns of this district are: —*Ripollet, San Cugat* and *Rubi*. This region lies behind the Tibidabo mountain fringing the town of Barcelona itself. Its wine is white and fruity in flavour.

«LA ANOIA»

La Anoia stretches along the Noya river between *Martorell, Los Bruchs,* and *Igualada*. Its wines are mild red and white of 11º to 13º.

«LA ANCIA»

La Ancia stretches along the Noya River between Martorell, los Bruchs and Igualada. Its wines are mild, red and white of 11º to 13º.

«LA SEGARRA»

La Segarra and the Bages makes *tintos* and *blancos* of between 11º to 13º. which have a fruity taste.

GERONA

«EL AMPURDAN»

Its towers pointing up to Eeaven, the fortified monastery of San Pedro de Roda is just visible on the distant horizon. Nearby is the castle of Perelada surrounded by the flourishing vineyards of the beautiful Ampurdán. This area is one of the most characteristic of Catalonia and of which the Catalonians are justly proud. Within its domain are the mountain slopes of the Pyrenese, La Costa Brava, the Gabarras and the many fortified *«masías»* or country houses recalling the times of Old Catalonia when baronies and landed estates were in evidence everywhere. It is the Monastery of San Pedro de Roda, however, which has come to symbolise the art of vineyard cultivation and perfect winemaking. The chief wine makers in the Ampurdán are found in the municipal districts of: *Pont de Molins, Campany, Masarchs, Mollet de Perelada, San Clemente de Sasebas, Espolla, Rabos, Villamaniscle, Llansá, Falau-Sabardera, Rosas, Pau, Pedret* and *Marsá, Garriguella, Vilajuiga, Perelada, Cabanas, Palafrugell, Figueras* and *Ripoll.*

The principal grapevines are: *Barceloní, Monastrell, Moscatel, Pausá, Picapoll, Xarel-lo, Cariñena, Garnacha, Lladoner* and *Cardinal.*

Each year in the castle of D. Manuel Mateu Plá, a former Spanish ambassador, is held a wine harvest feast together with the traditional chapters of LOS CABALLEROS DEL VINO.

El Ampurdán makes *blancos, tintos, claretes* and *rosados* of 11.5º to 13º and sometimes 14.5º.

LERIDA

On the plains of Urgel, the mild and aromatic white wines of Lérida are made. They are *corriente* wines, pleasant tasting but difficult to come by as the vineyards lie far to the North.

A LIST OF THE NAMES WRITTEN INTO THE «DENOMINACION DE ORIGEN PANADES»

Aquila Rossa, S. A.	Villafranca del Panadés
Cavas Albertí	Villafranca del Panadés
Codorniú, S. A.	San Sadurní de Noya
José Alegre Sanromá	Villafranca del Panadés
Cooperativa Agrícola	Vendrell
J. B. Berger, S. A.	Villafranca del Panadés
Batlle y Monserrat, S. L.	Monjos. Barcelona
Bodegas Bosch Güell, S. A.	Villafranca del Panadés
Bodegas Hill	Villafranca del Panadés
Bodegas Rubio	Villafranca del Panadés
José Freixadas & Cía., S. L.	Villafranca del Panadés
José Freixadas Bove	Villafranca del Panadés
Freixenet, S. A.	San Sadurní de Noya
J. Font	Castellví de la Marca. Barcelona
Cavas Hill	Moja. Barcelona
Luis Marcé & Cía., S. L.	Villafranca del Panadés
Antonio Mascaró	Villafranca del Panadés
Juan Montaner Montané	Villafranca del Panadés
Domingo Monserrat	Villafranca del Panadés
Domingo Olivella	Villafranca del Panadés
Destilerías Virben	Villafranca del Panadés
Francisco Olivella	Villafranca del Panadés
Cavas Parés Beltá, S. A.	Pachs del Panadés
Cavas Raventós Catasús, S. A.	Villafranca del Panadés
Bodegas J. Robert	Sitges
Ginés Rovira	Villafranca del Panadés
Heredad Segura Viudas	San Sadurní de Noya
José María Sogas Montaner	Villafranca del Panadés
Bodegas Juan Solé	Villafranca del Panadés
José María Tetas Vendrell	Villafranca del Panadés
Miguel Torres Carbó	Villafranca del Panadés
Vinos y Champanas de Cava Marqués del Monistrol	Monistrol de Noya
Cavas Conde de Caralt, S. A.	San Sadurní de Noya
René Barbier, S. A.	San Sadurní de Noya

ARAGON

«El vino a rajavaso»

Already the old wine shines,
The wine of Aragón, the Cariñena
That in the cool bodega
Six summers has matured and its fragrance
With old age announces fresh exuberance.

JOSE DE URCULLU.

INTRODUCTION AND
GEOGRAPHIC
SITUATION

It is not the first time that the wine of Aragón has been praised by the Spanish poets, but Aragón, to use a metaphor is the Ebro, for this masculine and noble river gives life and substance to this ancient kingdom, and enriches the land lying along its right and left banks. The river Jalón, one of its tributaries, brings with its waters the murmurs of those labouring in the vineyards.

Marcial, the Roman poet, sang of the Aragonese wines. And it was at the end of the Spanish Reconquest after centuries of struggle against the Arabs that the Aragoneses, faithful in their dedication, went back to the cultivation of their vineyards.

The statistics are clearly indicative: 247,500 acres of vineyard, having a density of 300 vines per acre. In the province of Sarragossa there are 1,050 winemaking bodegas and 45 cooperatives which shows their, commercial importance on the vitivinicular map.

The main vines are: *Bobal, Cariñena, Juan Ibáñez, Garnacha, negra, Ribote, Blasco, Vidadico, Aorastel, Arcos, Macabeo, Malvasía, Mazuelas, Paret* and *Viura*, all of which produce TINTOS and for the BLANCOS they are: *Moscatel, Crujidera, Miguel de Arcos, Valencí, Garnacha blanca* and *Macabeo* are used.

THE CARIÑENA

The district of Cariñena is protected from the northerly winds by the Massif Sierra de la Muela. Its sunny lands facing south are ideally situated and reflect the good quality of these wines in general. The places under the DENOMINACION DE ORIGEN «CARIÑENA» are: *Alfamen, Aguarón, Almonacid de la Sierra, Alpartir, Cosuenda, Encinacorva, Lomgares, Tosos, Villanueva del Huerva* and *Paniza*.

The most abundant wine in the district is the ordinary *tinto* used for blending. There are also the *rosados, claretes* and the **Pajarilla,** a pale wine obtained from the white grape. And finally the red and white *mistelas* very rich in sugar.

The **Cariñena** is renowned for its **valentía.** It is an ordinary wine of 16º to 20º and has a large quantity of dry extract very essential in the blending process. Its average total acidity is 5 grams per litre and its total volatile acidity goes from 0.70 to 0.80 grams per litre. There is no doubt about this wine for it is «un vino muy serio», as they say.

WINE, WOMEN AND SONG
(Photo J. M. Ruiz.)

The sweet *licoroso* Málaga type wine has a brilliant concentration of rosado must which is mixed with the natural must in the proportion of one part concentrated for every two parts unfermented must. Once mixed it is left to stand until the fermentation has started at 9º Beaumé and 15º alcohol. Then it is filtered two or three times until it becomes clear and transparent.

THE CHARACTERISTICS OF THE CARIÑENA WINES

Class of wine	Beaumé degree	Alcoholic degree	Dry Extract reduced	Fixed acidity of tartaric acid	COLOUR
Tinto (dry)	—	13-18	22-32	3.5-6.5	Red, dark ruby or pale
Clarete (dry)	—	13-18	21-30	3.0-6.0	Pink, yellow
Blanco (dry)	—	13-18	21-31	3.0-6.5	Colourless and very pale yellow
Tinto (sweet)	1- 5	13-17	22-32	3.5-6.5	Red (dark) ruby
Clarete (sweet)	1- 5	13-17	21-30	3.0-6.0	Pink
Blanco (sweet)	1- 5	13-17	21-31	3.0-6.0	Colourless, yellow
Rancio (dry)	—	14-18	20-30	2.5-5.0	Old gold
Rancio (sweet)	1- 5	13-17	20-30	2.5-5.0	Old gold
Mistela (red)	8-12	14-18	22-32	2.5-5.0	Red (dark) ruby
Mistela (rosada)	8-12	14-18	21-31	2.5-5.0	Pink amber
Mistela (blanca)	8-12	14-18	21-31	2.2-4.0	Colourless, slightly yellow
Muscatel	8-12	14-16	20-30	2.4-4.5	Amber

The region of *Calatayud* and *Ateca*, adjoining the provinces of Soria and Guadalajara, is soon expected to have its own «Denominación de Origen». Its *blancos, claretes* and *tintos*, are excellent and range from 13º to 16º. Its mistelas are 15º.

The *Daroca* district bordering the provinces of Saragosa and Teruel, like Calatayud and Ateca, is not yet protected by the «Denominación de Origen» and makes good tintos and claretes of 13º to 16º.

There are **three other districts:** the BELCHITE, RIBERA DEL JALON, along the said river and BORJA. The BELCHITE, near the river Ebro, makes *tintos* and *blancos*.

The RIBERA DE JALON includes the districts of *Rueda de Jalón, Epila, Salinas del Jalón* and *Morata del Jalón*.

BORJA, in the extreme north of Saragossa touching Navarre, produces *tintos, blancos* and *claretes* of the *valiente* type going as high as 18º.

HUESCA

Although the province is located far to the north, it does produce some wine in the districts of Barbastro, Litera, Lanaja, and Somontano. These wines are dry *tintos* of 14º and *blancos* of 12º to 13º. Being light of colour and body, they are ideal as table wines.

There are a few wines such as the *Secreta* of Novés, the *Somontano* of Alto Aragón, and the *Garnacha* of Sayabes, as well as the home made **rancio** wines which date back to the 12th century.

TERUEL

Teruel consists of three districts: *Valderrobles*, *Lecera* and *Daroca*, although a dry *tinto* and *rancio* wine also exists in the *Sierra del Albarracín* and *Cellax*.

The vine varieties that are cultivated are the Alcañón, blanco, Macabeo Monastrel, Marcheli, Garnacha and Cariñena.

Owing to the severe winter conditions each year, a great part of the harvest is lost. To remedy this, experiments are being carried out to delay the vegetative cycle of the vines.

The Daroca district includes the municiple areas of Calamocha, Luco de Jiloca, Martín del Río and Baguena. It produces «tintos» and «claretes» of 12 to 16º.

The Lecera district is abundant in tintos, blancos, and claretes of 13 to 15º and takes in the areas of Híjar, Muniesa, Alacón, Oliete, Ariño, Cortes de Aragón, Plou, Blesa and Maicas.

Finally, there is the district of Valderrobles which makes «tintos» and «claretes» of 14º to 16º and includes the areas of Valderrobles, Alcañiz and Castellote.

A LIST OF AUTHORIZED COMPANIES FOR BOTTLING WINE UNDER THE DENOMINACION «CARIÑENA»

Bodega Coop. Sindical Agraria «San Valero» — Avda. del Ejército, 22. Cariñena

Joaquín Soria Marquet — Hermana Matilde, 12. Cariñena

Genaro Tejero Abad — Primo de Rivera, 1. Cariñena

Santiago Morte Sanz — San Valero, 12. Cariñena

Cariñena Vitícola; G. S. de Colonización, 8833 — Carretera de Valencia. Cariñena

Vicente Suso y Pérez — Las Peñas, 2. Cariñena

José Vicente Juan — José Antonio, 65. Cariñena

Bodega Coop. Vitícola «San José» — Aguarón

Aragonesa Vinícola, S. A. «Arvin» — Avda. de la Hispanidad. Zaragoza

Bodegas Monteviejo, S. L. — Paseo María Agustín, 65. Zaragoza

Francisco García Blanco — Paseo María Agustín, 89. Zaragoza

Sucesores de Jerónimo Paricio — Coso, 186. Zaragoza

Balbino Lacosta Tello — Coso, 5. Zaragoza

Bodegas Carivin, S. A. — Camino Ibon, sfn. Huesca.

Bodega Coop. Sindical Agraria Nuestra Señora del Aguila — Camino Aladrén, 1. Paniza

Manuel Martínez Pescador — Almonacid de la Sierra

Bodega Coop. Sindical Agraria de San Roque — Alfamen

BODEGAS UNDER THE DENOMINACION «CARIÑENA»

Agustín Perdiguer — Cariñena

Sucesores Jerónimo Paricio — Villanueva del Herva

Cooperativa Virgen del Aguila — Paniza

Cooperativa San Roque — Alfamén

Cooperativa San Valero — Cariñena

Francisco García Blasco — Zaragoza, Cosuenda, Aragón

Arvin, S. A. — Zaragoza, Cariñena, Aguarón

Joaquín Soria — Cariñena

Viuda de Martín García Gil — Zaragoza, Longares

Ernesto Gasca Ubide — Encinacorba

Bodegas Carivin — Cariñena

Pedro Royo — Longares

Juan Polo — Cariñena

Joaquín Cebrián — Cariñena

Ramón Pérez Juan — Cosuenda

Francisco Burillo — Paniza

Cariñena Vitícola — Cariñena

EL RIBO DE OJA

**PRODUCT OF SPAIN
12/1 RED WINE 1955
RIOJA**

Already in the old statute laws of Miranda de Ebro, from 1099 onwards, mention is made of the Rioja and in other medieval documents, it is called the Ribo de Oja. Even legend has it that a son of Darius, Opo, was the founder of Oca from which are derived the names of so many towns, rivers and families in the region.

One thing certain is it takes its name from the river Oca whose source can be traced up into the Sierra de Ezcaray. It is rough land, through which the river Ebro winds its way to the Mediterranean. Half way down just where the river begins to widen the Ebro begins its 150 miles journey through the charming Rioja, a land of history, charm and historic interest.

The Rioja includes not only the geographic region of Logroño but also the surrounding provinces of Alava, Burgos and Navarre. The people from here have always been very attached to their land and emigration to other parts has been small compared to the rest of Spain. It has a total area of 5,800 square kilometres and a population of 270,000 inhabitants.

The centre of La Rioja is situated along the Way of St. James which in medieval times began at the tower of St. James in Paris and led the pilgrim across France to the shrine of St. James in Santiago de Compostela. Kings, nobles, bishops, and priests, rich and poor often set out on this great trek south and west. It was in the Rioja that the pilgrims were put up in the many abbeys, hostals and simple country barns. It is along this pilgrim route that some of the best examples of Romanesque architecture are to be seen together with the gothic, mudejar and baroque.

The Way of St. James in the Rioja has been called **The Romanesque Cooking Route** where food holds equal honour with the wine. King Alfonso

HARO, THE WINE CATHEDRAL,
CAPITAL OF THE RIOJA ALTA
(Photo Paisajes Españoles.)

the Wise said of this land: «God bestowed on it everything that one could desire».

The *Riojanos* do not know when the first vineyard was planted but the truth is that the grapevines grew and multiplied within the proximities of the river Ebro to such an extent that during the reign of the Spanish monarch Charles III, they were considered an indispensable part of any royal banquet.

The contrasts of mountain and plain, barren rock, land and cordillera, low hills and woodland, together with the river Ebro which fertilises the very rich valleys, have made this land a privileged one.

THE RIOJA
(LAND OF WINE)

In this symphony of colours and contrasts the vineyards of the Rioja flourish and its many diverse wines are made. The *tintos* are regal, strong, and masculine The *blancos* are *serios* and aromatic; the «claretes», «alegres» (cheering) and picaresque.

THE RIOJA ALTA

In Haro alone, the chief town of the Rioja Alta, there are ten maturing *bodegas*. It is a coincidence that they should all be found very near the railway station for there couldn't be a better place for the advertisement of these great wines. Merely crossing the bridge just outside the town and there you are in the RIOJA ALAVESA.

THE RIOJA ALAVESA

On the left bank of the river, there are the vineyards of *Labastida* and on the right *Laguardia* the capital. Along the river *Samaniego* the districts of *Leza, Baños de Ebro, Yecora, Elciego, Moreda* and *Labranza* are representative of these deep red wines of the *Rioja Alavesa*. This is explained by the fact that the vineyards here face south. The bodegas of the Marqués de Riscal are in *Elciego*. This illustrious bodega was founded by Don Camilo Gonzalo de Amézaga en 1860 and since that time its wines have aged and matured in Canadian oak barrels which eventually go to make the great solera wines.

THE RIOJA MEDIA

Cenicero in the Rioja Media is situated on the right bank of the river Ebro and encompasses 5000 acres of vineyard. Each acre has an average of 4,000 vines. Its production is in the region of 5,000 hectolitres.

It is in the beautiful country houses on whose walls are displayed the family coat of arms that the illustrious Rioja bodegas are located.

THE RIOJA BAJA

The bodegas of Calahorra on the Cidacos hillside are literally buried underground to keep the temperature cool and constant. A former Roman town, it was Quintillian who sang the praises of her excellent wine.

The RIOJA ALTA, with its capital in *Haro,* produces bright coloured red wines of 10.5° to 12° of slightly acid flavour which are essential qualities for the light and aromatic wines. The *Calagraño, Viura, Malvasía,* and *Torrontés* grapes produce the white and dry wines of a palid green tint of 11° to 12°. The vines used to make the *tintos* are the *Garnacha, Graciano, Tempranilla* and *Mazuela.* In the RIOJA ALAVESA, the same varieties are found together with the *Blanco Gordo, Tempranilla* and *Moscatel* wines of between 13° to 14°, and having their own peculiarities of taste, smell and colour. In the RIOJA BAJA the wines are stronger (16° or more) and are of the classical **valiente tintorro** kind.

Their shade of colour goes from pale white to cool amber and then from smooth claret red to an intense *tinto* red.

This variety is a product of careful and harmonious breeding of wines of very contrasting quality and exquisite «bouquet» as well as live and bright colours. Even the common *corriente* wines have a perfect composition in so far as alcohol, acidity and dry extract is concerned.

The same *tinto* has a smooth «bouquet», which has very often been compared to the Bordeaux wines whose drinking is particularly recommended for meats, sausages and good cheese. Speaking of the Rioja and its afinity with the Bordeaux wines, it is logical and natural for this wine to be highly regarded internationally.

However, this doesn't mean to say the white wines are inferior. Their diversity gives each one its own peculiarities and they are almost always compared to the white Sautern and Chablis wines.

From Haro to the district of Alfaro where the Rioja ends, the people call the wines of a year old **vinos tiesos.** To acquire their fullest quality they need to rest 3 to 4 years in the barrel and to become reserve wines they should ~~mature~~ *age* for at least 6 years.

AREAS OF PRODUCTION

The production area of the Rioja wines is composed of the lands situated in the municipal districts controlled by the CONSEJO REGULADOR (Regulating Council). The said municipal districts, encompassing the provinces of Logroño, Alava, and Navarra are classified into three subregions called the RIOJA ALTA, RIOJA ALAVESA and the RIOJA BAJA.

The municipal districts in the RIOJA ALTA consist of:

Abalos, Alesanco, Alesón, Arenzana de Abajo, Arenzana de Arriba, Azofra, Badarán, Baños de Río, Tobía, Bobadilla, Briñas, Briones, Camprovín, Canillas, Cañas, Cárdenas, Casalarreina, Cellórrigo, Cenicero, Cihuri, Cordovín, Cuzcurrita, Etrena, Fonzaleche, Fuenmayor, Gimileo, Haro, Herramélluri,

Hornilla, Hormilleja, Hornos de Moncalvillo, Huércanos, Leiva, Logroño, Manjarrés, Medrano, Nájera, Navarrete, Ochanduri, Ollauri, Rodezno, Tricio, Uruñuela, Ventosa, Villalba de Rioja, Villar de Torce, Zarratón and the municipal district of *Miranda de Ebro*, called «*El Ternero*» situated to the south of Haro.

RIOJA ALAVESA

Baños de Ebro, Barriobusto, Elciego, El Villar de Alava, Labastida, Labraza, Laguardia, Lanciego, La Puebla de Labarca, Leza, Moreda de Alava, Navaridas, Oyón, Salinillas de Buradón, Samaniego, Villanueva de Alava and *Yécora*.

RIOJA BAJA

Agoncillo, Alberite, Aícanadre, Aldeanueva de Ebro, Alfaro, Andosilla, Arnedo, Ausejo, Autol, Azagra, Calahorra, Corera, El Redal, El Villar de Arnedo, Galilea, Grávales, Lagunilla de Jubera, Mendavia, Murillo del Río Leza, Ocón, Pradejón, Quel, Ribaflecha, Rincón de Soto, San Adrián, Santa Engracia de Jubera, Sartaguda, Tudelilla, Viana, and *Villamediana de Iregua*.

The Rioja **tintos** are made with the *Tempranilla, Garnacha, Graciano* and *Mazuela* grapes and the **blancos** with the *Malvasía, Garnacha blanca* and *Viura*.

The **maturing areas** under their respective «Denominación de Origen» have the following municipal districts:

Rioja Alta

Briones, Cenicero, Fuenmayor, Gimileo, Haro, Logroño, Navarrete, Ollauri, San Asensio and *San Vicente*.

Rioja Alavesa

Elciego, Labastida, Laguardia, Lanciego, Oyón, and *La Puebla de Labarca*.

Rioja Baja

Alcanadre, Aldeanueva, Alfaro, Arnedo, Ausejo, Autol, Calahorra, Murillo, Quel, San Adrián, Tudelilla.

The ageing process of the reserve wines lasts for at least two years of which one is spent maturing in barrels of 225 litres. During this period the traditional methods, among them the necessary decantations, are employed until the wine matures.

The Rioja wines are many and for every dish there is a suitable wine. There is the **Rioja Blanco** which is especially indicated where light Hors d'oeuvres, fish and seafood generally are served. Its fine quality and varying degree satisfies the most demanding palate.

The **Rioja Rosado** goes well with all the meat dishes and is an excellent **aperitive** wine.

The **Rioja Tinto,** «*corriente*» or ordinary wine, is served with duck, turkey, etc. The majority of winemakers offer two types: a claret of the Bordeaux kind, light and deep in colour, and a strong Burgundy kind of good body and strength.

Wine	Density (minimum)	Acidity	Alcoholic degree (minimum)
RIOJA ALTA:			
Tinto	0.9935	3.5-9.5	10
Rosado	0.9915	4.0-6.5	10
Blanco.	0.9910	4.0-6.5	10
RIOJA ALAVESA:			
Lágrima (tinto). . . .	0.9935	3.5-6.5	9
Corazón	0.9905	3.5-6.5	12.5
Medio.	0.9905	3.5-6.5	12.5
RIOJA BAJA:			
Tinto	0.9920	4.0-6.0	12.5
Rosado.	0.9915	4.0-6.5	12.5
Blanco seco	0.9910	4.0-9.5	12.5

OLD WINE PRODUCERS IN THE RIOJA

In Haro: the Rioja Alta, Bodegas, S. A.; López Heredia, R. Viña Tondonia, S. A.: Martínez Lacuesta Hnos. Ltda.; Bilbao R. Bodegas. Herederos de Enrique Bilbao; Gómez Cruzado, Bodegas, S. A.; Rioja Santiago, S. A. Serrés Carlos; «Bodegas» founded respectively in 1890, 1877, 1895, 1924, 1886, 1898, 1904 and 1896. Bodegas Bilbaínas, S. A. founded in 1909 and Compañía Vinícola del Norte de España (CVNE) founded in 1879.

In Ollauri: Federico Paternina, S. A. founded in 1898.

In Cenicero: Lagunilla Bodegas, S. A. founded in 1885 and Bodegas Riojanas, S. A. Borisa, founded in 1890.

In Elciego: Vinos de los Herederos del Marqués del Riscal, S. A. founded in 1860.

In Logroño: Franco Españolas, Bodegas, S. A. founded in 1890.

In San Adrián, Muerza, Bodegas, founded in 1882.

In Alfaro: Torre y Torres, Andrés de la. founded in 1889.

In Fuenmayor: Bodegas del Romeral, S. A. founded in 1881.

In Laguardia: Bodegas Palacio, S. A. founded in 1894.

IMPORTANCE AND WORLD FAME OF THE RIOJA WINE

The nobility and prestige of the Rioja wines is partially explained by the type of vine cultivated and partially by the careful blending with the solera wines. Some of the most important bodegas were founded in the 19th century such as the Marqués de Riscal and these wines were to be seen in the role of honour on any great social occasion.

A WINE-CELLAR IN THE RIOJA

(Photo Yago.)

When the phylloxera desease killed off the French vines the Rioja which survived the crises became the chief source of wines for the rest of Europe.

It wasn't by pure chance that the illustrious winemakers settled along the banks of the river Ebro to survive this difficult period and maintain their prestige. Of course the techniques employed by the French in the making of these wines improved their taste, bouquet and colour, and soon the quality of these great wines opened up the way for them on the international market rivaling even the Burgundy and Bordeaux from which the noble breeding of these wines originally came.

It is not a question here of comparisons or parallels, the excellencies of each wine is made possible by a series of external factors such as the quality of the soil, sunlight, altitude, and winds.

The Spanish wines have not had the publicity of the French wines and consequently their reputation abroad has suffered with the exception of the sherries whose great name has been linked with British importing houses for centuries.

The old mature Rioja wines are found in all first class restaurants throughout Spain. If there is any criticism of these wines it is that their very essence makes them strong in body, taste and alcoholic degree.

With time the making of these wines has been perfected and through careful maturing and blending, the

coarse flavour has been refined. Today the «valiente» wines have become much milder and of a more fragrant bouquet and finer texture.

In France the enormous publicity which her wines have received, has given them a reputation comparable to any other luxury article. The slogans, inviting tourists to taste wine along the journey together with the collaboration of writers and politicians have created a national conscience. This can best be appreciated by looking at some of the wine lists of the first class establishments for they are beautifully illustrated and displayed. The gastronomical maps and menus are likewise drawn and decorated by well known artists.

The very same could be done respecting the wines of Spain and the wines of Rioja in particular. The time and effort spent on some good publicity would do an immeasurable amount of good with regard to their prestige abroad. It is not enough to say it is a Rioja wine but its locality, properties bodega, vine and year of bottling should be made known. The French wines are always distinguished by their taste, bouquet, degree, and class as for example the Côte d'Or in Burgundy, la Côte de Dijon, La Côte de Nuits and the Côte de Beaune.

CHARTS AND GUIDES
TO THE RIOJA WINES

FORENOTE

It is difficult to write about the Rioja wines without mentioning the many commercial brands. All of the Rioja wines are very good but those bottled commercially deserve a special word since the majority of them have a long history «solera». They vary according to the wine-cellar or bodega and of course the diverse kinds found within each. The following charts give an idea of the range and class of the Rioja wines existent together with their essential characteristics. The «tintos», because of their complexity and prestige in Spain and abroad, are described in greater detail than the «blancos» for which there is a separate section. The «rosados» are included in the final column of the charts for the VINOS BLANCOS.

These are the wines that the visitor drinks in Spain.

Some are exported and others are not. Some, however, are re-exported with a different label and to avoid confusion, the following charts give the Spanish name exclusively.

DESCRIPTIVE
TABLES

R I O J A

BODEGAS	BRAND	AGE
LOPEZ DE HEREDIA VIÑA TONDONIA, S. A.	VIÑA CUBILLO	3 years
	VIÑA TONDONIA	6 years
	VIÑA BOSCONIA	5 years
	VIÑA TONDONIA GRANDES RESERVAS	1942 vintage
		1934 vintage
LA RIOJA ALTA, S. A.	CLARETE RIOJA	6 years
	VIÑA ARDANZA	6-7 years
	RESERVAS «890» and «904»	More than 8 years old
FEDERICO PATERNINA, S. A.	BANDA AZUL	3 years
	BANDA ROJA «VIÑA VIAL»	6 years
	GRAN RESERVA 1928	More than 10 years old
BODEGAS BILBAINAS	CLARETE FINO	5 years
	VIÑA ZACO	6 years

WINES

CHARACTERISTICS	SUITABLE DISHES	REMARKS
Light and fresh 11.5º	*Soups, stews, rice, croquettes, sandwiches and pies*	All these wines have a characteristic acidity
Great «bouquet» and aroma. Ruby colour 12º	*White meats, poultry, stews, rice dishes with meat and sausages*	
With body. Velvet colour.	*Red meats. Dry and fermented cheeses. Mushrooms and sausage. Fillets. «Chateaubriand»*	
With body and «solera»	*Roasts*	
Magnificent «bouquet» Brick colour; outstanding quality wine	*All meats, roasts, cold meats, «churrasco», «cochinillo», liver and sausages*	
Light and dry claret 11.7º	*Soups, boiled dishes, paellas, vegetables, omelettes and fritters*	
Plenty of body and slightly fruity 12.7º	*Roasts, game, dry and fermented cheeses*	
Aroma and solera 12º	*Main dishes, braised meat, cheese, partridge and meat pies*	Very constant quality. Some acidity
A dark claret with body 12.5º	*All meats and vegetables*	
Burgundy type. Mellow. Fine taste and aroma 13º	*Red meats, roasts and all game*	
Great «bouquet» Very well balanced 12.5º	*Cold meats, poultry, game cheeses. Main dishes*	
Claret 12º	*Vegetables, soft cheese, white meat, and light dishes*	
Select and balanced 12.5º	*Selected meats*	

BODEGAS	BRAND	AGE
BODEGAS BILBAINAS	VIÑA POMAL	6 years
	POMAL RESERVA	At present on the market 1952 vintage
	RESERVA	At present on the market 1950 vintage
	VENDIMIA ESPECIAL	At present on the market 1953 vintage
COMPAÑIA VINICOLA DEL NORTE DE ESPAÑA, S. A. C. V. N. E.	CUNE 3.º AÑO	3 years
	CUNE 5.º AÑO	5 years
	IMPERIAL RESERVA	15 years
	IMPERIAL GRAN RESERVA	18 years
	VIÑA REAL PLATA	4 years
	VIÑA REAL ORO	20 years
RIOJA SANTIAGO, S. A.	YAGO 1966	4 years
	YAGO 1962	8 years
	YAGO CONDAL 1948	21 years
	YAGO CONDAL GRAN RESERVA 1835	35 years
	ENOLOGICA	1904

CHARACTERISTICS	SUITABLE DISHES	REMARKS
With body. Slightly fruity taste 13°	*Stews, poultry, game and cheese*	
Dry. Plenty of body 13°	*Game and red meats*	There are some outstanding vintages. 1924 supply exhausted
A very fine «bouquet»	*White meats, raviolis, Spanish cured cod and snails*	
Well balanced	*All kinds of meats, rice dishes cuba style, curry, pickled goose*	
A light but vigorous claret 11,5 to 12°	*Boiled vegetables, eggs, light meals, hors d'oeuvres*	Bordeaux type
Strong and great «bouquet» 12°	*White meats, roast suckling pig, pot of lamb*	
Fragrant, great «bouquet» Violet, ruby colour 12°	*White meats, cheese of La Mancha or Roncal*	Similar to the Bordeaux
Old aromatic, ruby colour 11.5° to 12°	*Sausage meats and hors d'oeuvres*	Similar to the Bordeaux
Balanced, dry, with body 13° to 13.5°	*Red meats and game*	Burgundy type
Body and «solera» Ruby colour 13.5°	*Red meats, roasts, game, boar, deer*	Burgundy type
Fine	*Meats, snails and «patés»*	
Fine	*Meats, light game dishes, croquettes and brains*	
Mellow	*Roasts, game, chicken, partridge and pickled red sausage*	
Old gold ruby colour	*Cold meats and roasts*	
«Siena» ruby colour	*Cold meats, green vegetables and Italian «paste»*	

BODEGAS	BRAND	AGE
FRANCO ESPAÑOLAS, S. A.	CLARET	3 years
	RIOJA BORDON	8 years
	ROYAL	8-9 years
MARQUES DE MURRIETA, S. A.	ETIQUETA BLANCA	5 years
	YGAY RESERVA	1950
	RESERVA, CASTILLO YGAY	1942, 1940, 1937
BODEGAS RIOJANAS, S. A.	VIÑA ALBINA	1960 vintage
	MONTE RRAL	1960 vintage
PALACIOS	RIOJA ALAVESA	4 years
	GLORIOSO	6-9 years
	RESERVA ESPECIAL «BODAS DE ORO»	1923 vintage
MONTECILLO	TERCER AÑO	3 years
	ALAMBRADO 5.º AÑO	5 years
	VIÑA MONTY	1960 and 1955 vintages

CHARACTERISTICS	SUITABLE DISHES	REMARKS
Light and mild 12°	*Green vegetables, boiled dishes, paellas, paste and hors d'oeuvres*	
Burgundy type	*Roasts and game*	
Old with a fine «bouquet»	*Roasts, game and stews*	
Mellow with body	*Stewed meats*	
Violet red colour. Great flavour	*Red meats*	
A claret of exquisite aroma and taste 12°	*White meats, poultry and vegetables*	
Good body. Dark colour	*Cheeses, game, all kinds of meats*	
Light claret with a fine aroma	*Green vegetables, paellas and rice dishes*	This firm sells its wines to the public in Bordeaux barrels of 220, 225 and 100 litres
Old with body and aroma. Bright ruby colour	*All kinds of dishes, particularly meats*	
Ruby colour. Very old	*Sausage meats, strong cheeses and game dishes*	
Slightly fruity. Aromatic	*Boiled dishes, red beans, poultry and meats*	
Aromatic. Ruby colour	*Poultry and white meats*	
A velvet intense red colour. Body and fragrance. Slightly fruity.	*Red meats*	

BODEGAS	BRAND	AGE
HEREDEROS DEL MARQUES DEL RISCAL	NORMAL	4 years
	RESERVAS	Vintages 59, 58, 57, 56, 55, 54, 52, 47, 38 and 1925
MARTINEZ LACUESTA	CLARETE SELECTO	
	CLARETE FINO 4.º, 3.º and 2.º año	4, 3 and 2 years
	SUPERIOR CAMPEADOR	4 and 5 years
	ESPECIAL 1928	More than 8 years
A. G. E. (Azpilicueta, G. Lafuente, Entrena)	SEGUNDO AÑO	6 months
	SIGLO	6 years
	SIGLO COSECHA 59	11 years
	A. G. E., TIPO 28	
FAUSTINO MARTINEZ	VIÑA CAMPILLO	1970, 69, 66, 64 vintages
GOMEZ CRUZADO, S. A.	PREDILECTO	3-4 years
	VIÑA MOTOLLERI	5 years

CHARACTERISTICS	SUITABLE DISHES	REMARKS
A mellow red wine	*Hors d'oeuvres and most meals*	The old vintages are of an extra-ordinary quality
Ruby, old gold colour. More golden with time	*Meats, game, cheeses and cold meats*	
Claret	*Hors d'oeuvres, broths, consommé, fish, stews and eggs*	
Mellow. Exquisite aroma 13º	*Roast, stews and game dishes,*	
Ruby colour. «Bouquet». Old	*Hors d'oeuvres and cold meats. Game*	
A lively young red wine	*Boiled and stewed dishes and light meats*	These four have been chosen as the most characteristic. Other brands are: Viña Tere, AGE,
Body and «bouquet»	*Poultry and meats*	Blend of «garnacha» and «mazuelo» grapes
Body, aroma and well balance	*Roasted dishes, red meats and game*	Wrapped in sacking
Well balanced. Red velvet colour	*Poultry, roasts, sausage meats and game*	Wrapped in sacking
Fragrant	*Foie-grass, game, meat, cheese and dry fruits*	
Light claret Fine aroma 12º	*Soups, rice, omelettes and most dishes*	
Ruby colour. Balanced. Extraordinary «bouquet» 12º		

BODEGAS	BRAND	AGE
GOMEZ CRUZADO, S. A.	VIÑA DORANA	More than 10 years
	REGIO HONORABLE	More than 15 years
CARLOS SERRES HIJO	RIOJA FINO EXTRA	5 years
	RESERVA ESPECIAL	1962 vintage
C. O. V. I. R. I. A. (Cooperativa Vinícola Rioja Alavesa)	PEÑASOL	2 years
	TERCER AÑO TINTO	3 years
	BESANA	6 years
	GRAN RESERVA	Very old wine
VINICOLA VIZCAINA, S. A. BILBAO	VIÑA DEL OJA	
BODEGAS CAMPO VIEJO LOGROÑO	TINTO CAMPOVIEJO	
BODEGAS LAGUNILLA CENICERO	VIÑA HERMINIA, VALLERZARZA, LAGUNILLA	
HEREDEROS DE ENRIQUE BILBAO HARO	VIÑA TURZABALLA	
BODEGAS BENES LOGROÑO		
COOPERATIVA VINICOLA DE LABASTIDA	FINO MONTEBUENA	
	DON GONZALO	
BODEGAS COOPERATIVAS DE SANTA MARIA LA REAL DE NAJERA		
BODEGAS MUERZA SAN ADRIAN		

CHARACTERISTICS	SUITABLE DISHES	REMARKS
Ruby colour. Balanced. «Bouquet»	*Red meats, roasts and game*	
Old. Ruby colour	*Roasts, cheeses, sausages and cold meats*	
Light 12º		
With body 12.7º to 13º	*Roasts and game*	1958 vintage is still on the market
Red, white and rosé 12.7º		
Red or white		
Mellow red wine with body		
Light red wines. Fine «bouquet»		
Claret		
Slightly sparkling		
Red wines of body		

WHITE

BODEGA	EXTRA DRY	DRY	FRUITY DRY
BODEGAS BILBAINAS		VIÑA PACETA 12º Pale *Hors d'oeuvres, fish*	
C. V. N. E.	MONOPOLE 11.5º to 12º *Oysters and light shell-fish*	C. V. N. E. 4.º YEAR 11.5º to 12º *Cheese, fish*	
PALACIOS		SEMILLON 12º «Bouquet» *Hors d'oeuvres, fish*	
BODEGAS RIOJANAS		MEDIEVAL 12º *Seafood*	
A. G. E.	SIGLO V. 1959 *Seafood*	AGESSIMO *Rich shellfish*	FUENMAYOR Very fine *Fish soup, smoked fish*
GOMEZ CRUZADO		SELECTO 3.º year *Fish, and cheese*	VIÑA MOTULLERI (1934 reserve) Aromatic *Rich dishes*
LA RIOJA ALTA	METROPOL 12º in its sixth year *Light shell-fish, fish*		RESERVA ESPECIAL BLANCO 12º *Smoked fish*
LOPEZ HEREDIA	VIÑA TONDONIA 1942 *Fish*	VIÑA TONDONIA 12º in its sixth year *Hors d'oeuvres*	VIÑA GRAVONIA *Fish soup and «bouillabaisse»*
PATERNINA	RINSOL 12º - 6 years old «Bouquet» *Light shell-fish*	BANDA DORADA Gran Reserva 12º - 4 years old *Hors d'oeuvres*	

WINES

MILD	SEMI SWEET	ROSÉ	OTHERS
CEPA DE ORO 12º Soft. «Bouquet» *Consommé, fish*	BRILLANTE 12º *White fish*	IMPERATOR 12º *Fish and simple meals*	The heirs of «Marqués del Riscal» have a magnificent rosé wine
	CORONA «SEMI» 11.5 to 12º *White fish*		
REGIO «Bouquet» *Creams. Seafood*			
	VIÑA ALBINA 12º in its 5th year *Sweet, soft and aromatic*	BORISA 11º *Blue fish, cheese*	
	SIGLO «PRECIOSO» *Consommés and desserts*	LAS ACACIAS *Green vegetables. Asparagus*	
	RIOJA ANAMELY *Desserts and pastries*	ROSADO *All meals*	
	RADIANTE 11º in its 5th year *Fish and desserts*		
VIÑA ZACONIA 12º in its sixth year Aroma *Consommés, creams*	VIÑA ROMANIA 11.5º *Fish and desserts*	ROSADO 5th year All *foods*	
	MONTE HARO 12.5º in its 5th year *Fish and desserts*	BANDA ROSA *Asparagus, green vegetables, white cheeses.*	

WHITE

BODEGA	EXTRA DRY	DRY	FRUITY DRY
RIOJA SANTIAGO	YAGO 1935 «Bouquet» *Shellfish*	YAGO 1955 *Seafood*	YAGO 1858 *Soups.*
FRANCO ESPAÑOLAS		CASTIL-CORVO 12º and 5º *Topaz shellfish, oysters*	VIÑA SOLE Pale gold. Aroma *Smoked fish. Cheeses*
MARQUES DE MURRIETA		MURRIETA 12º *Fish-Hors d'oeuvres*	
MONTECILLO		RESERVE - 62 *Stewed fish dishes. Cheeses*	
MARTINEZ LA CUESTA			
FAUSTINO MARTINEZ		VIÑA CAMPILLO 1970, 1969, 1966, 1964 vintages *Shellfish, ~~fisth~~* fish	

WINES

MILD	SEMI-SWEET	ROSÉ	OTHERS
YAGO 1948 *Assorted, fish*	YAGO 1949 Straw colour *Consommé, creams*	ROSADO 1945 Ordinary meals ROSADO 9158 Hors d'oeuvres	
	DIAMANTE (Sauterne type) 12,5º. Amber colour *White fish and consomme*	ROSADO (DRY) *All dishes*	
		ROSADO (DRY) *Asparagus, green vegetables*	
	SEMI-DULCE ALAMBRADO 6th year *Desserts and fruits*	HOJA DE PARRA DOS BANDAS 60 PETILLANT *Blue fish*	
	RIOJA SUPERIOR VIÑA DELYS *Consomme, fish*	RIOJA ROSADO 3rd year Light aroma «Bouquet» *Fish, cheese*	
	VIÑA SANTANA 1969 vintage	VIÑA CAMPILLO Fresh, aromatic 1970, 1969, 1966, 1964. Vintages *All kinds of dishes*	
	RIOJA FINO BLANCO TOPACIO 6th year *Fish, desserts*	RIOJA GRAN ROSADO 11,5º to 12º ~~Fruiti~~ Fruity All meals, *and* in hot weather	

DECALOGUE OF THE GOOD DRINKER OF RIOJA WINES

I.   *Each dish requires the right wine which should be chosen personally.*

II.   *Wines of different quality and kind should never be mixed.*

III. *The «tintos» and some of the «blancos» of some age require special attention and should be served without being shaken.*

IV.   *It is not bad form to try the wine to see if it is the right one.*

V.   *Each wine has its own temperature. Before uncorking a bottle see that it is at the required temperature.*

VI.   *Once the wine is served (neither under or overfilled) make sure that the bottle is visible for there is no better adornment than the presence of a good wine at the table.*

VII. *Never drain the bottle of wine. The dregs should always remain at the bottom as proof of the good wine that has been drunk.*

VIII. *It is better to drink small quantities of good quality wine than a lot of cheap wine.*

IX.   *Before choosing the wine, always remember to ask your guests what their preferences are.*

X.   *Selecting good wine is an art and the Rioja wines provide a wide range for every kind of dish.*

BODEGAS UNDER THE DENOMINACION «RIOJA»

NAME	ADDRESS	BODEGA
AGE, Bodegas Unidas, S. A.	Fuenmayor (Logroño)	Fuenmayor
Andrés de la Torre y Torres	Alfaro (Logroño)	Alfaro
Bodegas Berberana, S. A.	Alda. San Mamées, 49. Bilbao	Ollauri
Bodegas Bilbaínas, S. A.	Apartado 124. Bilbao	Haro
Bodegas Franco Españolas, S. A.	Cabo Naval, 1. Logroño	Logroño
Bodegas Gómez Cruzado, S. A.	Haro (Logroño)	Haro
Bodegas Gurpegui	San Adrián (Navarra)	San Adrián
Bodegas Lagunilla, S. A.	Cenicero (Logroño)	Cenicero
Bodegas Marqués de Murrieta	Apartado 175050. Madrid	Logroño
Bodegas Montecillo, S. A.	Fuenmayor (Logroño)	Fuenmayor
Bodegas Muerza, S. A.	San Adrián (Navarra)	San Adrián
Bodegas Palacio, S. A.	Colón de Larreátegui, 13. Bilbao	Laguardia
Bodegas Riojanas, S. A.	Cenicero (Logroño)	Cenicero
Bodegas Rioja Santiago, S. A.	Haro (Logroño)	Haro
Braulio Benés Cañas	Avda. Primo de Rivera, 6. Logroño	Briones
Cía. Vinícola del Norte de España	Navarra, 8. Bilbao	Haro
Carlos Serres Hijo	Haro (Logroño)	Haro
Federico Paternina, Vinos Rioja	Haro (Logroño)	Haro
Francisco Canals	Fuenmayor (Logroño)	Fuenmayor
Francisco Viguera	Ruavieja, 29. Logroño	Logroño
Herederos de Enrique Bilbao	Haro (Logroño)	Haro
La Rioja Alta, S. A.	Haro (Logroño)	Haro
Martínez Lacuesta Hnos., Ltda.	Haro (Logroño)	Haro
R. López Heredia, Viña Tondonia, S. A.	Haro (Logroño)	Haro
Savin, S. A.	Paseo Urumea. San Sebastián	Aldeanueva de Ebro
Vinos Hered. Marqués del Riscal	Elciego (Alava)	Elciego
Bodegas Faustino Martínez	Oyón (Alava)	Oyón
De la Torre y Lapuerta, S. A.	Alfaro (Logroño)	Alfaro
Rojas & Cía., S. R. C.	Alhóndiga Municipal, Bilbao	Laguardia
Vinícola Vizcaína, S. A.	Bilbao	Bilbao
Bodegas Campo Viejo	Logroño	Logroño
Bodegas Benes	Logroño	Logroño
Coop. Vinícola de la Bastida	Labastida	Labastida
Bodegas Coop. Sta. María la Real	Nájera	Nájera
Bodegas del Romeral. F. A. Martínez	Fuenmayor	Fuenmayor
Bodegas Estrena, S. A.	Navarrete	Navarrete
Bodegas Las Veras. Cruz G. Lafuente	Fuenmayor	Fuenmayor
Bodegas Ramón Bilbao	Haro	Haro

NAVARRE

Drink the purest wine you can get,
for true wine strengthens and heartens.

POPE. LEON XIII

The province of Navarre is bound by France along the north, the Basque provinces of Guipúzcoa and Alava in the northwest and the river Ebro and Logroño in the south. The geography and history of Navarre are interesting as they tell us a great deal about her relations with France and Spain in Medieval times.

Her history begins with the Vards and Vasconians, a people of great spirit and independence who were never conquered by either the Romans or Visigoths. The Latin penetration was of relative importance only. There was a period when Navarre was united to Aragón and the French civilisation and influence were particularly strong. However, during the reign of Ferdinand and Isabel, Navarre became a part of Spain.

Navarre is hard and noble like the Pyrenese that created her. Streams cascade down the mountainside, rivers flow down into the valleys of singular beauty and finally merge with the wood and farmland. Everything has a pastoral note about it. The monasteries, and castles of antique legend, mystery and romance are there to remind one of the holy pilgrimages to the shrine of Saint James. To the south lies the river Ebro and to the southeast the plains of the Bardenas Reales merge and are lost in the distance.

But nowhere is Navarre better known than at the Fiestas of San Fermín, for it is this occasion more than any other that has attracted writers, bullfighters and personalities from far and wide. Hemingway was inspired by this atmosphere of pomp and bright colours, the running of the bulls through the narrow streets and the «encierros».

VINEYARD AND SETTING

The 100,000 acres of vineyard are cultivated mainly in the south of Pamplona where the woodland and fields give way to open lands. The changing character of the land is particularly suitable for vine cultivation and has given these wines their rank and prestige. The stronger wines of higher alco-

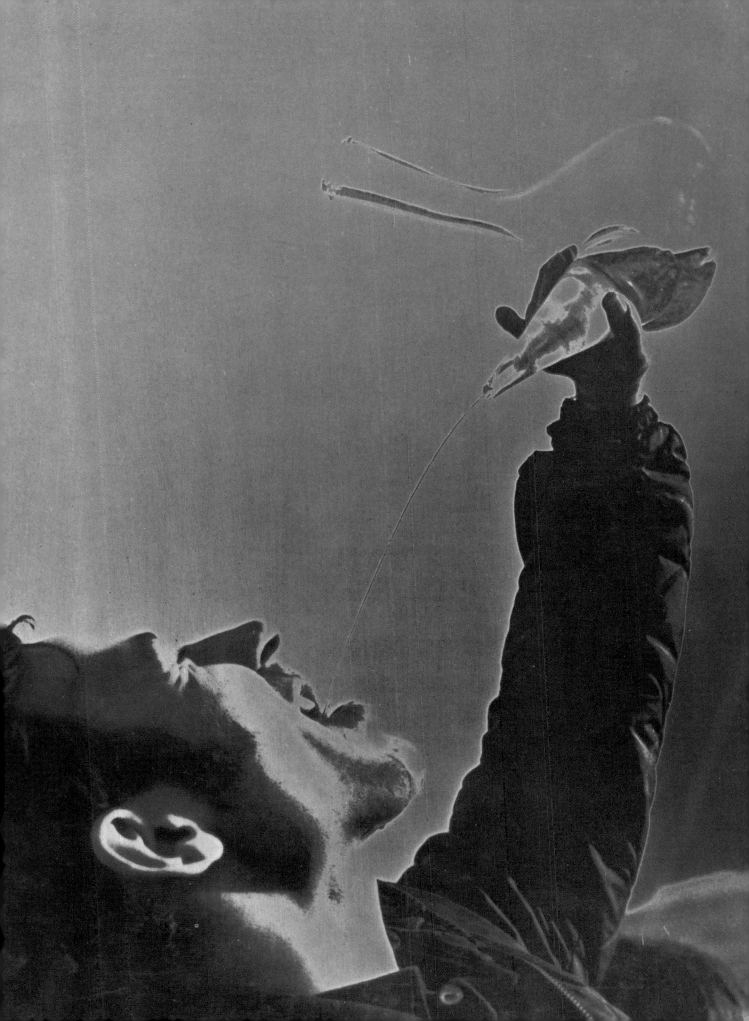

«PORRON» DRINKING

(Photo by Courtesy of La Semana Vitivinícola.)

holic content are made from the Garnacha grape, which are suitable for «coupage». Among them, the *finos*, milder red wines, are a masterly preparation.

In the north, the *vino verde* is made very similar to the popular Chacolí of the Basque country. This wine is the fruit of the rain, drizzle and damp atmosphere of the Cantabrian north together with a minimal amount of sunshine which seems essential in the preparation of this good wine.

THE DIFFERENCE IN LATITUDE AND THE STRENGTH OF WINE

In Navarre, the farther north one penetrates, the sparser are the vine yards and consequently the wine production much less. In the Guasalaz valley the wines have a sharp taste and are delicious. However, to the south in the lands lying along the Ebro valley and the Ribera is the real vinicular area. There the wines of a very fine quality, colour and body, are worthy of their renown.

Similarly, the wines of *Cirauqui, Puente la Reina, Artajona* and *Mendi gorria* deserve to be mentioned. The church of Mendigorria, so the local people say, was built with mortar and wine as this was more plentiful than water.

THE WINES

Navarre is a land of vernacular traditions and the secrets and ancient arts of wine making are still passed down from father to son.

The most highly prized grapes are the *Carasol* and the *Secano*. The wines produced from these were already known in the XVI century and gave fame to such names as *Puente la Reina, Mendigorrea, Manera, Cirauque, Artoze, Artajona* and *Solana*. In the district of *Corella* and *Cintruénigo* the wines are fairly strong and enhanced by their agreeable sharpe taste. The Russians, who were the chief importers in the past, had a very special preference for these wines.

In *Las Campanas, Pitillas* and *Falces* ordinary *tintos* and *claretes* vary from 11º to 15º.

In the proximities of Pamplona the *tintos* and *blancos* can be compared to any French wine from the Côte du Rhone.

In the district of Estella, the dark *clarete*, referred to as the *ojo de gallo* has a penetrating «bouquet» and serves well as a *fino* table wine.

The *rancio Peralta* wine, made in the area of *Las Campanas* and *Villafranca*, is very popular. It has a pleasing taste, golden colour and a fairly high alcoholic content.

As has been said already, the northern part of Navarre makes the sparkling «*chacolí*» class of wine, the *Chacolí tinto de Ezcaba* as it is called. It is not for nothing that Navarre has so many parallels with the adjacent Basque country.

The Navarese have a splendid reputation in the ageing and blending of their *claretes* and *blancos* which combined with the excellent arrangements between growers and cooperatives makes them some of the first in Spain.

It might be well to remember that some of the wines produced in the Ribera district bordering the Rioja can and do use the name of Rioja on their labels.

WINE BOTTLERS UNDER THE
REGULATING COUNCIL OF NAVARRE

Name	Address	Locality
Bodegas Camilo Castilla	Santa Bárbara, 40	Corella
Bodegas Carmen Uguet de Resayre	Postiguillo, 1	Ablitas
Bodegas Cayo Simón Magaña	Mayor, s/n	Murchante
Bodegas Coop. Ntra. Sra. del Romero	C. de Tarazona, s/n	Cascante
Bodegas Coop. Vinícola de Tafalla	C. Estella, s/n	Tafalla
Bodegas Corellanas, S. A.	Santa Bárbara, 29	Corella
Bodegas Félix Chivite Marco	Cascajera, s/n	Cintruénigo
Bodegas Julián Chivite Marco	Barón de la Torre, 2	Cintruénigo
Bodegas Delfín Pérez Lahera	B. Jacoste, 1	Tudela
Cooperativa Vinícola Navarra	Ciudadela, 5	Pamplona
H. Beaumont y Cía., S. R. C.	Señorío de Sarría	Puente la Reina
Vinícola Navarra, S. A.	Avda. Roncesvalles, 2	Pamplona

THE FOUR WINEMAKING AREAS IN NAVARRE

In 1967 **four areas** were formed with the right to use the Denominación de Origen «Navarra»—MONTAÑA, VALDIZARBE, RIBERA ALTA and RIBERA BAJA. Each one of these includes the following place names:

MONTAÑA

Aibar, Aoiz, Eslava, Ezprogui, Javier, Leache, Liédana, Lumbier, Lerga, Sada, and Sangüesa.

VALDIZARBE

Aberín, Adiós, Añorbe, Artajona, Artazu, Ayegui, Barasoain, Biurrun, Cirauqui, Elorz, Enériz, Estella, Garinoain, Guirguillano, Lagarda, Leoz, Mañeru, Mendigorría, Muruzábal, Obanos, Olóriz, Orisoain, Pueyo, Puente la Reina, Tiebas, Tirapu, Ucar, Unzué, Uterga, Villatuerta.

RIBERA ALTA

Allo, Arellano, Armanarzas, Arróniz, Barbarín, Bargota, Baire, Berbinzana, Caparroso, Cárcar, Carcastillo, Cáseda, Dicastillo, Desojo, El Busto, Falces, Funes, Gallipienzo, Larraga, Lazagurría, Lerín, Lodosa, Los Arcos, Luquín, Marcilla, Mélida, Miranda, Morentín, Murillo el Cuende, Olite, Oteiza, Peralta, Fitillas, San Martín de Unx, Sansoain, Sansel, Santacara, Sesma, Tafalla, Torres del Río, Ujué and Villafranca.

RIBERA BAJA

Ablitas, Arguedas, Barillas, Cascante, Cintruénigo, Corella, Fitero, Monteagudo, Murchante, Tudela and Tulebras.

THE BASQUE COUNTRY

Drinkers of Distinction

THE CHACOLI

Along the green and moist coast valleys of Vizcaya and Guipúzcoa, the chacolí vineyards are a cheerful sight indeed. You do not need to be a Basque to appreciate the excellence of this wine, a *vino verde*, of fine quality and flavour. The climate is the cause of this singular wine for the Cantabrian region is very wet and a fine drizzle known as the «sirimiri» falls constantly during the early Spring delaying the ripening of this grape. The vines are normally to be seen growing around old farm houses or «caseríos» as they are called.

The wine is as digestible as it is agreeable and ideally suited for the drinking of the **chiquito**—the classical Basque measure of a glass of wine. Being a particular sensitive, fragrant wine, it should be drunk in the country where it is made. Like all good things there is little of it. Baquio, Valmaseda and Murueta in Vizcaya hold primacy in the production of this *vino verde*.

In contrast to the sparing measure of the *manzanilla*, which is normally sipped in a wine glass, the «*chacolí*» is drunk down with one tip of the glass. However, like her distinguished lady friend, the «*chacolí*» is cooled under running water and is first tasted in a shaded place.

What the Andalucians think is confirmed by the Basques when they say there is no better wine for shellfish. As for the colour, some like it white, others, red; the «Txakolin zuri» and «Txakolin gorri» as it is called in Basque.

THE PRICE WAR OF THE CHIQUITO

From time to time throughout the Basque region, the usual calm atmosphere is broken by the war of the **chiquito.** It only needs a slight rise in the price of wine to change the visiting habits to certain taverns. But the curious thing is there is no bad feeling on either side. It is all part of the game and provides a certain amount of amusement. Time is spent in harmless argument, although the public appears to be up in arms because of the rise in price of a glass of wine, «el chiquito».

THE «CHIQUITEO»

It is around the aperitive time, just before lunch and going home in the evening that the «chiquiteo» goes on. It consists simply in buying rounds of

GOOD BASQUE WINE DRINKERS

drinks of *blancos* or *tintos* drunk out of a thick stubby glass filled to three quarters capacity. The taverns are usually packed with people and human chatter. Although the basques are held to be short of words—«breve en palabras»—once you get them talking, they are very amusing and prove to be the best of friends. The *chiquiteo* is just a pleasant and agreeable way of passing the time and of being simply sociable without being snobbish or sophisticated. The *chiquiteros* are wine drinkers exclusively and will have

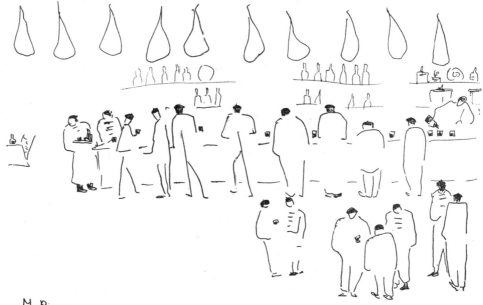

M. Roger

nothing to do with whiskies and cocktails. The seasoned drinkers handle their *chiquitos* with great care unconsciously fondling and caressing their glasses. The *chiquiteo* is a way of life and it has often been said that the «bilbaino» would rather shoot himself than miss his *chiquiteo* after seven. Of course, he never resorts to this thank God, and that is why he always «chiquitea» as the Basques put it in their humorous way.

THE CANTABRIAN
CORNICE

With the passing of time some important economic changes have taken place respecting vine cultivation and winemaking. These changes have been brought about by rising labour and production costs to the extent that the independent growers and the smaller bodegas have been forced to reduce their expenses or go out of business. To remedy this state of affairs, large co-operatives have been formed over the past few years to enable the smaller business to survive.

The vineyards of the northern provinces are not really sufficient to satisfy the demand. In Guipúzcoa, there are 75 acres of vineyards and in Vizcaya, 575 acres. The vineyards are usually found around the «caseríos» and the total production does not exceed 50,000 hectolitres. As a consequence, a lot of wine is brought from the south and southeast. In Asturias, for example, the wine supplies come principally from León and Zamora. In Vizcaya, it is the Rioja wine which takes precedent above all the others. The great wholesale house of «**Alhóndiga**» in Bilbao is well known and has generations of experience in providing excellent table wines not only from the Rioja but also La Mancha, Levante and Andalucía.

The number of bars and taverns in San Sebastián is impressive for in 1968 there were 44 bars for every 10,000 inhabitants compared to Madrid's 93.

THE CIDER OF ASTURIAS

The traditional **apple feast of Villaviciosa** is held in the month of September. It has to be Villaviciosa, as the Asturians and the connoisseurs of good cider know full well for this town conjures up all sorts of beautiful associations. There are her patron saints: *San Juan de Amondi, San Mamés de Arguero, Santa María de Arroes, San Juan de Camoca* and *San Miguel de Mar*. San Miguel would have to end with Mar for there is a beautiful river which runs down to it reflecting the grandeur of the romanesque churches and convents. Not far off on the steep green hills are the apple orchards reaching to the river bank itself. Finally, there is the dock of Espuncia where the ships come in to anchor and load up with cider.

The apples are of three basic sorts: the sweet, semisweet and bitter. The work involved in the making of these ciders is long and just as complex as winemaking, taking into account the picking, washing and bottling process. It is easy to mistake the ciders as each region has its own brand with its particular characteristic smell and taste and does not depend on its reputation as the wines do. This golden refreshing drink is either in stock or it isn't.

The drinking of cider has its own ritual regarding the pouring, drinking and also the manner of the *cata* or the moment of tasting it. The cider master who officiates with great solemnity carefully makes a hole in the barrel with a very fine drill while everyone present waits silently for the spouting of the first drops.

GALICIA

The Wine and the Rain

And Satan said to Our Lord
«All this I will give you
except Fefiñanes, Cambados
and San Tome.»

(ANONYMOUS.)

THE VINEYARDS

What is surprising about the Galician wines is their abundance. In Galicia 87,000 acres are used for vineyard cultivation and 1,200,000 hectolitres of wine is made. Some Galician wines produce up to 24 hectolitres per acre.

The damp weather, the very few frosts, the constant temperature, the short and dry Summers are causes of the high returns. The vines are thick and clustered together. They do not stretch their branches out over the dry parched land as in Castille, instead they clasp the stone cut posts, and reach upward in search of the sun.

In the valleys of the interior, low growing vines are frequently seen «a la castellana» as the Galicians say. When the coast is approached the wines go upward as if to escape from the excessive humidity. In Pontevedra las *parras*, vines that creep and grow overhead and along parallel wires, are typical.

Between Castile and Galicia, near León, is the *Bierzo* district which is rather like a pleasant portico before entering the Galician land.

THE VALDEORRAS VALLEY

The Valdeorras valley watered by the river Sil is surrounded by high ground and mountains that open into deep valleys wherever the vineyards rise up from the hollows of the valley below.

THE MONTERREY VALLEY

This valley to the south of Orense almost touching Portugal is washed by the Támega river. *Castrelo, Monterrey, Verín* and *Oimbra* are the four most important villages in the area. The vines produce excellent *tintos* and tradition has it that the natives of Verín in bygone days used to take baths to calm the after effects of drinking it. The vinestocks are grown and arranged close together in the Castilian way so that at harvest time the hillsides are one mass of green. In *Monterrey* it rains less than in other parts of the province and consequently the wines are some of the strongest in Galicia reaching 14º. The *tintos* are made from the *Negreda, Godello, Albarello, Bastardo, Verdello* and *Gran Negro* grapes and the *blancos* from the *white or Jerez type* grape.

THE TERRACES OF THE SIL AND THE MIÑO

The picturesque Galician villages are usually found high up on the steep hillsides and thereby dominate the valleys and rivers below. The Miño, and Sil are typical of this. To go down to the river banks, «socalcos» have been made. These are terraced steps often cut out of the rocky terrain. Sometimes ropes are needed to get up and down especially during the harvest period.

In the middle of each vineyard, the villagers, and this includes nearly every one, have their wine presses where they make their own wine. In this way, much of the labour involving the carrying of the baskets to and from the bodega is reduced and made easier.

The land lots are usually small and narrow and invariably spread out around the outskirts of the village. This system of land lots divided up among various families is very medieval and continues to be practised even today. It is known by the name of «minifundio». In this soil, the white wine is almost nonexistent, however, the *tintos* from the Sil gorge such as the *Amando* and *Pombeiro* are popular. They are wines of little alcoholic strength (9º to 10º). The traditional wines are the *Albarello, Brancellao, Mouraton,* and *Tinta Femia* and not forgetting *San Fiz* and *Chantada.*

The truly great bodega of Galician wines is situated in the **Ribero** of *Orense* and *Avia.*

THE RIBERO OF ORENSE

In Orense the vineyards widen along the banks of the Miño and its tributaries the Barbantino, Pungin Amoeiro. The vineyards are not so steep as in the Sil valley but have a greater density of 2,000 vinestocks per acre. The majority are grown in the way of «parras» which means that the vine is raised on sticks and stone columns with wires going along and across them. This protects the vine against the humidity and sees to it that the grapevine gets plenty of air and sun. To behold these «parras» is to contemplate real pieces of artwork. There is an old refrain that is pertinent here: *«He who has not stone or sticks has not wine».* In the proximities of Orense the capital, the wine is of the «tinto» kind prepared from the *Alicante, Mencia* and *Gran Negro* vines. On the other side of the river the grapes are white: *Torrontes, Treixadura, Albarino* and *Gudello.* These are wines of pleasant «bouquet» and stronger than the *tintos.*

THE SECRET OF LIVING
(Photo Guillén Franco.)

**THE RIBERO
DE AVIA**

The wines from this area are praised throughout Galicia. The vineyards are situated along the Avia river and occupy about 80 % of the fertile land. Apart from the ideal conditions prevailing for the making of good wine, there is a healthy rivalry in the area which enhances their quality even more. *Alvarellas* and *Pazos de Aventeiro* know a lot about all this.

The vines are clustered together to make the most of the available land. One acre produces from 3 to 4 thousand vines which converted into liquid measure makes 250,000 hectolitres. The vines are held up by simple sticks in small lots called «minifundio». (See The Terraces of the Sil and Miño.)

Both *tintos* and *blancos* are produced. Although the *tintos* are not so strong, they are equally as good as the *blancos*. The *Jerez, Palomino, Treixadura, Torrontés, Silverina, Albillo, Albariño*, vines abound. The connoisseurs assure us that the varieties *Brancellao* and *Caiño* are gradually being replaced by the *Alicante* which has a stronger colour, contains more tannine and is particularly suitable as a table wine.

The art of cultivating and making these wines has been inherited through the monastic orders who took advantage of the warm soft climate, the light winter rains and ideal soil conditions. The musts, however, need very special care as they are especially used to the damp atmosphere.

Near the Portuguese frontier the quality of the wine in the *Valle de Limia* is much lighter but none the less agreeable to the palate.

**THE WINES
OF PONTEVEDRA**

The vineyards are cultivated in «*parrales*» to separate them from the damp ground. They are usually about a metre or two high and even higher when seen growing up the walls of the enchanting country *Pazos* (Villas).

The three most important vinicular regions are: *El Condado, El Albariño* and *El Rosal*.

El Condado de Salvatierra on the north shore of the Miño bordering Portugal includes *Puenteareas, Arbo, Salvatierra* and *Las Nieves*. The vineyards cover one fourth of the total arable land and blend perfectly with the maize. fields. In the valley of *Puenteareas* itself the land is used for growing both cereal and grapevines.

THE ALBARIÑO

This area is situated between the Ría de Arosa and the Ría de Pontevedra including the peninsular land of La Toja. This part is called also the *Peninsula de Barbanza* and is here that wild young colts can be seen gamboling and running wild. Here in the valley of *Salnés, Cambados* is found.

Cambados holds the traditional **feast of Albariño** in August. It is not difficult to explain the origin of its name since it comes from the word «albariza».

José María Castroviejo, a native son and writer on Galicia, thinks that the vines were brought there by the monks of Cluny in the 12ᵗʰ century when Gelmirez was archbishop of Santiago and that they are of the same stock as the Moselle and Rhine wines. Others hold that it was the Templars who on their way to the shrine of Santiago brought the vines with them. The occasion of this feast is held in the palace of Fefiñanes and the wine from *Fefiñanes* is highly considered in Galicia and matured in the bodegas of the Marqués de Figueroa.

The area of Albariño includes the following districts: *Sanjenjo, Meano, Cambados, Ribadumia, Meis Villanueva* and *Portas*.

The *Alvariño blanco* like the *Espadeiro tinto* are alcoholically weak. The *tinto* has only 8° and is an ordinary wine that contrasts with the select *blanco* of 10° having a delicious flavour and aroma.

The Rosal Valley, lying along the banks of the Miño, is the last of the Spanish valleys for across the river Miño lies Portugal. Old father Miño, as it is often called, is full of nostalgic spirit and celtic poetry. From the high prominence of Santa Tecla, there is a magnificent panorama of the ruins of the Celtic war camps of «Puebla Celta», the Rosal valley, the river Miño and the Atlantic Ocean.

The vineyards are cultivated to the very limits of *Laguardia, El Rosal* and *Tomiño*, bordering the Atlantic and the glistening vines waving in the seabreeze look like so many white handkerchiefs. This valley, sheltered from the Atlantic winds by the coast hills, produces wines of 12° made from the *Albariño* and *Jerez* vines.

In the Miño Valley, not far from the Bay of Bayona, a mild red wine and the *Albariño blanco* is made. On the far side of the Ría de Vigo, in *Redondela, Sotomayor*, and the peninsular of *Morrazo*, grapevines and cereals are both cultivated.

The most common vines in this area are: *El Espadeiro, el Cairo, el Tintarrón, La Tinta Femia*, and the *Albariño*.

Further northward, the vineyards become sparser which is to be expected as the climate and land is noticeable harder. On the north side of the Ría Arosa there are about 1,500 acres of vineyard near *Noya* and *Boiro*. To the east the vineyards stretch along the Ulla river where they are tendered in little sequestered valleys separated by ravines covered with pine. The wine is very light but easily spoilt by exposure to sunlight and therefore should be drunk fairly quickly. The «*Racimo Catalán*» is the most popular.

Before bidding farewell to the Galician wines, a word should be said about La Coruña. Even in the far north in the Ría de Santa Marta, the vines grow and thrive in *Estaca de Vares*, *El Cabo Ortegal*, but the vines in the valley of *Mandea*, in the district of *Betanzos*, are better known. In this part of the country the «parras» are rarely seen and the white wines of *San Vicente de Aronera* are no longer to be had.

In Orense there are four specific winemaking areas:

1. *Ribero*

Composed of 12 municipal districts among which the Ribera Alta and the Ribera Baja are of particular importance.

2. *Barco*

Located along the Sil river, consisting of 7 municipal districts whose grapevines make the Barco wine especially appreciated as good red table wines.

3. *Monterrey*

This region includes the area of the whole Monterrey valley giving name to the wines under that Denominación de Origen.

4. *Orense*

This region belongs to the Ribero area.

The average production in hectolitres is approximately 3,601,580 hecto-litres for the total productive area of the province.

THE STRENGTH
OF THESE WINES

In the *Ribero* area there is a greater pro-portion of white wines of between 10º to 13º than *tintos*—9º to 12º.

In *Valdeorras* the «*blancos*» vary between 10 to 12º and the *tintos* from 9º to 11º. In *Verín*, the *tintos* go from 9º to 12º and the *blancos* waver around the 11º to 13º degree mark.

In *Orense* the wines are of a much lower degree, the *blancos* varying from 10º to 11º, and the *tintos* from 8º to 10º.

THE MAIN BODEGAS AND BOTTLING PLANTS IN THE PROVINCE OF ORENSE.

Bodega Cooperativa Nuestra Señora del Portal, del Ribeiro de Avia. Ri-badavia.

Bodega Cooperativa Monterrey, de Albarellos de Monterrey (Verín).

Bodega Cooperativa Jesús Nazareno, de Barco de Valdeorras.

Bodega Cooperativa Virgen de las Viñas, de la Rúa.

Bodega Cooperativa Nuestra Señora de los Remedios, de Laroca.

Bodegas Gallegas, S. A., de Orense y Los Peares.

Bodegas Campos, Sáez Díaz, 73. Orense.

Bodegas Magín Alberte Méndez, Castrelo del Miño.

Bodegas Antonio Nieves Iglesias, Castrelo del Miño.

Bodegas Luciano Eiroá y Cía.

Bodegas Alanís. Radica en Barbantes.

Bodega Rivera. En Barbantes.

Comercial Rofemar, S. L. En Borral (Castrelo de Miño).

Bodega Cooperativa Ribairo. En Ribadeira.

Bodega Manuel Méndez Villanueva. En Prado del Miño.

THE LORRY LOAD BOUND FOR THE «BODEGA»
(Photo Paisajes Españoles.)

THE WINES OF CASTILE AND LEON

The old Castilians say that their wines are not that prodigal for Castile and León are very cold regions and the sun is often insufficient for maturing the grapes. With some notable exceptions in the provinces of Zamora and Valladolid, Castile and León produce less wine than other areas although this insufficiency is made good by the abundant bread supply.

The province of Santander grows vines only in the *Potes* area. Segovia produces a little more than Santander, especially around the river *Eresma*, in the districts of *Rapariagos* and *San Cristóbal*. Soria, which has some good *clarete* and *tinto* wine, is a rather more productive than either Segovia and Santander.

Austere Avila, which doesn't pretend to be a vitivinicular area, provides a continuous supply of wine from *Cebreros*, ideal for drinking with the roast lamb and suckling pig. There are *tintos* and *blancos* mild and aromatic particularly suitable as table wines. The *clarete* wines of the *Valle del Tiétar*, located near the village of *Mombeltrán*, are also good table wines that are served with the «cabra hispánica» that curious animal which lives up in the sierras and provides such succulent meat.

In the province of León near *La Bañeza* and *Sahagún*, the *Pajarete, Perdiz, Jerez and Verdeja* grapes require a method of fermentation with «la madre». This is a slow fermentation process carried out by adding bunches of unsquashed red grapes to the must. It is a sharp mild wine of the type called *agujas*. In the *Cacabeios* area the *blancos*, «claretes», and *tintos* range from 12º to 14º and are very popular.

BURGOS

Burgos is the land of the Cid Campeador and the cradle of Castile. It has a good reserve of wines and a suggestive way of cooking. The wines of the Duero enjoy great prestige in the south of the province within the proximities of *Aranda de Duero* and *Peñafiel*. There are also to be had a few wines of noble ancestry, however, the struggle for survival between vine and vegetable produce goes on and the creation of new irrigation systems is destroying the cultivation of the grapevine in a merciless way. If as they say there are vineyards lying within the irrigation zones which made vine growing very difficult, it could be also said there are vineyards favourably sheltered from the prevailing northerly winds and whose soils and climate were favourable for the making of good wine.

The following statistics are indicative. In 1928 the total surface area of vineyard was 68,750 acres which today doesn't even have 50,000 acres.

Here are the villages which produce wine in the province of Burgos: *Aranda, Fuentecésped, Gumiel de Hizán, Gumiel del Mercado, La Herra, Olmedillo, Nava de Roa, Sotillo de la Ribera and Aguilera.*

The above wines of «mucha capa» have a sharp taste and agreeable smell.

Near the Cantabrian foothills in the north, the Burebe Vine is cultivated around Villarcayo and Miranda de Ebro. This makes a delightful *vino verde* very similar to the «chacolí».

VALLADOLID

In the province of Valladolid, vine cultivation has an area of 74,813 acres and produces wines of a very special quality for here is found the wine of *Vega Sicilia*, one of the most sought after wines on the international market. The vineyards of this wine are situated in the *Valbuena de Duero* area.

THE WINE MAKING DISTRICTS

The wine making districts are numerous, for on leaving the capital of Valladolid and veering northward, just beyond the Pisuerga river, the Tierra de Campos is approached. This is the region of *Cigales* whose main wine producing districts are: *Fuensaldaña, Mucientes, Cigales, Corcos, Trigueros del Valle and Cubillas de Santa Marta.* They are very light wines of 12° to 14°. The blending of the *Verdejo, Albillo, Jerez* and *Blancas* with the *Tinto* aragonés and *Garnacha* makes a *clarete* wine of 11° highly prized throughout the province.

In the south, between *Medina del Campo* and *El Duero,* is the region of *Nava.* The vineyards occupy 21,250 acres and include the districts of: *Serrada, Rueda, Nava del Rey, Medina del Campo, Villanueva de Duero, Rodilana,* and

Pozaldez. These easily maturing wines of 13º to 17º with a sweet aroma and taste were the white wines of kings and have often been mistaken for the Montilla wines.

The wine of *Rueda* is a white wine not in the least inferior to the *Toro* red wine. It is a wine that has been often quoted in the Spanish literature of the 16th and 17th centuries. It was considered fashionable at the time to

have this wine available on hunting occasions and open air parties. A traditional wine of secular breeding is made from the Castilian *verdejo blanco* vine which is aromatic and rather golden in colour, varying from 13º to 17º.

The grapevine requires a great deal of attention and care especially in the higher altitudes where it is exposed to the cold winds and frosts. Then they are covered until such time as the spring and summer is well under weigh. Each vine is surrounded by a bank of soil in the shape of a bell so as to catch the rain water in the hollow. This is what is known as *atetillar*.

The Medina del Campo vineyards between Valladolid and Zamora produce some excellent white wines from the *verdejo* grape variety. The extension of these vineyards covers the area from the banks of river Duero up to Tordesillas. The winters are severe here and the valley or depression tends to be cold and hard. The wine used to be clarified with a very fine earth. The other districts in the area are: *Madrigal, Ló Seca, Alaejos, Robledillo San Martín* and *Descargamaría.*

Quevedo, the illustrious 17th century Spanish writer, said: «*This French cloth doesn't keep warm half as much as a holy wineskin from Alaejos*».

The reputation of this wine lies mainly in its quality and strength.

In these higher and colder climbs, the vines grow very low as if to escape the biting chill of the Sierra winds that sweep down into the Duero valley and La Mancha.

Further to the South of the Segovian border in the Tierra de Pinares, Olmedo, Portillo, and Cuéllar, some excellent wines are made from the Verdejo and Albillo vines.

THE RIBERA DEL DUERO

The *pagos* lie on both sides of the river following the old encampments from Valladolid to Peñafiel. The districts most worthy of mention are: *Tudela del Duero, Sardón, Valbuena del Duero, Peñafiel, Castrillo de Duero, Quintanilla de Arriba, Quintanilla de Onésimo, Olivares del Duero* and *Traspinedo.*

The Ribera wines, mostly *tintos* and *claretes*, have an exceptional texture and alcoholic content of 13°.

The wine of *Vega Sicilia*, previously mentioned, enjoys an extraordinary prestige both in Spain and abroad. It is made in Valbuena del Duero, a small village of 1400 inhabitants situated along the Duero. There are only 150 acres of this vineyard which is cultivated with the utmost care. These «*pagos*» were planted at the beginning of the last century after the phylloxera desease had all but destroyed the then existing grapevines.

It was Don Eloy Lecarda who remedied this misfortune by introducing, planting and cultivating stocks from Bordeaux and Burgundy. The first *bodeguero*, Don Domingo Garrariola, known as «*Chomin*», knew how to mature this wine and very soon its reputation began to spread until it was heading the wine lists in all the first class restaurants. The knowledge and techniques of «*Chomin*» inherited by the present owner and bodeguero Don Martiniano Renero have become proverbial. It is a claret wine of «*mucha capa*». It ages in oak vats and is then bottled. Its special vintage goes under the name of Reserva Especial Unica. The Valbuena type is a five year old wine.

The varieties of grapes to be found in the province of Valladolid are: the *Palomino, Verdejo, Godello, Cañorroyo, Blancazo, Garnacha blanca*, these for the *blancos* and *Tempranilla, Garnacha tinta, Tinta de Madrid and Mollar* for the *tintos*.

Peñafiel produces a good quality *tinto*. The vine is «*tinto fino de la Tierra*» and now the *Tinto aragonés* and *valenciano* are cultivated. The villages of *Peñafiel* are: *Quintanilla, Langayo, Bojete de Monte, Olivares, Valbuena, Pesquera, Boco, Castrillo and Canalejas*.

ZAMORA AND SALAMANCA

Along the Duero Valley and crossing into the province of Zamora is the Tierra del Vino. Salamanca shares with Zamora this land of red soils.

THE WINE OF TORO

The town of **Toro,** a very Spanish name indeed, is always a point of reference where the Zamora wines are concerned. It produces a **robust wine** of between 24 and 25 grams of dry extract and of between 13° to 15°, the strongest in the region. Its hard colour is like the land itself and creates the conditions for the making and maturing of the wine.

«Toro wine is gold and as thick as the moors».

«I have a Toro (bull) who makes wine and a León (lion) who drinks it up».

WINE HARVEST MAID
(Photo Guillén Franco.)

The last refrain was said by a Catholic king of León, in the Middle Ages, when the Toro wines were famous.

These *tintos* are very like the Aragonese wines as they have the same type of soil and climate. They are ideal for blending, strong in tannine and have a long tradition jealously guarded by experts at the Enological School of Toro.

The vineyards of Toro sweep down on both sides of the river Duero around Zamora, *Cigales*, *Benavente*, *Fuentesauco*, *Toro* and *Villalpando*. These wines were carried by the Cid Campeador and the ancient counts of Castile to fire the energies of their soldiers.

Very near the Portuguese border there is another region renowned for its wines, *Vitigudino*.

Talking about the valley of the river Duero, let it not be forgotten that many vinicular regions on the Castilian «Meseta» are found at an elevation of more than 800 metres.

FERMOSELLE

The wine of *Fermoselle*, a stone's throw from the frontier, is consumed almost exclusively in Portugal. The wine strip begins on the very banks of the Tormes river. The vineyards are terraced and the vines grow very close together. There are 500 grapevines per acre. It is in this area that the wine barrels are made and there is a flourishing wine market.

Fermoselle has a good *tinto* wine of 13º to 14º that is a result of the blending of various vines among which prevails the so named «*Juan García*».

A little farther North, in Salamanca, *Aldeadávila*, *Villariño*, *Mazueco*, *Pereña* and *Corporario* make a good *tinto*, almost a claret wine, reaching 13º

PALENCIA

Palencia because of the severe winters and scarcity of suitable land for vine cultivation produces only a limited quantity of wine. These come mainly from *Mollar*, *Mencía*, *Malvasía*, *Negro aragón*, *Jerez* and *Garnacha* vines. They are medium clarets of 10º and have a special taste of their own. In *Dueñas de Villamuriel*, the wines are made from the same kind of grape and have the same strength as those from Valladolid.

EL BIERZO

El Bierzo is located on the northwestern side of León where the Galician foothills and the Sil Valley have their beginning. The Sierra de León acts as a protective wall to the wide open valley below. On the western slopes lie Los Picos de Ancares. Surrounded by these sierras is the Bierzo region, over which presides the township of Ponferrada. In Ponferrada, an ancient castle built by the Templars rises up as a memorial and reminder of the «Camino de Santiago».

Villafranca del Bierzo is the other capital of the district. This is a hard rugged land, green and mountainous with plenty of irrigated land. The vines are terraced on the slopes themselves and each terrace is held up by stone walls.

In the main *El Bierzo* produces excellent table wines of 12º to 14º which can be aged and bottled easily. The *Cacabelos* wine is very famous indeed as well as the wine from *Camponarraya* and *Toral de los Vados*.

The vines are *Alicante* and *Garnache*, which make the best *tintos*, and the *Mencía* vine for the *claretes*. In the region of *Arganza* a *blanco* is made from the *Jerez* and the *Valenciana* vines.

It is the early spring, the good quality of the soil, the westerly or Galician wind, as well as the «savoir faire» of the people which have made these wines so popular. The above conditions hasten the ripening process of the grape by at least a month.

This wine fills the Galician and Asturian bodegas. Its wines are more and more in demand throughout the peninsular region especially the *Cacabelos* wine. The vineyards of Bierzo have much in common with those of Valdeorras.

THE WINE OF THE CONQUERORS

Who was Sentia Amarantia? According to the inscription on a grave stone which Sentius Victor dedicated to his wife, she was a Roman matron in the flower of her life. With her right hand she is caressing a small barrel and in the other, she is holding a jug in a serving posture. The oak barrel

is a symbol of the *solera* of the wine. It could well be a wine from the sierra, a *tinto* of *Montánchez*, a *blanco* of *Almendralejo*, or a *clarete* from *Vera de Plasencia*.

Because of their variety of colour, the *Extremeño* wines have nearly every shade of colour ranging from parched brown and green through to amber and topaz and finally to deep red. In Roman times these wines from *Tierra de Barros*, *La Serena*, *La Vera* and *El Arañuelo* were considered just as highly as the Falerno and Ligurian wines from the Peloponessus.

The chronicles of the time of Charles V say that during the retreat of the Emperor to the monastery of Yuste, he was accustomed to giving away a variety of wines ranging from pale green to deep *tinto* red matured in the bodegas of the monastery. And this he did despite his gout and all the wordly vanities he had left behind him.

CACERES

The vinicular areas of Cáceres are located around the periphery of the province. Near the neighbouring lands of Salamanca and Portugal is *Cilleros*, a region sheltered by the Sierra de Gata to the South west of the Urdes which produces a full bodied white wine of around 15º. Within the proximities of the Portuguese frontier, there are the *Tintos* of *Ceclavín* of 14º. Bordering Avila in the north and to the south of the Sierra de Gredos are the two vinicular belts of *Hervás* and *Jertes*, producing wines of 14º to 15º respectively.

On the Badajoz border is the region of *Cañamero* in the Sierra of Guadalupe that produces tintos of 14 to 15º of good body. There are some extraordinary monastery wines in Guadalupe. In *Montánchez*, sheltered by the sierra bearing its name, there are some **valiente** wines of 14 to 15° of a deep red colour.

In *Cáceres*, there are a number of typical *«punches»* worth mentioning as for example the *Chapurral de Ahigal*, a mixture of wine and lemonade and the *«Poncha de Jaraz de la Vera»*, a refreshing drink made with wine, water, oranges, sugar, and sometimes eggs. It is especially popular with the ladies where it is taken as a cocktail instead of wine.

The commonest grapes are the *Lairén*, *Cayetana* and *Azaria*. Among the *tintos* the commonest are: *Aragonés*, *Albilla negra*, *Escobera* and *Pinta*. The *Mantúa*, *Moscatel*, *Torrontés*, *Jaén*, *Palomino* and *Pedro Ximénez* are also abundant.

The cultivated surface is 29,000 acres with a proportion of 1,200 vines per acre.

BADAJOZ

The province of Badajoz is very extensive but unfortunately there is only a fraction of this territory which can be used for vinicular production. The white grapes used are: *Eva*, *La Cayetana*, *Baladí*, *Guaraña*, *Macabeo*, and **the aristocrats** *Pedro Ximénez* and *Palomino*. The red grapes used are: *La negra de la Almendralejo*, *La Garnacha* and the *Morisca*.

It is in the central region of the province that most of the vine growing is done.

LA TIERRA DE BARROS

The Almendralejo district includes the following villages. *Villafranca de los Barros*, *Villalba de los Barros*, *Santa Marta de los Barros*, *Solana de los Barros*, *Torremejías*, *Acebuchal*, *Corte de Pelea*, *Fuente del Maestro*, *Los Santos de Maimona* and *Zafra*. They are wines of 13.5° to 13.8° and between 3.8 to 4.5 grams of tartaric acid. The ordinary wines range from 12° to 13.5°.

LA SERENA

To the north of the Guadiana river is *Don Benito*, *Guareña*, *Santa Amelia*, *Villanueva de la Serena*, *Quintana de la Serena*, *Magacela* and the other villages.

The *Llerena* region includes the villages of *Llerena*, *Puente de Cantos* and *Medina de las Torres* which borders on the provinces of Sevilla and Huelva.

LATE AUTUMN IN THE VINEYARD
(Courtesy of La Semana Vitivinícola.)

THE WINE AND THE WIND

LA MANCHA

Today in La Mancha, there are still to be seen the «*tapias*» or mud walls, the wood sheds, farmyards, open fires, long spiked gables, rustic huts as well as the inns with their large spacious stables. There is the immemorial well and oven for bread baking. Then, there are the old nags perhaps descendent of Don Quixote's Rocinante, the lean gaunt faces of aquiline nose, the Don Juan's, Diego's, Alvaro's and Alfonso's. Finally, there are the rustic characters themselves immortalised by Cervantes. The short pot bellied Sancho Panzas of ruddy complexion, cunning philosophy and open laughter. The eternal «bachilleres», the Sanson Carrascos caught between good reason and wreckless failure. Those who contemplate the growing grass and above all those in whom simplicity and humility prevail as tasty and good as the cheeses and *aloque* wines.

Indeed La Mancha is as simple as its language, clear and frank, unspoilt by the times. Although farming methods have been modernised and there is a small amount of light industry still the people have not really changed, and their life continues much as it always has. If modern life has had any effect at all, this has been for the good as the villages have been done up and the people are more hospitable than ever.

What remains unchanged are the traditions and customs, the bell shaped chimneys that so fascinated the writer and traveller AZORIN; the rush chairs and shining earthenware vessels and «*botijos*».

The fundamental produce of the economy is its cereal, saffron, olive oil and wine. There is a fair deal of sheep raising as well.

«*Wine a la antigua Artesania*» is the old way of making wine got by treading on the grapes with primitive grass matted sandals which give it the required flavour. Each vintager makes his own wine and the secrets of making it is passed down from father to son. In this way wine possesses some unique characteristics where its density, transparency, aroma and taste are concerned. The same is true in the making of cheese, and one can honestly say that the bread, cheese and wine have the same taste as they had in the time of Cervantes.

On the 3rd September, the fiesta of «*Poesía*» and «*Vendimia*» (Poetry and Wine harvest) which is one of the most important in the year, takes place. The wines from La Mancha cannot be treated lightly for they include not only the flat-lands of Toledo, Ciudad Real, Cuenca and Albacete but a large part of New Castile. All of these regions have a similar climate, landscape and grapevine as well as the white chalky «albariza» soil.

The most common grapevines in La Mancha are *Bobal*, *Jaén*, *Jarcibera*, *Marisancha*, *Pardillo*, *Aragón*, *Castellan*, *Cirial*, *Crujidera*, *Garnacha*, *Hebén*, *Mencía* and *Tortozón*.

If «Spain is different», then, each region and district has a marked personality. This is no more clearly apparent than in the wide variety of wines so mysteriously and magically prepared. The process of *encabezar* (adding alcohol to the wine) *abocar* (sweeten), the way of maturing and maintaining the brand i. e. freshening the solera with new wine to obtain a pure wine of a required «bouquet» in harmony with the taste, in short, to make a «*redondo*» wine—this is no mean task and needs a long apprenticeship and even more essential, an innate sense of smell, taste and perception.

La Mancha is an open expanse of golden land which gave renown to the exploits and adventures of the knight errant, Don Quixote. It is the land of military orders, for example, the Templars of Calatrava, Santiago, Montesa, and San Juan. It is the land of renowned hunting grounds, windmills, wheat and above all a great area of winemaking.

THE REGION

This region includes a large part of New Castile, taking in considerable areas of Ciudad Real, Cuenca, Toledo and Albacete. In the west, it reaches as far as Extremadura. In the east, it reaches the fringe of Alicante and Valencia. Up to the north, the Mancha borders the Serranía de Cuenca and to the south it touches the Sierra Morena.

LA MANCHA ALTA

La Mancha Alta includes the provinces of Albacete and Cuenca. La Mancha Baja, which is much more extensive, spreads over the remaining provinces of Toledo and Ciudad Real. The intensity of the sun and the hot summers, combined with the good soil conditions, favour the complete ripening of the grapevine. The Arabs on calling the land «*Tierra Seca*» certainly found the appropriate words. These vines have existed since time immemorial especially in the undulating hills facing the west. This privileged position was praised by the poet Horacio on more than one occasion.

WINE PRODUCTION

La Mancha's wine production makes it one of the first in Spain. Ciudad Real has 592,500 acres of vineyard. Toledo 280,000, Albacete 242,500 and Cuenca 210,000 acres according to the 1968 statistics. Vine cultivation takes third place after the wheat and olive production.

In the spring, the immense stretches of vineyard offer the visitor an unforgettable perspective. As the summer passes, the landscape takes on a reddish golden colour and the chalky white towns of La Mancha are immersed and lost in the green covered land. Along the outskirts of each town, the innumerable *bodegas* and cooperatives are always visible.

La Mancha offers a good selection of fine table wines used for the «*copeo*» which are very popular in the bars and taverns of Madrid. It also offers an abundance of good «corriente» wines. These wines have centuries of experience behind them. In the seventeenth century, the *aloque* of Valdepeñas was well known. It is these classical clarets that have given the good reputation to the wines of Valdepeñas. However, the common *blancos* and *tintos* are the basis of the great market wines.

In the making of the white wines, it is the *Lairén* grape that prevails. They have an average alcoholic content of 13º to 14º, pale colour and are ideal for blending.

Among the red wines, the following grapes are common: *Cecibel, Monastrel* and *Tintorera*, which is highly regarded for its quality and body. Other vines that are particularly frequent are: the *Garnacha, Alarife, Bobal, Aragón* and *Castellana*. The «tintos» range from 14º to 16º and have an exquisite taste and brilliant colour.

THE WINE
PRODUCING AREAS

In the province of CIUDAD REAL, the following districts are to be found: *Alhambra, Albadalejo, Alcázar, Almoradil, Almagro, Argamasilla de Alba y la de Calatrava, Almedina, Almodóvar, Aldea del Rey, Arenas de San Juan, Alcolea, Bolaños, Ballesteros, Calzada, Campo de Criptana, Carrión, Caracuel, Castellar, Garrizosa, Ciudad Real Daimiel, Fernán Caballero, Fuente del Fresno, Fuenllana, Granátula, Herencia, La Solana, Las Labores, Miguelturra, Malagón, Manzanares, Membrilla, Montiel, Piedrabuena, Poblete, Porzuma, Pedro Muñoz, Santa Cruz de Mudela, Pozuelo, Puerto Lápice, San Carlos del Valle, Puebla del Príncipe, Socuéllamos, Tomelloso, Torralba, Torre de Juan Abad, Torrenueva, Terrinches, Villamayor, Villamanrique, Villahermosa, Villanueva, Valdepeñas, Villarta, Villar* and *Valenzuela*.

In the province of TOLEDO, the manchego wines include the districts of *Ajofrín, Almonacid, Cabezamesada, Camuñas, Consuegra, Corral de Almoguer, Chueca, El Romaral, El Toboso, Dos Barrios, Huerta de Valdecarábanos, La Guardia, Lillo, Manzaneque, Mascaraque, Madridejos, Majaliza, Miguel Esteban, Noblejas, Nambroca, Los Yébenes, Mora de Toledo, Orgaz, Ontígola, Ocaña, Puebla de Almoradiel, Quero, Santa Cruz de la Zarza, Talavera de la Reina, Villa de Don Fradique, Villafranca, Villarrubia, Villamuelas, Villanueva de Bogas, Villatobas, Villanueva de Alcardete, Villacañas, Villaminaya, Quintanar de la Orden, Urda, Yepes, Cabañas de Yepes, Turleque, Templeque* and *Esquivias*.

The region of MENTRIDA includes the districts of: *Almorox, Arcicolar, Aldea en Cabo, Alcabón, Camarena, Camarenilla, Casarrubias, Carranque, Castillo de Bayuela, Carmena, Carpio de Tajo, Chozas de Canales, Cardiel de los Montes, Escalona, El Casar, Fuensalida, Escalonilla, Hambrán, Illescas, Garciatún, Hormigos, Hinojosa, Los Cerralbos, La Sagra, Máqueda, Méntrida, Nombela, Novas, Nuño Gómez, Otero, Portillo, Paredes, Puebla de Montalbán,*

Quismondo, Real de San Vicente, Santa Cruz de Retamar, Santa Olalla, Val de Santo Domingo, Venta Retamosa, Valmojado, Villamiel, Domingo Pérez, Huescas, Torre Esteban and *Torrijos.*

The districts found in the province of CUENCA are: *Ucles, Fuente de Pedro Navarro, Villa Mayor de Santiago, Puebla de Almenara, Villarejo de Fuentes, Osa de la Vega, Los Hinojosos, Mota del Cuervo, El Pedernoso, Las Pedroñeras, Villar de Cañas, Las Mesas, Santa María del Campo, Rus, Castillo de Garcimuñoz, Vara de Rey, Sisante, Casas de Benítez, La Almarcha, Olivares del Júcar, La Hinojosa* and *La Alberca del Záncara.*

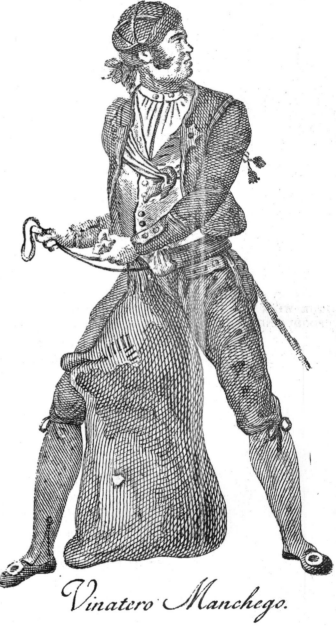

Vinatero Manchego.

THE BODEGAS

The wines of *Valdepeñas* are the first thing that come to mind wherever La Mancha is mentioned. Its very name is a guarantee of the prestige of its wines. They are smooth, well balanced and range from 13º to 15º. The *claretes* are a ruby colour, slightly acid but very dry with a fruity flavour. The *tintos* are a little thicker and softer than the *blancos.*

The «aloques» and «ojos de gallo» supply the bodegas, bars and restaurants of Madrid and the provinces outside. As has already been said they are frequently used for blending and a considerable quantity of them are exported to France every year.

«TINAJAS» IN LA MANCHA
(Photo Guillén Franco.)

Valdepeñas has come to be the wine emporium of La Mancha with its hundreds of huge wine cellars and the countless family wine presses. The typical bodega is characterised by the belly shaped «*Tinajas*» which are large earthenware amphoras where the wines are fermented and matured.

The experience, knowledge and «savoir faire» enables these people to detect the slightest signs of adulteration.

THE ANCIENT RANK OF THE MANCHEGO WINES

In the novel of Quijote de la Mancha there are several allusions to the bodegas of the region. What gives status to the «manchego» wines is that they were taken to the Low Countries and Germany by Carlos V and the predilection of the Emperor for these wines was handed down to his son Philip who always had this wine at the Escorial. The manchego Fray Diego de Yepes, confessor to the king, made his fastings a little lighter with this village wine.

Within the lands of La Mancha there are a series of towns and villages intimately connected with the wine industry. They are *Valdepeñas, Daimiel, Campo de Criptana, Herencia, Ocaña, Pedro Muñoz, Manzanares, Alcázar de San Juan, Río Záncara, Socuéllamos* and *Tomelloso.*

The making of alcohols reaches considerable figures. These alcohols are obtained from burning and distilling wine. Most of this production is sent to Jerez de la Frontera.

In *Valdepeñas*, there are also companies which make Anisette, Chartreuse, etc.

In *Alcázar de San Juan* **concentrated musts,** thick and highly alcoholic, are obtained to make the «*arrope vínico*». This concentrated must is the base for the preparation of the sweet wines, mistelas, vermouths, etc., products highly valued in the north of Europe.

EXPORTERS UNDER THE DENOMINACION «VALDEPEÑAS»

Abarca Pascual, Andrés.
Bodegas Castañeda, S. A.
Bodegas Ciudad.
Bodegas Canchollas
Bodegas Espinosa, S. A.
Bodegas Guerola, S. A.
Bodegas Navarras.
Bodegas Ortiz.
Canuto Gómez, Vicente.
Carmelo Madrid, S. A.
Cepesa.
Cooperativa del Campo «La Invencible».

Cruzares, S. A.

Delgado Cámara, José.

Galán Sánchez Molero, Salvador.

González Bustos, Ambrosio.

González Escudero, Rogelio.

Hidalgo Peñuelas, Ramón.

Jiménez Lucas, Juan.

Jiménez Martínez, Bibiano.

López de Lerma Moreno, Francisco.

López Morales, Juan.

López Tello Pérez, Rafael.

Luis Megía, S. A.

Maroto Maroto, Martín.

Márquez Jiménez, Viuda de Valentín.

Martín García, Miguel.

Martín Sevilla, Ana María.

Matías Brotóns, S. A.

Medina Madrid, Antonio.

Megía Cornejo, Hijo de Francisco.

Megía Fernández, Filomena.

Megía Maroto, Blas.

Merina Utrera, Antonio.

Miguel Calatayud, S. A.

Morales Yunta, Luis.

Navarro Martín, Antonio.

Pérez Texeira, S. A.

Pintado Ortega, José.

Pró Rosendo, Juan.

Quintana y Moreno.

Redruello Hermanos.

Rodero Jiménez, Luis.

Rodero Rodero, Félix.

Rodríguez de Lamo Ruiz, Miguel.

Ruiz Ruiz, Israel.

Sánchez Alcaide, Agapito y Luisa.

Sánchez Delgado, Francisco, «Bodegas 6 de Junio».

Sánchez Gómez, Alfredo, «Bodegas Alfredo».

Sánchez Gómez, Gerardo, «Bodegas Morenito».

Sánchez Ordóñez, Manuel.

Sánchez Ruiz, Manuela, «Vinícola Pinarejo».

Sánchez Rustarazo, Gerardo, «Bodegas Iberia».

Solís Fernández, Félix.

Tarancón Rodero, Abel.

Videva.

Vinícolas Manchegas, S. A.

ALBACETE

The province of Albacete has large areas which are used for vine cultivation with the exception of Alcaraz and Yeste, a mountainous region often referred to as the Swiss Manchega.

The districts that come under the DENOMINACION «LA MANCHA» are: *Villarrobledo, La Roda, Minaya, El Bonillo, Casa de Montiel, Munera, Fuensanta, Lezuza, Montalvos, La Herrera* and *Barrax*.

The wines are pale white of 12.5º to 13º and clarets that tip the 13º mark.

LA MANCHUELA

This region takes in part of the province of *Albacete* and the unfolding plains of the north bordering Cuenca and Valencia, and includes: *Villamalea, Madrigueras, Casas Ibáñez, Tarazona de La Mancha, Alborea, Mahora, Navas de Junquera, Fuentealbilla, Cenizate, Alcalá del Júcar, Casas de Ves, Valdacete, Abengribe, Motilleja, Albacete, Vilatoya, Balsas de Ves, Jorquera, Galosalvo, Casas de Juan Numez, Alatoz, Carcelén, La Gineta, Recueje, Pozolorente, Villar de Ves* and *Villavaliente*.

The above wines generally have much body and the ordinary «tintos», clarets and «rosados» of 12º to 14º are the most common.

THE «TINAJAS»
EARTHWARE
VESSELS

On approaching *Toboso*, the immortal town of Don Quijote's Lady Dulcinea, the *«tinajas»* or wine vessels, those round voluminous clay containers have given a special atmosphere to this place where good ordinary wine is produced of the white and claret type. They are made from the very subsoil of the district composed of clay and fresh earth. This mixture of ocre coloured soil has just the right texture for the making of these «tinajas», as well as for growing grapes.

It is in the town of our Lady of Toboso, the beautiful Dulcinea and along the trails of Don Quixote, especially in Villarrobledo, that the *«tinaja»* industry flourishes. At one time, these vessels were used to transport wine and olive oil all over the Mediterranean. Today the *«tinajas»* have been replaced by oak barrels and the oak is brought from Canada. These tend to make a highly aromatic solera wine although the *«tinajas»* are still to be seen around and have come to be very decorative ornaments which the tourist likes to take home with him as a souvenir.

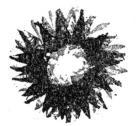

«EL RIÑON DEL VINO TINTO»
The Heart of the Red Wine Country

LA MANCHA,
LEVANTE AND
SOUTHWEST

The four regions of La Mancha, Levante, Murcia and Albacete intersect at a certain point and all four of them are famous for their noble, «valiente» wines, of high alcoholic content. The *tintos* are heavy and as the Cante Hondo says are a meal in themselves. They are excellent for strengthening and colouring other wines.

The production of these wines, whether domestic or foreign, reached its peak in the 17th century, when great quantities were exported abroad. It is at this time that *Alicante, Valencia, Utiel, Requena, La Manchuela, Almansa* and *Alpera* wines, that is to say «**El Riñón del Vino Tinto**», gained their popularity.

In this part, New Castile and Levante border each other. It is a region broken by gentle slopes beginning on the lower Meseta and continuing to the coast hills and river valleys of the Júcar and the Segura.

JUMILLA

A part of the province of Murcia in the south comes under the DENO-MINACION DE ORIGEN **Jumilla.** Jumilla is protected from the north wind by steep ground. A third of its total area is used for growing vines and olive orchards exclusively. The climate is variable due to the changes in altitude and the sierras that surround it on all flanks. It is the high concentration of pyrite, copper, sulphur and salt in the subsoil which produces strong wines.

It is important to understand the struggle of these vines to survive as they have to put their roots deep down into the seams of the subsoil to extract the necessary minerals and food which are later converted to give the wine its flavour and taste.

YECLA

Very much the same thing happens with *Yecla* as it has a similar topography and history. Villages and farms are scattered throughout the land

THE GRAPE CLUSTER
(Photo Guillén Franco.)

which have come to make up the main *pagos* and guarantee the «valiente» type of wine of high alcoholic degree.

Throughout the whole region of *La Mancha*, located on the Murcian side, prevail the vines of the *Monastrel, Legrén, Aledo, Tintorera* and *Bobal* variety. In *Yecla* the *tintos* and *claretes* range from 14º to 17º and in *Jumilla* from 14º to 18º. They normally have 4 to 6 grams acidity per litre and are thick, heavy and strong.

ALMANSA

This region forms a bridge from the heights of the Meseta to the Alicante and Valencia lowlands. It includes the municipalities under the DENOMINACION **Almansa**, an area with a long history. Ever since the 17 century, wine making has been one of its chief occupations. Under *Almansa* are the following vineyards *Alpera, Bonete, Corralrubio, Higueruela, Hoya Gonzalo, Pétrola, Chinchilla de Monteargón, Pozo Hondo, Caudete* and *Villar de Chinchilla.*

It produces tintos and claretes of 12º to 17º, a large number of which are ordinary wines and many of an intense colour almost black. Because of their rich high extract, fixed acidity and good taste, they are considered fit for blending and export.

The province grows 265,000 acres of vineyard and the total wine production is around 1,813,200 litres and 70 % of the total production is shared among 36 cooperatives. There are 16 distilleries.

The DENOMINACION DE ORIGEN-**Albacete, La Mancha** and **Manchuela** come under «El Riñón del Vino Tinto» and have already been mentioned.

WINE AND THE ISLANDS

Baleares and the Canaries

... «*Wine, wine, wine red wine.*» — *The Nightingale cries to the Rose.*

OMAR KHAYYAM.

The small landowners of these islands show a marked interest in the growing of grapes and the making of wine although their small lots of land are not really economically productive. The traditional methods of growing and cultivation still continue and the harvests are not as fruitful as they might be using modern plants and better equipment.

The vineyards of the islands of Mallorca are mostly on the eastern side of Levante which is the plainland found between the two bays of the vinicular area of *Palma* and *Pollensa*. There are two main regions: The first of them is *Benisalem* including the town of this name, the villages of *Consell*, *Santa María*, *Santa Eugenia* and *San Cellas*.

The vinicular district of *Felanitx* begins in the same area very near the caves of Mallorca and includes the districts of *Lluchmayor*, *Manacor*, *Porreras* and *Villafranca*. It is the most extensive area and harvests 60 % of the total production.

The island of *Menorca* has the eastern half of its area reserved for vine cultivation including *Mahón Bay*. The principal vinicular districts on the island are *San Luis* and *Alayor*.

The island of *Formentera* is located integrally within the wine growing region and four fifths of the island of Ibiza on which there are included the municipal districts of *San Antonio*, *San José* and *San Juan Bautista*.

The Balearic wines are of the *rosado* and *dry tinto* variety. The *rosados* are produced in greater abundance and have a slightly acid flavour. Their alcoholic content ranges from 13° to 15°.

The district of *Benisalem* produces coarser wines of an intense colour. The district of *Felanitx* has, on the other hand, «*tintos*» and claret wines of lesser strength rarely passing 11° and of little acidity. In *Manacor* the wines have similar qualities and like the *Felanitx* are ideal for serving as a table wine. In the region of *Buños*, some white wines are made from the *Malvasía* grape that do very well in the local wine markets.

In *Ibiza* and *Formentera*, the wines gravitate between 12º to 13.5º. They are excellent **corrientes,** made in the traditional way. The main varieties of grapes found of the Balearic type are: *Manto Negro, Batista, Callet, Ciró, Fogoneu, Calop, Parellada, Sumoll, Xarel-lo, Pepita de Oro, Vinater, Balisch, Blanch, Bogacén, Gargallosa, Malvasía, Moscatel, Panzal* and *Sabaté.*

The amount of alcohol produced in the year 1967-68 was 794 hectolitres. The firms involved were local ones: *Inca, Manacor, Porreras* and *Felanitx.*

The *Felanitx* region is the most important and consequently the four alcohol industries are grouped in the same area. Over the last few years they have formed cooperatives which now have some 400 members.

The 1968 vine production was 88,000 hectolitres from a growing area of 19,385 acres.

THE CANARY ISLANDS

On the Canary Islands the following varieties of grapes are to be found: *Moscatel, Jaén, Malvasía, Listán, Pedro Jiménez, Verdejo, Negramosel, Tintilla, Bermejuela* and *Forestera*. These grapes ripen very well indeed in this excellent climate where the sun is fairly constant throughout the year.

The archipelago of the Canaries produces good class genuine wines which go particularly well with the typical dishes of these blessed isles. The continual flow of visitors from season to season has brought prosperity to the region and the proof of this is seen by the number of hotels and first rate restaurants in existence today.

Wine experts have said that the wines of these islands so longed for by northern Europeans have become the best complement to the Andalucian wines.

The select wines *los vinos generosos*, **las Malvasías,** were already known in the 16th century and are often compared with the Hungarian wines.

The *Malvasías de la Orotava* valley are of a little earthy colour and are very like the *Gorgolana* and *Santa Ursula* variety, found on the Island of Tenerife.

Among the good white wines are found *El Vidueño*, a mild wine, mainly from the *Valle de Guerra* and *Las Arenas*. The wines produced in *Valsequillo* and *La Matanza, Entende* and *La Atalaya* also taste well.

The «*seco blanco*» or dry white of *Palma*, in *Barranco Seco y Gran Canaria* is likewise enjoyed.

It was in the 17th and 18th centuries that these very carefully cultivated vineyards reached their peak. In *Lanzarote*, each wine is normally enclosed by a circular trench. The *Muscatels of Lanzarote* are becoming more and more popular and so is the *Muscatel of Las Palmas*.

The ordinary wines, for the most part *tintos*, are made in the districts of *Agulo, Chiparbe, La Gomera, Palmar* and *Icod*, called *Icod de los Vinos*. These wines of 11º to 12º are fortified with wine alcohol until they rise to 14º or 15º.

According to the statistics, the annual production of wine in the Canary Islands is 50,000 hectolitres of which 50,000 hectolitres are ordinary wines, *blancos* and *tintos* and the remaining 10,000 are clarets.

Whenever speaking of the Canary wines, the *Tacoronte* wines must not be forgotten. They are called locally *mountain wines*. Other wines worthy

THE «GARRAFAS» (CARAFES)
(Photo Guillén Franco.)

of mention are those of Hierro and the *rosado* of *Taganana* and *Garafia* with a raisin taste similar to these antique Grecian wines of bitter flavour.

CHARACTERISTICS
OF THE CANARY
WINES

Area	Type	Alcoholic Degree	Colour
Tacoronte	Ordinary	12-14	Tinto
Orotava	Ordinary	11-13	Blanco
Icod	Ordinary	11-13	Blanco
Arafe	Ordinary	11-12	Blanco
Fuencaliente	Ordinary	12-15	Claret
Hierro	Ordinary	12-15	Blanco

THE REMAINING WINES
THAT WE DRINK AND THE FEW
THAT WE REMEMBER...

They are usually *corrientes* and smack of the earth and air of the country where they are made. They are found along the routes which take us along the highways and byways of the unexplored wine routes of the Spanish hinterland—by the rivers, over the plains and into the mountains. No matter which route you choose, any one will lead you on a happy gastronomical tour of good eating and drinking.

Let us begin with the lands in the middle southwest, the EXTREMADURA, for here is the much sought after «*aloque*» of *Hervás*, a clear red wine, and the *Lagaret* of *Ahigal*. Along the banks of the river Eresma is the white wine of *Rapariegos*. In the *Bierzo* region, the favourite and most blessed land of León, are made the *Villamañán* fine wines of which a good proportion are sent up to bars and restaurants in Madrid.

To the south, there are: the fair *Pedro Ximénez* in *Jerez;* the smooth old and fragrant wines in *Castilleja de Guzmán;* the clarete of *Aljarafe;* the golden *Pajareto of Bornos;* the *Blancos* of *Alanís* in the county of *Niebla;* the *Pajarete* of *Cádiz;* the *Jaloque* of *Sanlúcar;* the *blancos* of *Chiclana;* the *Moscatel* of *Chipiona;* the *Tintilla* of *Rota;* the *Tinto* of *Calonca* and the *Alpujarreño* of *Purchena*.

In JAEN, where Baltasar de Alcázar made famous the «Taberna de Castilla», there are the pale wines of *Andújar* and *Martos*, and the tintos and clarets of *Ubeda* and *Baeza* which more than once quenched the thirst of Antonio Machado, the Spanish poet.

There are the wines that he sung of

«*And they don't know the hurry*
not even in fiesta days».
Where there is wine, they drink wine,
Where there isn't wine, fresh water.

In LEVANTE, each wine has its own flavour, name, vineyard and «*pago*».

THE «FERIA» IN JEREZ
(Photo Guillén Franco.)

There are the sweet wines of *Albiflor*, the sweet and dry *Morsi* of *Levante*, the *tintos* of *Campo de Salinas*, the land where Azorín's family had their country home and *about* of which he wrote ~~about~~:—the wine presses, grapes and wines, the red wines of the *Cañada de Benejama* and *Biar* in *Alicante*; the *tinto Amargoso* de *Moratalla* in *Murcia*; the *Pardillo* of *Cuenca*; the *Aloque* of *Garcimuñoz*, and the *Rojo* of *Belmonte*, which they say Fray Luis de León drank in his student days.

In VALENCIA, the *Moscatel* and the *Rancio* wines of the *Cartuja de Porta Coeli* can be tasted up in the Serra Mountains. The *dorado* of *Sagunto* and the good strong white wines of *Benicarló* that furnished and stocked the bodegas of Pope Luna at the time of the great Schism between the Oriental and Occidental Churches.

In CATALONIA, the *blancos* of *Valle*, and *Campo de Tarragona* are found amidst a landscape of almond trees and bean fields, as well as the sweet *finos* of *Paniza*, and the *tintos* of *Calatayud*. Further eastward, there is the *Somontano* and ALTO ARAGON and the *claretes* of the *Sonsierra* NAVARRA.

No matter where you go, anyone of these routes provides a range of wines as distinct in «bouquet» as in variety. In the VASCONGADAS, the *Chacolís of Zarauz*, *Baquio* and *Valmaseda* are becoming more and more scarce. In SANTANDER and ASTURIAS, the *tinto* of *Lebeña* and *Candamo* are there for the asking.

The wines from BURGOS, the *tintos* of *Aranda del Duero* and *Tordesillas*, dating back to the XV century could be noted down in a very personal way for they were wines drunk by the Emperor Charles V himself.

In MADRID, the *tintos* from *Colmenar de Oreja* and *Coca* are as easy to come by as the Rioja and La Mancha wines.

The *clarete* de *Santo* from the *San Saturnino* farm property of the Escorial monastery, and the *Aloques* of *Guadalajara* close this by no means exhaustive list.

THE «TASCA»
(Water colour by Valentín Moragas.)

GASTRONOMIC AND VINICULAR MAP OF SPAIN
(Courtesy of the Ministry of Tourism.)

GASTRONOMY AND WINES

Part ~~Tree~~ Three

INTRODUCTION

The regions of the **guisados** or stewed dishes are located to the north of the Cantabrian Cordillera stretching from the river Bidasoa at the French border to the river Miño in the west. Among the most popular of these dishes are: —the «bacalao» (codfish), «chipirones» (cuttlefish), «merluza» (hakefish), «la fabada», and the «pote gallego» (Galician broth).

It is the higher elevations of the «Meseta» land in New Castile that constitute the region of the **asados** or roasts. In Madrid, Burgos, Segovia, Salamanca, Avila, to mention only a few of the famous places, the **asado** is the king dish, especially in the winter when the weather turns very cold.

The region of the **gazpachos** is found in Andalucian and falls more exactly on the southern side of the Sierra Morena.

To the east, two gastronomic regions can be clearly defined—that of the **paella** along the Mediterranean coastland reaching northward into Tarragona and southward to Murcia and Valencia and that of the **escudella** in the old kingdom of Catalonia.

Spanish gastronomy is in perfect keeping with the wine growing areas. The gastronomical regions of the «pote gallego» and the «fabada asturiana» coincide with the Rosal, Ribero, Albariño and Monterrey wine growing areas. For the «asados» of the Duero, there are the *Toro, Rueda, Medina,* and *Cebreros* wines and for La Mancha, the wines of *Valdepeñas*. Extremadura lies partly in the «asado» and partly in the «gazpacho» region.

The gastronomy of the Basque provinces is much more complex since it not only has its own typical roast dishes but **guisos** (stews), which go very well with the Rioja wines.

In Valencia, the «paella» goes well with the wines made there, while Murcia partakes of both the «paella» and «gazpacho» gastronomy.

Finally, Catalonia has within its province the **escudella** and **Carn d'olla** dishes and the great *Panadés*, *Alella*, *Priorato* and *Tarragona* wines to go with them.

MALAGA ayer...

MALAGA «CANTAORA»
(Water colour by Rodríguez Miranda.)

A WINE-CELLAR IN ANDALUCIA
(Photo Foat)

THE REGION OF THE GAZPACHOS
ANDALUCIA

The Olive orchards, the «serranías», the Guadalquivir valley, the extensive coastline, provide an infinite variety of possibilities where wine and food are concerned. There are two basic elements in the Andalucian gastronomy: —**olive oil,** the base of its cooking, **and sherry wine,** as old as its history.

Andalucia is always spoken of as the region of the **gazpacho andaluz** where there are as many ways of making it as there are districts. The «cocido andaluz» varies in the same manner. As for the celebrated cured ham, it is worth noting the difference between the hams of Trevelez, cured in the snow, and those of Jabugo, cured in the open air.

The Andalucian dishes, generally speaking, have become part of the menu in any of the first-class restaurants and hotels found along the «Costa del Sol».

HUELVA

The «serranía», as the Sierra de Aracena is called, is one of the main staples of the gastronomy of Huelva. The famous «serrano» hams of black or Iberian pig, which are bred there, are best eaten in Jabugo, Cortegana and Repilado

The Costa de la Luz or Costa Colombina named after Columbus contributes to the high ranking prestige of the seaford and shellfish and fish generally. The «Coto de Doñana», a famous hunting reserve for migratory birds, is also important in the gastronomy of this region.

TYPICAL DISHES:

«Choquitos» (baby squid) cooked in their own juice; hake cooked in white wine; sword fish «en amarillo»; «caballa» oven style; «langostinos» (crawfish); partridge «Odiel» style; «gazpacho andaluz».

SWEET DISHES:

«Hornazos», «tocinillo» and figs from Lepe.

WINES:

All of the wines under the «DENOMINACION» HUELVA and the very palid ordinary wines of 11º to 14º. Also included are the *Finos* and *Palmas* of a pale straw colour reaching 14º to 16º.

SEVILLA

TYPICAL DISHES:

The typical «cocido sevillano»; eggs «flamencan style»; «sopa de mariscos» (shell-fish soup); «sopa de ajos tostados» (toasted garlic soup); «garbanzos con bacalao» (cod with spanish brown peas); «habas con jamón» (beans with ham); «gazpacho»; «pescado frito»; (fried fish); «pez espada en adobo» (swordfish and special dressing); «lenguados del estero» (estero sole); dressed boiled roes.

SWEET DISHES:

San Leandro candied yolks; «alfajores» (a paste made of nuts, honey and spices); «mostachones» (macaroons) and «torrijas» (fried bread and milk pudding).

WINES:

Include all the Andalucian wines and especially the *select table wines.*

CADIZ

The art of frying fish is unexcelled here.

TYPICAL FISH DISHES:

Estero fried fish; oven cooked fish with parsley; giant perch in this various styles; bonito with olives; fried «calamares» (squid)and roast mackeral.

MEAT DISHES:

Tripe «Andalucian style»; kidneys «Sherry style»; beefsteak «Andalucian style»; cocido «Andalucian style»; «carne mechada» (larded meat); meat with anchovies.

DESSERTS:

«Turrón»; «tejeringos»; candied yolks; candied coconuts and «tocinillo de cielo» (caramel flan).

WINES:

All the Sherry wines.

CORDOBA

TYPICAL DISHES:

The «olla de los cortijos» (a kind of andalucian stew); «salmorejo» (made with bread crumbs, tomatoes and olive oil); «sopa de maimones»; «cordobés» fillets of steak; stewed bull's tail; «cochifrito» (fried young goat).

SWEET DISHES:

«Mostachones»; «alfajores de Montilla and Rute; «polvorones»; «mantecados»; coffee meringues and «membrillo de Puente Genil» (Quince preserves).

WINES:

Those from *Montilla* and *Moriles*. Also *Lucena, Aguilar, Cabra, Puente Genil* and *Córdoba*.

JAEN

Although Jaén is fundamentally an olive producing province, it has some good hunting and fishing reserves.

TYPICAL DISHES:

«Gachamiga»; «tallarines» with hare; «serrana» omelette; ham and eggs dressed with green asparagus; oven cooked head and leg of lamb; trout in almond sauce; «andrajo»; spinach Jaén style; stewed beans; «pipirana»; pepitoria chicken; roast boar.

DESSERT AND SWEET DISHES:

«Santa Ursula» candied yolks.

WINES:

White and red wines from *Despeñaperros* and *Torreperogil;* ordinary wines from *Bailén;* select wines from *Lopera*.

MALAGA

TYPICAL DISHES:

Fried anchovies; «chaquetes»; fried sardines; sardines in white wine; grilled sardines; angler fish soup «Málaga» style; stewed meat Andalucian style; Ronda style beans; turbot «a la Malagueña».

SWEET DISHES:

Málaga raisins; «polvorones»; candied yolks and «alfajores» (made with nuts, honey and spices).

WINES:

All the wines under the DENOMINACION MALAGA including the ordinary (CORRIENTE) wines of the province.

GRANADA

TYPICAL DISHES:

Trevelez cured ham; Sacromonte omelette; fried beans with ham; stewed suckling kid; sardines from Motril; chicken with tomatos; prawn omelette; beans and green peas omelette; Spanish omelette.

SWEET DISHES:

Almond cakes; «torta real» from Motril; cakes made by the Comendadores of Santiago and Santa Isabel and «piononos de Santa Fe».

WINES:

Red and claret wines from *Motril*, *Guadix* and *Baza*.

ALMERIA

TYPICAL DISHES:

Here, there is a great variety of fish and shellfish; «bullabesa» made of fish and shellfish; dressed needle-fish; Andalucian whiting; fried suckling kid with garlic; pot of lamb; cured ham of Seron; «ajo colorado»; «escabeche de sardinas»; rice «a la banda»; «aguasal de cordero»; «longaniza de Viator»; gypsy style snails; pot of green beans.

SWEET DISHES:

«Soplillos de Laujar»; «mantecados» (butter cakes); meringues and caramel flans.

WINES:

Red and white from *Berja*, *Dalias*, *Alhama*, *Laujar*, *Ohanes*, *Padules*, *Alharia*, *Fiñaña*, *Tabernas* and *Purchena*.

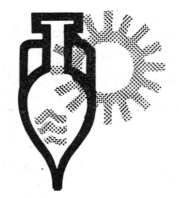

TYPICAL WINE-CELLAR IN JEREZ
WITH THE PATRON
SAINT OF SAN GINES DE LA JARA
IN THE BACKGROUND

(Photo Courtesy of C. R. Jerez & Grafibérica)

PEPPERS AND RED WINE
Murcia

THE COUNTRY

Murcia is a reflection of its vegetable garden. The peppers of Espinardo contribute largely in giving that special blending of the red and ground pepper which gives a special flavour to the stews as well as the sausages and salamies of hot taste and red colour.

Along the river banks is found the famous rice of Calasparra, a dark brown coloured rice selected in making a certain type of paella.

TYPICAL DISHES:

Murcian omelette made from peppers and tomatoes; beans omelette; Murcian potage made with rice and kidney beans. Another special dish is a kind of pie made with wheat flower and stuffed with meat, chorizo, hard boiled eggs and brains; lamb ribs with chips in «cabanil garlic»; roast lamb's heads; «caldero marinero», is a rice dish made from a broth of assorted fish, garlic, tomato, saffron, salt and parsley. Another broth or «caldero» is made in the country but with wild game meat.

Typical fish include: mullet, gilt head, and «dentón».

The pork sausage meats are typical and among them are found the white and red «Longaniza», the «blancos de cerdo», the pork cheese, «la guarra» and the «morcilla» or black pudding.

SWEET DISHES:

«Alfajores»; «Fanfarrona»; «Picardía de Lorca»; Cordiales de Torre Pacheco; «Yemas de Caravaca»; Marzipan de Alhama; Buttercakes.

WINES:

Murcia has very strong wines. The wine under the DENOMINACION JUMILLA reaches 19º. The wines of *Yecla* are very similar. Other wines include *Cieza, Caravaca, Moratalla, Mula, Lorca* and *Cartagena* which are heavy and range from 13º to 14º.

PAELLA AND CRAWFISH
Valencia

Along the Mediterranean coast, from the Costa del Sol to the Costa Dorada, the Costa Blanca stretches away until it merges with the Costa de Azahar.

Throughout this region, it is the **paella** which is lord. The «paella» here is at its most baroque and universal gastronomic expression. The **Paella Valenciana** has become popular everywhere because of its attractive appearance and also the delicious foods that go into making it. For example, the crawfish. History tells us that Hannibal introduced the crawfish from Africa where they multiplied throughout the Mediterranean.

Valencia cannot be excelled where the presentation of the Paella is concerned. But where the gastronomes differ is in the ingredients that the classical paella must have. There are some who tend towards the paella made in and around the Albufera region. They claim that it is the most genuine because it is made with eels, snails, and runner beans. Others say that the real «paella» allows for all sorts of fish and meats. However, the success of each variety of «paella» depends on the seasoning and good cooking.

ALICANTE

Alicante specialises in the «arroz abanda», a sort of watery rice, rice and cauliflower, rice and cod, rice and squid, rice and vegetables, and rice «marinera» style.

The «ali-oli», an exquisite sauce, is typical of the region and used to condiment the various meats. It is made with garlic and oil.

TYPICAL FISH DISHES:

Grilled, fried and oven cooked tuna fish; «salmonetes» (red mullet); «rape a la marinera»; turbot; octopus; Santa Pola crawfish; «mojama» (Alicante salted tuna fish) and mullet roes.

TYPICAL MEAT DISHES:

Grilled chops with «ali-oli»; black pudding and beans; pot cooked partridge; Maestrazgo ham; stuffed tomatoes; spinach pie and «nogada» (dish with potatoes and nuts).

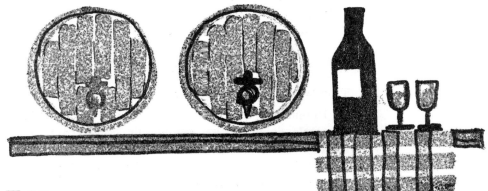

WINES:

The enormous variety of wines of the region satisfy even the most demanding tastes. The wines are those of the «Denominación de Origen» - Valencia, Cheste, and Utiel-Requena, as well as the wines of Chelva, del Arzobispo, Campo de Liria, Sagunto, Ayora, Carlet, Enguera and Onteniente and the Valle de Albaida.

In the province of Castellón, there are the «corriente» wines of Maestrazgo of 13º to 17º; the coast wines of Oropesa, Benicasín of 12º to 14º and the red, claret and white wines of San Mateo of 12.5º to 16º.

CATALONIA

«El Suquet de Peix, la Escudella y la Carn D'Olla»

The antiquity of Catalonian gastronomy is very much in keeping with the history of the old kingdom. Her commercial relations and contacts with the other Mediterranean towns and the Near East has influenced her cooking which with time has taken on a traditional character.

In the year 1470 the first Spanish cookery book the «Libro de Cozina» was printed. It was written by Roberto de Nola, chief cook to King Fernando of Naples to whom the book was dedicated.

Catalonia is well known for its **Escudella, Carn D'Olla,** the Bullabesa, whose origin is disputed between Genoa, Marseille and Barcelona, and any kind of stew done «a la marinera». In Catalonia, the «All-i-olli» is also very popular as in all the Mediterranean countries.

Her rich and diverse gastronomy is maintained by the infinite variety of fish and game available in the interior and mountain areas of the province. Each of the four Catalonian provinces provides some rather curious dishes.

GERONA

TYPICAL DISHES:

Pyrenese soup; «rape» soup; «Zarzuela marinera» (a mixed fish stew); «Zarzuela de mariscos»; «suquet de pescado»; «salmonete al «funolls»; «calamares rellenos» (stuffed squid); «pavo relleno asado» (stuffed roast turkey); pigs trotter with Cerdanya turnips; hare with chocolate; «butifarra» (pork sausage) with mushrooms; beans with «butifarra»; «Pernil de la Cerdanya» (ham).

SWEET DISHES:

Carquinyolis (dry biscuits); Cocas de San Juan with fruit and «piñones» (figs and «piñones» bread); «crema catalana» (very sweet custard with burnt sugar); «Menjar blanc» (made with almond milk).

WINES:

In the province of TARRAGONA is included the DENOMINACION TARRAGONA AND PRIORATO, together with the *Conça del Barbará, Bajo Panadés,*

THE VINEYARD IN WINTER
(Courtesy of La Semana Vitivinícola.)

Terra Alta and *Uldecona*. There is every sort of wine available from *blancos, tintos, rosados, claretes* (11º to 18º). Those of the Rivera del Ebro are of medium alcoholic strength. There are also a great variety of sweet wines and *«mistelas»*.

LERIDA

This bordering province that stretches from the river Ebro to the Pyrenese offers dishes from both the plain and mountain areas having a marked French influence.

The cooking of the mountain areas of Pallars, Ribagorza and the valley of Arán, based on game and river fish, goes back to Medieval times.

The «vega» of Lérida heads the nation in vegetable and fruit growing.

Among the typical dishes found in the region are the Pyrenese soups «lechones» and «tostones al horno», or «asados al espeto»; «truchas»; «Escudella», cheeses and «turrones» of Agramunt.

The wine of *Urgellet* and the hot wine of the valley of Arán complete the gastronomy of Lérida.

WINES:

Alp, Figueras, Palafrugell, Ripoll, Vilajuiga, all of between 12º to 13º; *Espolla, Gariguella* and *Llansá* wines of between 13º and 14º and red, white and claret *Perelada* wines.

BARCELONA

TYPICAL DISHES:

Fish and vermicelli soup; lobster «a la catalana»; turkey soup with egg and cheese; «suquet de pescado»; breadcrumb omelette; quail «Montseny» style; rabbit and snails Montseny style; stewed partridge; stewed meat with peas and peaches; butifarra catalana; Vich sausage and not forgetting the «Escudella» and «Carn D'Olla».

SWEET DISHES:

«Tortel» (ring); «crema catalana»; «panallets» (dry cakes) and «cocas».

WINES:

In the PANADES, the whites, clarets and reds as well as the sparkling wines. The *Malvasías* of *Sitges*, and the *red* wines of Bodegas Torres; in the MARESME, the wines of *Alella, Teia, Tiana, Masnou* and *Mongat* under the «DENOMINACION DE ORIGEN»-ALELLA. Among these are found the Marfil, whites, rosados and Lacre Gualda and Lacre violeta.

In the Valles near Barcelona are the magnificent *corriente* wines drunk by nearly everyone. They are the wines of *Ripollet, San Cugat* and *Rubi.*

TYPICAL DISHES:

TARRAGONA

Garlic soup a «la Catalana»; musce soup; great old fashioned soup; «suquet de pescado»; roast lobster; cod with «vomesco» (made with oil, garlic, and tomato); salmon «a la catalana»; eel with «all-i-oli» sauce; «parrillada de pescado» (assorted grilled fish); «romesco» with rabbit; lamb's rib with chocolate.

«¡Viva la buena vida!»

Aragón's gastronomy is as diverse as its natural districts. El Alto Aragón, El Bajo Aragón produces some of the best olive oils in the world.

Its livestock, big and small game, fishing and vegetable products are provident. It must be remembered that one of the great masters of international cooking, Don Teodoro Bardají, a native of Aragón, gave Spanish gastronomy its international prestige.

TYPICAL DISHES:

The garlic soups, which can be made in various ways either with green almonds, fried bread or eggs; soups made from the different parts of the

pig's trotter, ears and ham; crawfish, mussel and crab soups and the curious «sopa de gato» (cat soup made with cheese, oil, egg, bread and ground pepper).

Shepherd style roast chops and roast goat on the spit; back gammon Sarragosa style; eels and beans; partridge «a la aragonés»; suckling roast lamb of the Sierra de Guarra; Teruel cured ham; rabbit with «salmorejo» sauce; trout «a la aragonés»; snail omelette; «Caldereta de pastores» (typical shepherd style pie).

SWEET DISHES:

«Orejones»; «suspiros de monja»; «magdalenas», and «mantecados».

WINES:

Under the DENOMINACION-CARINENA, there are red, claret, and dry white wines of 13º to 18º. There are also a great variety of sweet wines, «rancios», «mistelas» and *muscatels*, many of these reaching as high as 17º. Other good wines are those of *Ribera del Jalón, Campo de Calatayud, Anillón, Villarroya, Fuentes, Ateca, Daroca, Campo de Belchite*, and other wines of less body and strength from *Albarracín* and *Trruel, Huesca, Granen, Robles* and *Lanaja.*

«The 7 July, Saint Fermin... to Pamplona we must go» (From a song).

The gastronomia of Navarre has been strongly influenced by the bordering French provinces, for it is found along the pilgrim's route to Saint James Its rivers abounding in trout, its thick woodland, historic valleys, soft grazing country, determine the type of food to be eaten in the same way as the grapevines determine the wine to be drunk.

DISHES:

«Ribera» soups (made with liver veal and grated cheese; «migas de las Bardenas»; crab tails; «menestra de Tudela» (a stewed vegetable dish); Bidasoa salmon, veal's tongue with nuts; «potage de castañas» (chestnuts); shrimp omelette; eels done in a spicy sauce.

The abundance of game in Navarre provides a number of exquisite dishes, usually made locally in the villages. Those particularly worthy of mention are dishes made from thrushes, larks, red wings, turtle doves, quails, par-

CANADIAN OAK BARRELS OF WINE

(Courtesy of La Semana Vitivinícola.)

tridges, doves, woodcocks, pheasants, wildducks, rabbits, «lobo de nieve» —snow wolf; hare, buck and head of boar and deer. These meats can be cooked in sauces, stuffed, stewed, roasted, and even grilled.

The cheeses of this area are excellent and the following are important: *Roncal, Aralar, Urbasa* and *Azama.*

WINES:

White, rose, claret and red. With game meat, red wine is taken and can be found in *Arroniz, Cintruénigo, Olite, Cirauci, Cascante, Dicastillo, Añorbe, Pitillas, Eneriz, Corella, Puente de la Reina, Bere, Tafalla, Los Arcos, Urbiola, Bergota, Obanos, Fitero, Lumbier, Artajona, Castillo de Tiebas.*

THE BASQUE COUNTRY AND ITS GASTRONOMY

THE LAND
The gastronomy of the provinces of Guipúzcoa and Vizcaya is identical, although Guipúzcoa has perhaps affinities with the cooking of her French neighbour. Alava likewise shares the cooking of Rioja and Aragón. However, there are a series of Basque dishes which are typical.

VIZCAYA
TYPICAL DISHES:

«Marmita-ko», a fishermen's dish made with tunny fish, onion, garlic, pepper, potatoes and olive oil; «Porrusalda» (Cod, leeks, potatoes and garlic); cod «Biscay style»; cod «al pil-pil», hake «Basque style» either in green sauce, fried or grilled; «Chipirones en su tinta» (squid in its own ink); «angulas»; stuffed red peppers; pork gammon country style»; Berriz beef steak; Villagodio (typical fat Basque steak); «revuelto de perrochiko» (scrambled mushrooms); «callos a la euskalerria» (tripe «Basque style»).

SWEET DISHES:

«Canutillos de Bilbao» (rolled wafer); rice pudding; «cuajada de Gorbea» (delicious curd of sheep's milk).

WINES:

White and red **Rioja** wines, **chacolí** and *cider*.

ALAVA
TYPICAL DISHES:

Garlic soup; «sopa migada»; toasts and peppers; cod «al ajo arriero»; sea-bream «Rioja» style; roast chicken and apples; partridge «con salsa Aperdigonada»; mushrooms omelette; watercress salad; pot of snails and ham; tripe and hot sauce.

SWEET DISHES:

«Ponche de Zurracapote»; Cold stewed fruit; puff-pastry pie and rolled wafers; «cuajada de Olaeta»; «arropes Yecora style» (concentrated boiled honey conserve).

WINES:

Chacolí and wines under the Denominación—Rioja from Laguardia, Labastida, Lanciego, La Puebla de la Barca, Leza, Navaridas, Pálamos, Oyón, Salinillas, Samaniego, Villabuena and Yécora.

GUIPUZCOA

TYPICAL DISHES:

Hendaya soup with fresh vegetables; fish soup «Koskera» style; «Kokotxas» of hake; «txangurro» (oven cooked spider crab); very good beef and veal steaks. Idiazabal and Urbia cheeses.

WINES:

Apart from the «chacolí» and *cider*, the fresh wines of the *vino verde* type go well with certain fish dishes and shellfish. On the other hand, the Basque has made the Rioja wines his own.

OLD CASTILE AND LEON

«*Con pan y vino se anda el camino.*»

Refrain.

SANTANDER

Santander is the only province of Castile that has a window on to the sea and consequently much of her gastronomy is accordingly affected.

SHELLFISH:

«Percebes», mussels, oysters, spider crabs, and lobster.

FISH DISHES:

Trout; stuffed hake; grilled sardines; «Cabracho del Tura».

MEATS:

Veal steaks «a la castellana».
The CHEESES are excellent, especially the «queso de nata» and blue cheeses like the «Treviso».

WINES:

The area around Potes in the Picos de Europa produces a very small quantity of good *vino verde*. The **Rioja** wines and those from *León* and *La Mancha* are also very popular.

LOGROÑO

LOGRONO is first of all **the capital of La Rioja** and also the region stretching across the Ebro valley. When cooking is the topic of conversation, *the Rioja wines* inevitably come to mind.

TYPICAL DISHES:

Roast lamb, «Rioja soups», sausage meats; tripe and snails. All pork dishes; red sausages; cured ham; «lomo adobado» (highly seasoned gammon). Also typical are the game and trout from the rivers. The two most popular ways of cooking hake are: «a la riojana» and «a la camerana».

VERY OLD CATALONIAN WINE CELLAR

(Courtesy of La Semana Vitivinícola.)

WINES:

All those under the «DENOMINACION RIOJA»:
Reds from the *Rioja Alta* (10º to 13º), **reds** from the *Rioja Baja* (13.5 to 16.5º), *Lagrima Rioja Alavesa* (11º to 12,5º), *Corazón Rioja alavesa* (14.5 to 15.5º) *Medio Rioja alavesa* (13.8º to 14.5º), *Rosados* (11º to 13º), and *whites* (10.8 to 13).

BURGOS

It would be impossible to speak of the gastronomy of Burgos without first mentioning the **lechazo** or suckling lamb, **tostón** suckling pig, the popular **chorizo** (red sausage) of Villarcayo, and the white and soft sheep cheese. The abundance of sheep, and pig assures a good supply for the home. In the streams and rivers teem the delicious crabs and trouts. In the north, where the Ebro has its source near the passes of Escudo and Los Tornos, the excellent hams are cured in the open air by the «cierzo» wind.

TYPICAL DISHES:

River crabs «Burgos style»; «Chanfaina» (ragout); stewed dried beans and «chorizo»; rice with chicken; Lam's tongue «Burgos style»; stewed pigeons; Hare with beans; partridge «a la castellana»; veal steaks «a la castellana»; young goat, roasted or barbecued.

SWEET DISHES:

Candied yolks; almonds covered in icing sugar; pastries made by the nuns of Las Huelgas.

CHEESES:

Fresh creamy or dry cheese and «requesón de Sedano» (a type of cottage cheese).

WINES:

Aranda, Roa, and the *Burgalese* are the most popular.

«SORIA PURA»

«*Silver grey hills, and opaline promontories*», Soria is the source of the Duero river and the high tableland immortalised by the poet Antonio Machado. It is also the place that inspired the «Cantares de Gesta».

The two chief sources of gastronomy are the famous «merina» lamb flocks and the river trout.

Big game is well represented by the bear and buck which can be seasoned in various ways. The pig is the base of a series of succulent dishes such as boiled tongue with hot sauce, cured gammon served with lemon, garlic, and mint and continental sausage or «chorizo» and «lomo embuchado» cured by the Moncayo winds.

The sweet butter of Soria is well known and so are the candied yolks of Almazán and the butter cakes.

WINES:

To accompany these «sierra» dishes, there are always the common red and claret wines of *Osma, San Esteban de Gormaz, Berlanga de Duero, Langa* and *Castillejo*.

SEGOVIA

Segovia is in the region of the what is called the **asados** or roasts. Together with Burgos, Avila and Soria, it has a wide range of cattle and game and completes its gastronomic table with sundry vegetable products.

As a shepherds dish, the «caldereta» (pot) of lamb, with plenty of ground peppers is typical. The livestock is roasted over the burning coals or in the oven.

As the livestock matures, the flavour becomes richer and the quality improves. The same thing happens with the veal and beef. At all times red meat is preferred to any other.

The cooking of Segovia has a direct relationship with the classical Spanish cooking of profound rural origin. As a result there is a **cocido** (main stew) as we saw in Catalonia, Andalucía and other regions. And so it is with the codfish which is cured before it is stored and eventually taken to the interior regions where it is consumed.

TYPICAL DISHES:

Tripe «a la segoviana»; river crabs «a la segoviana»; trout; frog's legs and the typical roasted lamb and suckling pig as mentioned above. The cheese of Cuéllar is highly recommendable.

SWEET DISHES:

Candied yolks; Segovia punch; curdled milk and «natillas» (very fine custard).

WINES:

In Segovia, there are very good wines made from the family vintages in the old fashioned way. The most important are the wines of *Santiuste* in the *Campo de Arévalo* along the rivers Voltoya and Duratón. All of these are red and claret wines with a fruity «bouquet». In the north, bordering on the provinces of Burgos and Valladolid, the famous vineyards of *Valtiendas* produce a good white and claret wine.

AVILA

Avila is the roof of Castile. It has been called «Avila de los Caballeros», the «Ciudad del Silencio» and the town of Santa Teresa. From the very gates of the ramparts, under a cloudless sky, Castile in all its grandeur of unfolding land can be contemplated.

Saint's and names of captains reminiscent of the Reconquest are to be seen everywhere. The name of Isabel the Catholic is just as present as Saint Teresa herself.

The cooking of Avila is Medieval and its dishes are as tasty as they are flourishing. The veal of the Valles de Ambles is renowned throughout Spain and so is the **cochinillo** and **corderito** (suckling pig and lamb) of Arévalo and Madrigal de las Altas Torres.

TYPICAL DISHES:

«Chanfaina castellana» (ragout); «chorizos a la olla» (red sausages); stewed hare; soup Castilian style; veal in «rebozo» (coated); crab soup; stewed fried partridge in its own juice; leg or head of boar; Spanish goat; «rebeco» (chamois), and trout from the Tormes river.

SWEET DISHES:

Santa Teresa candied yolks; «glorias de Avila»; «huesillos fritos»; «sequillos»; and twisted cake loaf.

WINES:

White and red wines of *Cebreros*, soft and aromatic (12º to 13º). Wines of *Arenas de San Pedro*, *Cuevas de San Beltrán*, *Madrigal* and *Mombeltrán*.

VALLADOLID

Valladolid partakes of the «Tierra de Campos» in the north and the «Tierra de Vino» in the southeast. The river Duero that runs across the province at its widest part marks out a wine region of ancient rank and extraordinary prestige even before the discovery of America. Here were the wines of the Royal Court when the Kings and nobles wandered from town to Castilian town

Situated in the gastronomic area of the roasts, its dishes deserve to appear on any menu.

TYPICAL DISHES:

Garlic soup with toasted bread; roasted suckling pig of Medina; suckling lamb of Peñafiel roasted «al ajillo» (seasoned with garlic); hen with «pebre» (sauce made of pepper, garlic and vinegar). Fried fishes from the Pisuerga river; river crabs with tomato; trout with ham.

SWEET DISHES:

Toasted pine nuts; «natillas» (custard); «tocinillo» (made with eggs and syrup); «mantecados» (butter cakes of Portillo); pastries of Medina de Río Seco; «Amarguillo de Tordesillas» (bitter almond sweetmeat).

WINES:

Tudela, Sardon, Peñafiel, Castillo de Duero, Valbuena, Traspinedo, and the *Vega Sicilia* of international fame. They are red and claret wines not exceeding 30°. In the *Cigales* region, the wines of *Fuensaldana, Mucientes, Corcos, Trigueros del Valle*, and *Cubillas de Santa María* are light wines of 14° to 15°. The region of *Nava del Rey* taking in *Serrada, Rueda, Medina del Campo, Rodilana* and *Pozaldez* make good wines going from 13° to 17°.

ZAMORA

The nature of this province is coarse and hard like its *valiente* wines which need some digesting by the way. The dishes of this area are as plain as they are tasty.

Each village has its own style of dish. In Sanabria, the trout and the veal are of the first order. The same can be said of the famous «adobados» (piglet) as well as the «garbanzos» (chick peas) and asparagus of Fuentesauco.

AREA PROVINCIAL DEL CULTIVO DE LA VID

LA CORUÑA
LUGO
ASTURIAS
SANTANDER
VIZCAYA
GUIPUZCOA
PONTEVE DRA
ORENSE
LEON
PALENCIA
BURGOS
ALAVA
NAVARRA
LOGROÑO
HUESCA
LERIDA
GERONA
ZAMORA
VALLADOLID
SORIA
ZARAGOZA
BARCELONA
SEGOVIA
TARRAGONA
SALAMANCA
AVILA
MADRID
GUADALAJARA
TERUEL
CASTELLON
CACERES
TOLEDO
CUENCA
VALENCIA
BALEARES
BADAJOZ
CIUDAD REAL
ALBACETE
ALICANTE
CORDOBA
JAEN
MURCIA
HUELVA
SEVILLA
GRANADA
ALMERIA
MALAGA
SANTA CRUZ DE TENERIFE
LAS PALMAS
CADIZ

MENOS DE 10.000 HAS.
DE 10.000 A 25.000 HAS.
DE 25.000 A 50.000 HAS.
DE 50.000 A 75.000 HAS.
DE 75.000 A 100.000 HAS.
MÁS DE 100.000 HAS.

THE WINES OF LEON
(Photo Paisajes Españoles.)

MAP SHOWING INTENSITY
OF VINYARD CULTIVATION
(Drawing by J. M. Castejón)

TYPICAL DISHES:

Wedding soup; «asado de Fermoselle» (roasted dish); «tostón» (suckling pig); Zamora style: «dos y pirgada»; «pulpo» (octopus); Sanabria style; cod «a la tranca» (typical dish of Toro); trout «al ajillo» (with garlic); hake «al ajo arriero».

SWEET DISHES:

«Rosquillas de Zamora»; «Eos de Benavente»; «empiñonada de Villar de Ciervo»; «melocotón albino» (a type of peach).

WINES:

The *Toro wine* comes to mind immediately. It is a rather heavy wine of 13º to 16º. The wines of *Fermoselle, Morales, Cañizal, Cavajales, Cabezón, Tordesillas* and *Simancas* are lighter and have enjoyed a fine reputation for many centuries. As table wines, those of *Benavente, Corrales, El Cubo, Moraleja, Madridanos, Villalazóa* and *Villalpando* are ideal.

PALENCIA

Palencia is really three things. Firstly, it is «La Calle Mayor» with its many pastry shops where the «candeal» bread is made and the «pan sobado» which are round loaves of about two fingers in measure.

Secondly, it is the «Cristo del Otero» sculptured by the Palencian born Victorio Macho... Here the Christ figure, his arms raised, is blessing the plainland stretching away in the distance.

Finally, it is the river Carrión surrounded by the white elms and waving poplars.

The Gastronomy of Palencia has a strong and definite tie with the «Camino de Santiago» and has been influenced accordingly.

Its culinary arts have been recorded and kept in the cookery books of its convents and monasteries and for this reason its cooking is fundamentally traditional.

TYPICAL DISHES:

Game, especially partridge, is to be found on nearly every menu list as well as the «Lechazo asado» (young suckling lamb). Other dishes are: Roast chicken with apples and onions; snails with ham and red seasoned sausage; «jijas» (fried sausage meat); vegetable stew; or «menestra», and eggs with peas.

SWEET DISHES:

Fried milk; «amarguillo» (bitter almond sweetmeat); trappist chocolate; butter cake; biscuits; and ring shaped fritters.

WINES:

Along the banks of the rivers of Pisuerga and Arlanzón that meet in the Cerato valleys, the vineyards grow. They are red and claret wines of exquisite bouquet and alcoholic content not exceeding 11º. The *Paramillo* wine leaves a fruity after taste in the mouth.

SALAMANCA   Salamanca is abundant in game and cattle and for this reason the province is located in the gastronomic area of the roasts. In Peñaranda the suckling pig and kid are very popular. In Calendario, Guijuelo, Ciudad Rodrigo, and also in Las Batuecas area, one of the most primitive regions in Spain, the sausage meats and cured hams have acquired an exceptional reputation.

El Farinato, a very popular dish, cannot be left out of this list. It goes particularly well with the English breakfast and it needs only a little Farinato to be taken with a couple of fried eggs on toast to give that «je ne sais quoi».

In Béjar, the «Calderillo», a well known shepherd's pot, is cooked over a slow flame. Its ingredients are: veal meat, potato, onion, pepper and ground red pepper. It is made in the «caldero», a sort of bucket with a curved handle at the top.

OTHER TYPICAL DISHES:

«Sopas de Freje», a soup made with liver, pig's blood and cumin seed, and «cabrito embuchado» (roast kid seasoned with pepper, salt and garlic).

SWEET DISHES:

In Alba de Tormes, the sugar covered almonds made by the Benedictine sisters are called «Garrapiñadas». The «Bollo Maimon» made with eggs, flour and starch is appropriate for any feast. «Las rosquillas» of Eresma and the «chocos» are all made in the capital.

WINES:

Along the river Tormes are the fertile vineyards and bodegas of *Cantalapiedra, Cantalpino* and *Villariño*. The *corriente* wines of between 11° to 12° have an agreeable bouquet.

LEON   The old kingdom of León offers one of the richest and varied gastronomies to be found in Spain, however, it is one of the least known. Its forever green pastures produce some of the best cattle in the land together with its fine cheeses and the butter cakes of Astorga. Finally, the proximity of Asturias and Galicia makes for a very varied gastronomy indeed.

TYPICAL DISHES:

Garlic soup; river trout soup; «cecina» cooked or raw dry beef; «cecina» of boar; partridge and cabbage quail and peppers; veal tails and sweetbreads; oven roasted lamb or kid; mountain black sausage; continental sausage; smoked ham; «empanadas» (Galician meat or fish pie); trout «Bierzo» style; trout in «escabeche» (a very oily sauce and laurel leaf); frog's legs in hot sauce; octopus «Bierzo» style.

SWEET DISHES:

Butter cakes of Astorga; «imperial de La Baneza»; «Suspiros de monja» (nun's sighs); imperial figs in syrup.

ASTURIAS

LA FABADA

The Picos de Europa and all of the Cordillera Cantábrica including its forest and fertile valleys provide a wide variety of game—mountain goat, buck, roe, deer, boar and even bear. Its rivers and rapids carry along their waters salmon, salmon trout and ray trout and the Asturian coastline is a fisherman's paradise. To the interior of the province, the soft pastures of the mountain valleys guarantee a flourishing cattle business from which come the cheeses, milk and butter. The famous «Cabrales» is also available for those who appreciate a really strong creamy cheese.

The Asturian gastronomy, like the Galician, has a great deal in common with that of Normandy, Brittany, and Ireland, and has been carried beyond the provincial and national frontiers to overseas areas and to South America in particular.

On feast days, the «cantelo», a round sugar loaf, is never wanting and is shared round with everyone. The **Fabada** is the most typical Asturian dish made with the «Longaniza» (sausage), black pudding, and beans. «La Caldeirada», a potato and fish dish, is just as popular as the Mediterranean «boullabesa».

OTHER TYPICAL DISHES:

Butter soup made with white bread crumbs; hazelnut soup made with ground hazelnuts and breadcrumbs; white beans soup; «pote asturiano»; «formigos» made with bread, milk, eggs and sugar; tripe; «lacon» (pork legs and pigs trotter).

SWEET DISHED:

Roast apples; Asturian toasted bread; rice pudding; «casadilles»; «maranuelas»; «frixuelos».

WINES:

Asturias is situated in the region of the *vinos verdes* and the little wine drunk is in *Cangas de Narcea*. The typical drink, however, is the **cider** and the real heart of the cider country is in the region of *Villaviciosa* and *Nava*.

WINES:

Rosados and clarets from *La Bañeza*, *Sahagún* and *Villaharta* of a fruity taste and between 10º to 12º; white and red *Bierzo* wine, the wines of *Oteros*, *Valdevimbre* and *Villafranca* of lower alcoholic content and the select table wines of *Cacabelos*, whites, clarets and reds of 12º to 14º.

WINEMAKING
(Courtesy of La Semana Vitivinícola.)

GALICIA

Land of the Pilgrims

The monasteries, abbeys, fairs and saint's days have made famous the cooking of this region. The University and the Galician writers are a testimony of this fact and it is they who have made famous the cooking. The prestigious pens of Alvaro Cunqueiro and José María Castroviejo have universalised the ancient «savoir faire» of Galician cooking. There is a popular slogan: «to eat, Lugo», meaning to say if you really want to dine well, Lugo is the place to go.

THE GALICIAN «MARISCO» OR SHELLFISH:

The Galician gastronomy begins with the very tasty shellfish found along the Atlantic coast and the «Rías» or inlets. Very common are: «Vieras», «navajas», «chocos» (cuttle fish); «lapas», oysters, mussels, squids, lobsters, «percebes», crawfish, Mediterranean shrimp, spider crab, prawns, «cigalas» (a smaller variety of Crayfish), crab, and «Santiaguiños».

RIVERFISH:

Salmon, ray trout, sea lamprey, eels, and «Angulas» from the river Miño

SEAFISH:

Sardines, hake «Galician style», grilled or oven roasted seabream, turbot, haddock, whiting, plaice, jurel.

OTHER DISHES:

Caldo Gallego (A Galician soup made with porkmeat and vegetables); shellfish soup; «lacón con grelos» (leg of pork and green tops of the vegetables, Galician style tripe; roast or stewed kidgoat; all the pork cuts which go to make up the traditional Galician dishes; partridge; hare; quail; stewed rabbit; «empanadas» (Galician pie) made either of sardines, hake, mussels, chicken, lamprey and wild birds.

CHEESES:

From Arzua, Curtis, Illana, all found in the province of La Coruña; the cheeses of fermented cow milk of Cebrero in Lugo; also in Lugo, the cheeses of San Simón, Friol, Palas del Rey, Guimaray and San Pantaleón de Vivero.

SWEET DISHES:

Carnaval pancakes or «Filloas»; Carnaval «flores» and «orejas»; Santiago almond pie; chestnuts roasted, boiled or with milk; Mondenero tart; cakes from Ordenes and Caballo; honey fritters and nougat from Puentedeume and Puenteareas; ring shaped fritters sold on feast days.

WINES:

The *vinos verdes* are to be found in all four quarters of the province. *Rosal* wines and those of *Cambados, Ulla, Ribero, Valdeorras, Ribadavia, Chantada, Amandi, Monterrey, Castrelo del Miño, Arnoya, Leiro, Albarellos, Lazas, Celeiros.* The white wines go from 10° to 15° and the red wines which are heavier, from 9° to 12°.

EXTREMADURA

Land of the «Conquistadores»

The two largest provinces of Extremadura have, in their splendid valleys, plains, evergreen oak forests «sierras» as well as in the spacious lands of Barros and La Serena, more than an adequate supply of food. It is said that one of the reasons why Charles V retired to the monastery of Yuste, was on account of the hunting and the beauty of the countryside itself.

Extremadura has a great tradition respecting the art of cooking. This tradition began in the monasteries of Alcántara, Tentudia, and Yuste. Among the dishes originating in this vast natural region, the Caldereta has a priority. It is the typical rustic cooking bucket always used for stewing lamb or goat's meat, and is always accompanied by other savoury foods such as mushrooms and snails, peppers and of course the hot paprika. As well as the pork specialities, there are the famous cured hams, sausages and salami, foie gras and the truffle. The trout and river fish are there for the asking.

The influence of La Mancha and Andalucía can be noted in the «Gazpacho de pastor», the celebrated «galianos» spoken about by Cervantes in Don Quixote. This dish is prepared with all sorts of meats and pieces of unleavened bread.

«El gazpacho extremeño», consisting of peppers, breadcrumbs, vinegar, oil, garlic, almonds and cucumber is distinct from the Andalucian in that the tomato is added after the dish has been made.

OTHER TYPICAL DISHES:

Sweetbread soup; lamb's tails; pheasant «Alcantaran style»; chicken «Padre-Pedro» style; rice with rabbit; «migas extremeñas»; hare of Villanueva del Fresno.

SWEET DISHES:

Stewed chestnuts with sugar; sugared round cake Nuedalo del Piñonate; «hernazo de Trujillo»; «tortas de Arroyo de la Luz» and «tortas de Alcuescar»; soaked cakes of Cáceres; «coco» cakes of Malpartida de Plasencia.

WINES:

Red wine of *Pasaron*, *Vino Verde* of *Ahigal*, *«Aloque»* of *Hervás*, *«Chinato»* of *Malpartida de Plasencia*. Wines of *Salvatierra*, *Medellín*, *Almendralejo*, *Cañamero*, *Montánchez*, *Ceclavín*, *Cilleros*, *Alburquerque* and *Jarandilla*.

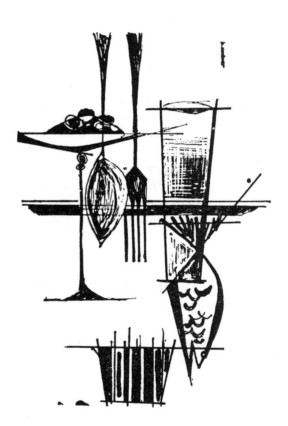

«BODEGA» DE CAMACHO
(From the painting by J. M. Sert.)

LA MANCHA

MADRID

The capital of Spain, indeed, has its manchegan dishes as it lies within La Mancha region between the Sierra de Guadarrama and the Sierra Morena. Nevertheless, the typical Madrileñan dishes take priority. The more important ones are: Seabream «Madrileñan» style; «cocido»; tripe; pork chops; veal steaks; stuffed hake; snails. All these dishes are prepared «a la madrileña».

SWEET DISHES:

Wind fritters, San Antón French rolls, egg custard, «tejas de San Isidro».

WINES:

White, red and claret wines from 13º to 15º, the wines of *Cadalso de los Vidrios, Navalcarnero, San Martín de Valdeiglesias, Pinto, Villaconejos, Villa del Brado, Mosteles, Morata de Tajuña*. Moreover all the Spanish wines in Madrid have their best market either as table or as popular «**chateo**» wines.

GUADALAJARA (LA TIERRA DE LOS MENDOZA)

This province has been linked all through its history with the Mendoza family. The Palace of the Infantado, built by Don Iñigo de Mendoza and the Palace of Pastrana of the Dukes of Pastrana have left in their chronicles interesting records of the sumptuous banquets held there. The ancient monasteries of the Benedictines and Geromites have written down in their cookery books all of their recipes and seasonings used for cooking game, riverfish, and vegetable produce. The Alcarria honey is the base for making most of the sweet dishes.

TYPICAL DISHES:

Partridge Castilian style; quail; oven cooked head of lamb; roasted or fried lamb or mutton chops; «migas»; fried frog's legs; beans with «chorizo» and paprika; fresh goat and sheep cheeses.

SWEET DISHES:

Egg custard; «rosquillas» (ring shaped fritters); candied yolks.

WINES:

This province produces very little wine. In the *Sacedon* area there are some vineyards producing a strong wine of 14º to 15º. In *Cifuentes*, a light family wine is made not exceeding 10º.

TOLEDO
(«LA IMPERIAL»)

Toledo is typical of La Mancha especially in its customs and traditions. This western part is influenced by the Extremadura and the north by the Sierra de Gredos.

TYPICAL DISHES:

Partridge, Toledo style; «morteruelo» (fricassés of hog's liver); «gachas manchegas» (a kind of porridge); «olla podrida»; Manchegan sausages; «ajo arriero»; «gazpachos» or «galianos». Manchegan cheeses.

SWEET DISHES:

Marzipan and sponge cakes of Toledo.

WINES:

The most common wines come from the *Mentrida* area and go under that name in the «DENOMINACION DE ORIGEN». They are rather strong dry red wines. Their names are *Almorox, Escalona, Santa Cruz de Retamar, Valmojado, Villatobas del Monte, Illescas, Esquivias, Yepes, Ocaña, Borox, Quintanar de la Orden, La Puebla de Almoradiel, Villanueva de Alcaudete, Noblejas, Villarrubia de Santiago, Dos Barrios, Santa Cruz de la Zarza* and *Uclés*. Also those of *Tembleque, Madridejos* and *Consuegra*.

CIUDAD REAL

Half of the province of Ciudad Real is used for vineyard cultivation. Most of the region comes under La Mancha gastronomy. To the south, in the Sierra Morena, the cooking has a distinctly Andalucian character, while the mountains of Toledo in the north have plenty of big game. In Ciudad Real, the majority of game reserves are used exclusively for hunting the partridge.

TYPICAL DISHES:

«Tojunto»; «pipirrana»; egg plants of Almagro and Valdepeñas; «pisto manchego» (a dish made of fried tomatoes, potatoes and vegetables); «Almagro omelette»; Manchegan partridge; «migas»; «gachas»; «gazpachos manchegos»; La Mancha cheeses.

WINES:

White, red and claret table wines of 12° to 13° under the DENOMINACION VALDEPENAS. They include the wines of *Campo de Criptana, Tomelloso, La Solana, Membilla, Villanueva de los Infantes, Herencia*. There are also white «corriente» wines of 13° to 15°.

CUENCA

About half of the food and wine supply of Cuenca comes from the Sierra and the other half from La Mancha according to the lay of country. Guadalajara, in the Alcarria and the Palameras de Molina districts, tends to be flat open land. Teruel and the sierras of Albarracín, in contrast, are rugged and hostile and the eating and drinking habits of the people change considerably.

TYPICAL DISHES:

Lamb «en calderete»; lamb chops «al sarmiento»; dressed trout; «Morteruelo» (fricassés of hog's liver); «gachas de almortas» (blue vetchs); «Pisto Manchego» (fried mixture of vegetables and eggs); «migas» or crumbs with bacon and grapes; «atascaburras».

WINES:

Red and *claret* of *La Mancha* type, ranging from 11º to 14º from *San Clemente, Belmonte* and *Taracón.*

ALBACETE
(THE CAPITAL OF
THE PLAINS)

More than three quarters of this province is used for wine growing. In the south, the Sierra de Alcaraz and Calar de Mundo are some of the most beautiful as well as some of the most unexplored country in Spain. It is an extensive area of rugged mountains, marshland and waterfalls. This province has a large number of game reserves and the partridge attracts many hunting visitors from far and wide.

TYPICAL DISHES:

Roast lamb «a la Manchega»; hare pie; «caldereta» or pot of lamb; «gazpachos manchegos» made with crumbs of unleavened bread and game meat, snails, mushrooms and «collejas» (a wild weed). This is a dish eaten by the shepherds and is centuries old. Sausage meats of all kinds; «paellas» Valencian style; different game dishes; cheeses from La Mancha.

SWEET DISHES:

Butter cakes; «tortas con chucharrones» (fried lard); special Santa Cruz Day cakes; «librillos de Montealegre» (made with wafers and honey); «alpera» rolls with eggs.

WINES:

Its wine producing areas are included under the DENOMINACION MANCHA, MANCHUELA, ALMANSA and JUMILLA. In the MANCHUELA area, there area *tinto, claret* and *rosé* wines of 12º to 17º and in ALMANSA, *red* and *claret wines* of 12º to 17º. In JUMILLA, the wines go from 14º to 18º and are the most powerful wines in the country. These are called **vinos de raza** meaning wines of good stock.

LAS BALEARES

The cooking of the Baleares has a well deserved reputation. It was through the strategic situation of these islands with the Mediterranean countries of the classical world that slowly they acquired the special knowledge where the art of cooking is concerned. These islands offer a wide variety of foods

as well as some much coveted game reserves which make them important within the Mediterranean gastronomy.

TYPICAL DISHES:

Mallorquín soup (a vegetable soup); Ibiza soup; Partridge Chaplain Style; back gammon with almonds, back gammon with mayonnaise; liver with almond sauce; chicken in «escaldums»; red mullet Spanish style; stuffed red mullet; «coquerrois», Mallorca pie; «tumbet» (made with egg-plants potatoes and tomatoes); «berenjenas» (egg-plants); grilled or with mayonnaise; grilled mushrooms; «sobrasada» (Mallorca sausage); «butifarra» (a type of pork sausage); cured ham, and Mahón cheese.

SWEET DISHES:

«Ensaimada mallorquina» (a kind of Bath bun); «alfeniques» (sugar paste); «concos de Inca»; apricot cakes; biscuits; «salsa Nadal» (Nadal sauce).

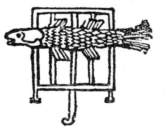

WINES:

Red and white wines of *Benisalem* of 14º and 13º. Red and rosé wine of *Felanitx* of 12º and 11º, and the *corriente* of 10º to 12º. In *Manacor*, there is a light white wine of 11º and a red wine of 10º.

A SEVENTEENTH CENTURY WINE DECANTER
(Photo Más.)

THE CANARY ISLANDS

«Las afortunadas»

The Canary Islands are characterised by their climate and exotic beauty for here are found extinct volcanoes, parched desert lands and vast white beaches. The palm and plane tree grow beside the cactus, pine, coconut and the legendary dragon tree.

The gastronomy of these islands is as diverse as its flora and vegetation.

TYPICAL DISHES:

Hen soup, country style, shellfish and fish soup. Every kind of game meat, poultry, lamb, prepared in the Canary way; also the pig and pork sausage meats, chorizo fried in its own fat or roasted in rum; steaks «en llamas», roast chicken with banana cream.

El Gofio is one of the basic products used in Canary cooking. It is a sort of flour made from toasted corn. There are many ways of serving it and it can be used as a supplement at all meals. It is similar to the maize of the South American countries with which the celebrated «tamales» are made. The «tamales» are hot cakes served and wrapped in tropical leaves.

«El mojo» is a sort of «gazpacho andaluz» with plenty of hot pepper and served as a complement to many dishes. The dressing of kidney beans is very like the American.

The most *typical dishes* to be found are: Halibut, squid, «cabrillas», «cherne», and «morena».

CHEESES:

Flor de Guía, Blanco de Hierro, La Palma, Sur de Tenerife, Quesadilla de Hierro.

WINES:

Red wines of *Agulo, La Gomera, Lanzarote, Hierro, La Palma, Monte, Tijarafe, Tacoronte, Arafo La Matanza* and *Icod de los Vinos.*

White wines of *Fuencaliente* and *Palma;* the rose wines of *Taganana* and *Grafia* which smack of «ea» pine; dry and sweet *Malvasías* and *Lanzarote.*

WINES AND CHEESES

LOCAL AND PROVINCIAL CHEESES

PONTEVEDRA: «Tetilla de Vaca», a slightly acid cheese with hollows and very little crust. The most famous are from Villa de Crucis, Lalin, Rodeiro and Estrada.
«Queso gallego» (also goes under the name of «Patela», and «Perilla»). It is the famous cheese of Ulloa.

LUGO: «El Cebrero» cheese. It is a soft cheese with a semi-dry crust shaped like a mushroom. It has an slightly acid flavour. It is better eaten when fresh and made in Caurel, Nogales, Becerrea and Triacastela.
San Simon is a creamy and hard crusted cheese made in San Simón de la Cuesta, Villapedre, Lanzón, La Nabiza de Friol, Palas del Rey.

LA CORUNA: «Tetilla de Curtis», Arzua and Illana.

BURGOS: Fresh cheese, «Pata de mulo» of Villalón, requesón de Sedano.

SEGOVIA: Cuéllar cheese.

SANTANDER: Cream cheese. Tresvijo blue cheese.

LA MANCHA: Villarrobledo and La Mancha and sheep cheeses.

EXTREMADURA: Sheep cheeses.

CANARY ISLANDS: Cheeses of Guía, Hierro, La Palma and Sur de Tenerife

BALEARES: Mahón.

NAVARRE: Cheeses of Roncal, Aralar, Urbasa and Urzama.

VASCONGADAS: Idiazábal, Urbia and Gorbea.

ASTURIAS: «Cabrales» and «Peñasanta» (both a type of French Rochefort).

WINE AND CHEESE GUIDE

	CHEESES	WINES	TEMPERATURE
1	Soft and fresh cheeses	White and rosé	10°
2	Soft and fermented (Cammembert type)	Strong red and full bodied	Room temperature
3	Semi-dry and compact	Strong red and full bodied	Room temperature
4	Cooked and hard	Clear claret	Normal
5	Soft creamy and fermented with blue and green streaks	Strong red and full bodied	Room temperature

ANOTHER TABLE OF WINES AND CHEESES

CHEESE	WINE
Soft fresh and creamy	White, semi-dry and mild (unsweet)
Cooked and melted	White and very dry
Fermented	Red (good body & alcoholic content)

FRENCH CHEESES AND SPANISH WINES

Not so long ago, in Barcelona, a banquet was held in the Hotel Diplomatic to test the French cheeses and Spanish wines. It was sponsored by a committee of Spanish wine importers from the Federation of Importers for Foreign Drinks, and the Lopexa, a society for the selling and promotion of French food products.

Certainly the most appropriate food to go with wine is cheese as it especially brings out its fragrance and bouquet. Consequently, a full range of French cheeses were brought forth and tried. Among them were the Brie, Rochefort, Saint Paulin, Gruyere, Compe, blue Ambert, and very fresh cheeses like the Petit Suisse, Fontainebleau, and Demisel. The saying goes that «a meal without wine is like a day without sun» and so the white and rosé wines were served with the Gruyere, and the red «tinto» wines with the Rochefort and the fermented type of cheeses. All of the wines served came from the Bodegas López Heredia, Franco Españolas, Torres, Rioja Santiago, Rojas and Compañía, Scholtz and Codorniu.

This banquet in the Hotel Diplomatic convinced and confirmed once again the fitness and appropriateness of French cheeses for the Spanish wines.

WINES OF SPAIN AND THE REST
OF EUROPE

ANALOGIES
BETWEEN CERTAIN
SPANISH WINES AND
THEIR EUROPEAN
COUNTERPARTS

It has already been said that the grapevine through its continual transplantation is the greatest and oldest traveller of the vegetable species. The history of the vines and wines of Spain goes back in some cases to the Middle Ages and the times of the Crusades, when they were brought from the Middle East.

It is not surprising therefore that the Catalonian vines are probably of Asiatic origin and were introduced by the Venetians and Greeks. The Malvasia and Muscatel vines of Sitges and Panadés also have their beginning in the Middle East. The Alella, as has already been said, originally came from the Moselle and Rhine valleys.

In Galicia, the same relationship exists between its vines and wines and those of Central Europe. Some experts argue that the vines planted in certain areas originated in La Rochelle and the «Tostado» wines have a lot in common with the Oporto wines of Portugal.

The wines of La Rioja and Navarre, like the Vega Sicilia in Valladolid, are intimately related with certain French wines from Burgundy, Bordeaux, and the Côte de Rhone.

White, dry, and light wines served at 10° centigrade	*Rioja, Mancha, Valdepeñas, Panadés, Manchuela, Moriles, Huelva, Cheste, Benicarló, Torreblanca, Oropesa, Albarinos, Cigales, Conça, de Barbará, Bajo Panadés.*
	In **France**: *Bordeaux, Graves, Alsace* and *Muscadet*.
	In **Germany**: *Rhine* and *Moselle*.
White dry wines served at 10° centigrade	*Rioja, Valdepeñas, Daimiel, Campo de Criptana, Alcázar de San Juan, Bajo Maestrazgo, San Mateo de Castellón, Panadés, Zona de la Nava, Ribera del Ebro, Serrada, Rueda, Nava del Rey, Medina del Campo, Pozáldez, Alicante, Tarragona, Alella, Requena-Utiel, Cheste, Chiva, Torrente, Jerez, Manzanilla, Montilla, Moriles, Peñafiel* and *Tordesillas*.

SPARKLING WINES
(Courtesy of La Semana Vitivinícola.)

In **Italy**: *Vernaccia* and *Ravello*.

In **France**: *Bourgogne* and *Côte de Rhone*.

In **Germany**: *Rhine*.

Semi-dry wines served at 8°	*Rioja, Panadés, Cuarte, Turis, Chiva, Alella.* In **Italy**: *Frascaty* and *Orvieto.* In **France**: *Bordeaux, Loire* and *Coindrieu.*
Sharp wines served cold	*Albariño, Ribeiro, Rosal, Ramallosa, Condado de Salvatierra, Ribero de Avia, Norte Navarra* and *Cornisa Cantábrica.*
Light red wines served at 16°	*Rioja, de la Vega del Guadiana, Tierra de Barros, Badajoz, Felanitx, Canarias (Agudo, Chiparde, La Gomera, Palmar), Bajo Panadés, Panadés Medio, Icod de los Vinos, Baleares (Benisalem and Manacor), Mancha, Alicante, Valencia.* In **Italy**: *Chianti.* In **Germany**: *Mosselle, Rhine* and *Johannesburg.*
Red wines of body served at 18°	*Navarra, Rioja, Valencia, Alicante, Almansa, Alpera, Panadés, Yecla, Jumilla, Cariñena, Priorato, Vega Sicilia, de la Selva, Villena, Alto Ampurdán, Panadés, Toro, Zamora, Fuentesauco, Villalpando, Benaventes* and *Corales.* In **France**: *Bordeaux, Burgundy, Chateauneuf* and *Hermitage.* In **Italy**: *Barolo* and *Gattinara.*
Sweet wines	*Málaga, Alicante, Tarragona, Malvasía, de Sitges, Moscatel, Rioja, Panadés, Tostado del Ribeiro* and *Valdeorras.* In **France**: *Sauternes* and *Coulée de Serrant.* In **Italy**: *Albana* and *Marsala.*
Sparkling wines	*San Sadurní de Noya, Codorniú* and the sparkling Catalonian are found in the *Panadés* region, as well as in the *Valle de Miño, Pontevedra* and in the province of *Orense.* In **France**: The CHAMPAGNE region of universal fame.

THE INTERNATIONAL WINE DECALOGUE

1. Never shake up a bottle of wine.

2. Never add ice to any wine.

3. Never mix up in the same jug or glasses, wines from different bottles.

4. Don't heat or chill red wine. It should always be served at room temperature. To do this never use artificial methods.

5. Be very careful when transferring red wine.

6. Serve wine in large glasses and only half fill them.

7. Serve the white wines with hors d'oeuvres, soup and fish.

8. Serve red wine with roasts, game, and red meats.

9. It's better to chill champagne. Never add ice. It can be served during the meal.

10. The order of preference for the white wines: Dry always before the sweet. As for the red wines, it is necessary to take into account the alcoholic content. The light wine is always served before the heavy.

APPENDIX

EL VILLAR IN THE PROVINCE OF ALAVA
(Photo Arbex.)

SPANISH WINE PUBLICATIONS

VID

Editorial Técnica Española, S. A. Doctor Castelo, 48. Madrid, 9.

LA SEMANA VITIVINICOLA

Mestre Racional, 8. Apartado 642. Valencia, 5.

EL CULTIVADOR MODERNO

Vía Augusta, 158, 6, 4. Barcelona, 6.

MESA Y VINOS DE ESPAÑA

Infanta Carlota, 151, 7. Barcelona, 15.

AGRICULTURA

Caballero de Gracia, 24. Madrid, 14.

LA REVISTA VINICOLA Y DE AGRICULTURA

Lapuyade, 23. Zaragoza.

LA PAMPANA DE BACO

Apartado 21. Socuéllamos (Ciudad Real).

ESPAÑA HOSTELERA

General Mola, 119, 6. Madrid, 2.

EL CAMPO

Servicio de Estudios. Banco de Bilbao. Bilbao.

APPENDIX II

BRITISH IMPORTERS OF SHERRY WINES

Clode & Baker Ltd.—Bearbrock House, Oxford Road, Aylesbury.

Batles Duval & Beaufoys Ltd.—Great West Road, Corner Syon Lane, Isleworth, Middlesex.

Williams & Humbert Ltd.—Sherry House, 39 Crutched Friars, London, E. C. 3.

Evans Marshall & Co. Ltd.—14 New Burlington Street, London, W1X 2BU.

Luis Gordon Wines Ltd.—9 Upper Belgrave Street, London, S. W. 1.

Giordano Ltd.—38-40 Windmill Street, London, W. 1.

CFbillo & Co. Ltd.—19 Eastcheap, London, E. C. 3.

Luis Gordon & Sons Ltd.—12 Hobart Ppace, London, S. W. 1.

Lindlater Mackie Todd & Co. Ltd.—92 Wigmore Street, London, W. 1.

Rutherford, Osborne & Perkin Ltd.—62 Dean Street, London, W1V 5HG.

González, Byass & Co. Ltd.—91 Park Jtreet, London, W. 1.

F. S. Matta Ltd.—21 Lillie Road, London, S. W. 6.

Wm. & Jno. Lockett Ltd.—665 Sefton House, Liverpool-2.

Mackenzie & Co.—20 Eastcheap., London, E. C. 8.

Edward Young & Co. Ltd.—14. New Burlington Street, London, W1X 2BU.

Montemar Ltd.—20-21 Suffolk Street, London, S. W. 1.

A. Cassinello.—La Riva House, South Molton Street, London, W. 1.

Western Licensed Supplies Ltd.—Royal Oak House, Royal Oak Avenue, Prince Street, Bristol-1.

Averys of Bristol Ltd.—7 Park Street, Bristol.

Barber & Co. Ltd.—Seaview Road, Wallasey.

Blumenthals Ltd.—Albert Bridge House, 127 Albert Bridge Road, London, S. W. 11.

Block, Grey & Block Ltd.—26 South Audley Street, London, W. 1.

Brown, Gore & Welch Ltd.—2 Seething Lane, London, E. C. 3.

Burton Sheen Ltd.—Vincent House, Vincent Lane, Dorking, Surrey

C. Buswell & Co. Ltd.—Devonshire Chambers, 146 Bishopsgate, London, E. C. D.

Capital Wine Agencies Ltd.—Central House, 32 Stratford High Jtreet, London, E. 15.

Christopher & Co. Ltd.—94 Jermyn Straeet, London, S. W. 1.

Churtons Ltd.—Eberle Street, Liverpool-2.

Converdale & Co. Ltda.—51 Cutched Frías, London, A. C. E.

Dale & Co. Ltd.—The Broadway, Farnham Common, Buckinghamshire.

Davis & Co. Ltd.—97 Commercial Road, London, E. 1.

Dempsey, Kelly Ltd.—26A Church Gardens, Rathmines, Dublin-6.

Fox & Beames Ltd.—Morrison Flats North, 35 Commercial Road, London, E. 1.

W. A. Gilbey Ltd.—Harlow, Essex.

Grants of St. James's Ltd.—31 Bury Street, St. James's, London, S. W. 1.

Roger Grayson Ltd.—Bond House, Goodwood Road, New Cross Gate, London, S. E. 14.

Greenall Whitley & Co. Ltd.—Warrington.

Grierson, Oldham & Adams Ltd.—25 Haymarket, London, S. W. 1.

Robert James Son & Co. Ltd.—15 Grape Street, London, W. C. 2.

Charles Kinloch & Co. Ltd.—Kinloch House, Cumberland Avenue, London, N. W. 10.

Mackenzie & Co. Ltd.—20 Eastcheap, London, E. C. 3.

Stanley Marlow & Son Ltd.—39 Hospital Jtreet, Birmingham-19.

Jhon Martin of London, Ltd.—Battlebridge House, Tooley Street, London, S. E. 1.

Martin, Silva & Co. Ltd.—19 Eastcheap, London, E. C. 3.

Norton & Langridge, Ltd.—Compter House, Street, Cheapside, London, E. C. 2.

Powell & Son Ltd.—108 The Broadway, Wimbledon, London, S. W. 19.

Reiver Sales Ltd.—180 New Bridge Street, Newcastle-upon-Tyne, 1.

Xigby & Evens Ltd.—Moreland Street, London, E. C. 1.

Pedro Roca & Co.—12 Henry Street, Liverpool-1.

Roma y Puerto Ltd.—2 Norfolk Place, London, W. 2.

Saccone & Speed Ltd.—32 Sackville Straet, Picaddilly, London, W. 1.

Second City Wine Shippers Ltd.—7 Little Bow Street, Birmingham-1.

E. Dudley Smith & Co. Ltd.—69 Queen Square. Brilstol

Southard & Co. Ltd.—56 Palace Road, East Molesey Surreu.

David Taylor & Son Ltd.—26 South Audley Street, London, W. 1.

Western Licensed Supplies Ltd.—Royal Oak House Royal Oak Avenue, Prince Street, Bristol-1.

BRITISH IMPORTERS OF OTHER SPANISH WINES

s. tw) Adams & Sons Ltd.—29 John Street, Bedford Row, London W. C. 1.

s) John Allnut & Co. Ltd.—(Bernal y Cía), 6 York Buildings, Adelphi, London W. C. 2.

s. sw) W. J. Atkinson & Co. Ltd.—(A. Deleyto-Juan Mory y Cía.), 29 John Street, Bedford Row, London W. C. 1.

s) Averys of Bristol Ltd.—7-11 Park Street, Bristol.

s) Bagots, Hutton & Kinahan Ltd.—Bagots Buildings, 27-28 South William Street, Dublín.

s. sw) Balls, Austin, Ltd.—379 Bethnal Gren Road, London E. 2.

s) Barham & Marriage Ltd.—(Ramón López y Cía.), 3 Mitre Street, aldgate, London E. C. 3.

s) John Barker & Co. Ltd.—Kensington, London W. 8.

tw) George Barnes & Co. Ltd.—129-131 City Road, London E. C. 1.

s) John Barnett & Co.)London) Ltd.—226-7 Blackfrías Road, London S. E. 1.

s) Bartlett & Hobbs Ltd.—Polo House, Prince Street, Bristol.

s. sw) Barton & Co.)Wine Shippers) Ltd.—Ocean House, Great Tower Street, London E. C. 3.

s) Thomas Baty & Sons Ltd.—16 Water Street, Liverpool 2.

---

a: altar wine (vino de altar)
b: brandy
s: sherry (jerez)
w: sweet wine (vino dulce)
tw: table wine (vino de mesa)

s) Beaufoys Wines Ltd.—16 Villiers Road, Kingston-on-Thames, Surrey.

s) Belloni & Co.—Belloni House, 52-55 Charlotte Street, London W. 1.

s. sw. a. tw) Bilbaínas (London) Ltd.—4 Hungerford Lane, 15a Strand, London W. C. 2.

tw) H. Billingham Ltd.—596 Coventry Road, Birmingham 10.

s) D. M. & A. Bishop Ltd.—Bentinck Buildings, Wheeler Gate, Nottingham.

s. tw) Blackett & Spedding Ltd.—(Luis Felipe-L. Viñas).—241 Lord Street, Southport.

s) Block, Grey and Block Ltd.—26 South Audley St. London W. 1.

s) Blumenthals Ltd.—125 Pall Mall, London S. W. 1.

s) Bouchard Aine Ltd. (Manuel de Morales).—3 Halkin Street. Belgrave Sq. London S. W. 1.

s) Bournemouth Wine Co. Ltd. (C. A. Munez).—4a & 4b Westcliff Road, Bournemouth.

s) Brega & Rossi Ltd. (A. Valdés y Hermanos).—1-3-Stephen St. Tottenham Court Road, London W. 1.

sw) G. E. Bromley & Sons Ltd.—31 London Street, Leicester.

s) Bulloch & Co. Ltd.—4, 6 & 8 Cadogan St., Glasgow C. 2

s) John Burnett & Co. (Wine Merchants) Ltd.—Highbridge, Somerset.

s) James Borrough Ltd.—29 Cale Distillery, Hutton Road, Lambeth, London S. E. 11.

s) Borroughs Ltd.—Smithfield Street, Liverpool 3

s. sw) **Buswell, C. & Co. Ltd.** (Florido Hnos.-Bodegas Salvat).—Devonshire Chambers, 146 Bishopsgate, London E. C. 2.

s) **Thos. A. Buxton Ltd.** (M. S. Cosio).—College Street, Dowgate Hill, London E. C. 4.

s) **Canova & Co. Ltd.** (Juan Vicente Vergara).—22 Buckingham Street, Strand, London W. C. 2.

s. tw. sw) **Capital Wine Agencias)Wholesale) Ltd.**—Finsbury Pavement, London E. C. 2.

s. tw) **Carter & Co.)Wines) Ltd.**—51 Dean Lane, Bristol 3.

s) **Cassinello A.** (Compañía Vinícola Jerezana- M. Antonio de la Riva, S. A.).—La Riva House, South Molton St., London W. 1.

s) **W. H. Chaplin & Co. Ltd.**—16 Deptford Bridge, London S. E. 8.

s) **Charnley, Abraham & Todd Ltd.**—33 St. Mary-at-Hill, Eastcheap, London E. C. 3.

s. sw. s) **A. & R. Chartres Ltd.**—Colonial Buildings, 18 Cope St., Dublín.

s. sw) **Sydney F. Chorley & Co. Ltd.**—72 Sanderstead Court Avenue, Sanderstead, Surrey.

s) **Christopher & Co. Ltd.**—94 Jermyn St., London S. W. 1.

tw) **Churchill & Williams Ltd.**—20-22 King St., Northamton.

s) **Churtons Ltd.** (Pedro Córdova & Co.).—Eberle Street, Liverpool 2 and Finsbury Court, Finsbury Pavement, London E. C. 2.

tw) **Cini Bros. & Co. Ltd.**—37 The Highway London Dock, London E. 1.

s. tw) **Clark, Matthew & Sons Ltd.** (Garvey, S. A.-El Sindicato Alella Vinícola).—Cannon Street House, 110 Cannon Street, London E. C. 4.

b. sw. s. tw) **Cock, Russell & Co. Ltd.** (A. R. Ruiz Hermanos-Juan y Co.).—60 Fenchurch Street, London E. C. 3.

s) **Constant, Mertens & Co. Ltd.**—19 Bury Street, St. James's, London S. W. 1.

s) **Copp, A. H. Ltd.**—7 Royal Parade, Jersey (Channel Islands).

s) **Coquantin M.** (M. Gil Galán, S. A.).—50 Hillside Crescent, Leigh-on-Sea, Essex.

s. tw. a. sw) **Coverdale & Co. Ltd.** (Arealva Ltd.-Federico Leal-Cía. Vinícola del Norte de España).—1 & 2 Rangoon Street, Crutched Friars, London E. C. 3.

s) **Crabb W. J. & Son.**—24 New Road, Brighton 1.

s) **Charles Crewe Ltd.** (Díez Hnos.).—Poulenoire House, Talbot Road, Blackpool.

s) **Cullen A. C.)Wines) Ltd.** (Destilerías Jerezanas).—Mount Street, New Basford, Nottingham.

s) **John Daly & Co. Ltd.** (Palomino y Vergara).—10-20 Kyrl's Quay, Cork (Irlanda).

s. tw) **D. J. Davis & Hammond Ltd.** (José Martínez Rodríguez & Berger, S. A.-J. B. Berger, S. A.).—Africa House, 44, 45 & 46 Leandenhall St., London E. C. 3.

tw) **Charles Day & Co.** (Hijos de Martínez Lacuesta). 62 Crutched Friars, London E. C. 3.

s. tw) **James Denman & Co. Ltd.**—Denman House, 20 Piccadilly, London W.

s) **Dent, Urwick & Yeatman Ltd.**—61 Mark Lane, London E. C. 3.

s) **Dobell, John & Bartholomew Ltd.** (Carbonell & Cía.).—419-420 High Street, Cheltenham.

s) **Dolamore Ltd.**—38 Baker St., London W. 1.

s) **Donnelly & Co. Ltd.** (Sánchez Romate Hnos.).—Portmahon, Church Gardens, Rathmines-Dublín.

s. tw) **Edward J. Doyle.**—13 Dartry Road, Dublín.

s) **Jules Duval & Co. Ltd.** (. Ruiz y Cía.).—7-17 Bermondsey St. Tooley St. London S. E. 1.

s) **John Egan & Son)London) Ltd.** (Emilio Lustau).—9-15 and 10-12 Crucifix Lane, Thomas Street, London S. E. 1.

s) **G. Epstein & Sons Ltd.**—179 Cheetham Hill Road, Manchester 8.

s) **Evans, Marshall & Co. Ltd.** (Bertola, S. A.).—6-7 Water Lane, London E. C. 3.

s) **Evans, Morris & Co. Ltd.**—78 Mosley Street, Manchester.

s. tw) **Frank Fehr & Co.** (Manuel de Argueso).—1-4 Bury Street, London E. C. 3.

s. tw) **John E. Fells & Sons Ltd.**—56 & 58 Tooley St., London S. E.

s) **Fergusons Ltd.**—116-7 Broad Street, Reading.

s) **Fuuerheerd, Wearne & Co. Ltd.**—23 Suffolk Street, Pall Mall, London S. W. 1.

s) **Fielding A. & Burchell Ltd.**—87-100 Queensbury Road, North Circular Road, Wembley, Middx.

a. s) **J. Lleming & Co.**—39 Dame St., Dublín.

a. tw. s) **John Forsyth & Co.**—119 Finsbury Pavement, London E. C. 2.

a. tw. s) **Fox & Beames Ltd.** (Dalmau Hnos.).—Billiter Buildings, 22 Billiter St., London E. C. 3.

s) **Gardner-Mc Lean, J.** (Wilson & Valdespino Ltd.). 114 Union St., Glasgow C. 1.

s) **Garnett Brothers Ltd.** (Domecq).—16 Howard St., Rotherham.

tw) **Gash & Zazzi** (Bodegas El Montecillo, S. A.).—24 Calthorpe Street, London W. C. 1.

s) **Gilbey, W. & A. Ltd.**—Gilbey House, Oval Road, Regent's Park, London N. W. 1.

EXPORT WINES
(Courtesy of La Semana Vitivinícola.)

sw. tw) G. M. Wine Co.—Victoria House, Vernon Place, London W. C. 1.

b. s) González, Byass & Co. Ltd. (Tío Pepe).—7-8 Gt. Winchester St., London E. C. 2.

b. s) Luis Gordon & Sons Ltd. (Pedro Domecq, S. A.).—28 Mark Lane, London E. C. 9.

s) Andrew Grahan & Sons.—10 Botolph Lane, Eastcheap, London E. C. 3.

s) Roger Grayson Ltd.—39-40 Mitre Street, London E. C. 3.

s) Gresham Wine & Cigar Co. Lt.—Copthall House, 13 Copthall Ave., London E. C. 2.

s) Grimbley, Hughes & Co. Ltd.—55-57 Cornmarket St., Oxford.

s. sw) Gulliver, Byron & Sons Ltd.—High Street, Baldock, Herts.

s) Samuel Gulliver & Co. Ltd.—13-17 Kingsbury Sq. Aylesbury.

s) Hall & Bramley Ltd. (González Byass & Co. Ltd.). National Bank Building, Fenwick, St., Liverpool 2.

a. s) Frank Halse & Co. Ltd.—Tower Building, 2 Wolborough St., Newton Abbot-Devon.

s. sw) Hancliff Ltd.—5 Monmouth Place, London W. 2.

s) William Hancock & Co. Ltd.—Crawshay Street, Cardiff.

b. s) Hay & Son Ltd.—95 to 101 Norfolk St., Sheffield.

s. tw) Hayward Bros (Wines) Ltd.—Joiner St., St. Thoma's Street, London.

s. tw) Head, George & Lawler Ltd.—63 Crutched Friars, London E. C. 3.

s) Hunt, Roope & Co. Ltd. (José de Soto & Co).—11 Eastcheap, London E. C. 3.

s) J. & J. Hunter Ltd. (Sánchez Romate & Co.).—38 Donegall Quay, Belfast.

s) C. F. Jackson & Co.—108 The Broadway, Wimbledon S. W. 19.

s) Andrew Jardine.—400 Duke St., Glasgow E. 1.

s) George Jones & Co. (London) Ltd.—24-26 Great Suffolk Street, Blackfriars, London S. E. 1.

s) Rober L. Kehoe & Co. Ltd.—48-9 William Street, Dublín.

a. s) T. W. Kelly & J. Ltd.—58 Upper O'Connell St., Dublín.

s. sw) Charles Kinloch & Co. Ltd.—Queensbury Road, Wembley, Midds.

s) A. J. Knowland Ltd.—4-7 Norris St. Haymarket, London S. W. 1.

s) Koppenhagens.—31-2 Haymarket, London S. W. 1.

s) Charles A. Labin Ltd.—53 Piccadilly, London W. 1.

s. sw) Lakeside Wines Ltd.—5 Monmouth Place, London W. 2.

s. sw) Lamb & Whatt Ltd.—48 St. Anne St., Liverpool.

s) Lamberts, Parkers & Gaines (Hull) Ltd.—78 Paragon St., Hull.

s) La Montagne (London) Ltd.—39 Elystan St., London S. W.

s) Lankester & Wells.—5 Mercers Row, Northampton.

s) Le Forestier, H. & C.—6 Buckingham St., Adelphil London W. C. 2.

s) J. J. Le sueur.—7 Bond Street, Jersey (Channe, Islands).

s) Luis Lladró.—10 Eastcheap, London E. C. 3.

s) John Lovibond & Sons Ltd.—Greenwlch, London S. E. 10.

s) Low, Roberston & Co. Ltd. (Manuel Fernández y Cía.).—10 Links Place, Leith.

s. tw) Lyttleton, Matthew & Co.—Room 202 B, 7-8 Idol Lane, London E. C. 3.

s) J. McCarthy & Sons Ltd.—35 Coog Street, Cork, 39 Dame Street, Dublín.

s) James McCullagh Sons & Co.—36 South Frederick St., Dublín.

a. s) Alex Macdonald & Co.—49-53 Church St., Inverness.

s) D. MacDougall Junr. (Agencies(Ltd.—53 Renfrew Street, Glasgow.

s) Macgregor, Caldbeck & Co. Ltd.—3 Lloyds Avenue, London E. C. 3.

tw) McIntoscsh, Palengat, Walford & Co. Ltd.—48 Mark Lane, London E. C. 3.

s) E. Marcus & Son Ltd.—233 Mile End Road, London E. 1.

s. tw) Stanley Marlow & Son Ltd.—18 Bath Street, Snow Hill, Birmingham 4.

s) Marshall Bros. (Wines) Ltd.—63-67 Linenhall St., Belfast.

s) Marshall, Taplow Ltd.—Whitehall Distillery, Stratford, London E. 15.

s) Mason B. B. & Company Ltd.—Prince Rupert House, 64 Queen St., London E. C. 4.

s) Martínez, Gassiot & Co. Ltd.—5 Fenchurch St., London E. C. 3.

s. tw) Mason, Gattley & Co. Lts.—137 Victoria St., London S. W. 1.

s) Maurice Meyer Ltd.—Palace Chambers, Bridge St. Westminster, London S. W. 1.

s. b)   M. Misa.—Corn Exchange Chambers, Seething Lane, London E. C. 3.

tw)   Molton & Co. (Wine Shippers) Ltd.—54 South Molton Street, London W. 1.

s)   William Mullar (Mark Lane) Ltd.—4 Cullum St., London E. C. 3.

s)   Mullins & Westley Ltd.—43 New Cavendish Street, London W. 1.

s)   S. Myers (Wines) Ltd.—16-20 Vernon Street, Manchester.

s)   Neilson's Black & Gold Ltd.—12-15 St. Andrew's Square, Glasgow.

s)   Cliffoerd Neville & Co. Ltd.—Panton House, Panton Street, London S. W. 1.

s)   Norton & Langridge Ltd.—Mitre Court, Milk Street, Cheapside, London E. C. 2.

s. sw)   J. R. Phillips & Co. Ltd.—18-19 Nelson St., Bristol 1.

s. tw)   Reid Stuart & Co. Ltd.—16 Deptford Bridge, London S. E. 8.

s)   J. C. Rennie & Co. (Wines) Ltd.—180 West Regent Street, Glasgow C. 2.

s. tw. sw)   W. & T. Restell (De Muller).—9 Union Court, Old Broad Street, London E. C. 2.

s)   Rodney, Watson & Co. Ltd.—10 Philpot Lane, London E. C. 3.

tw)   H. H. Roose & Co. Ltd.—13 Road Lane, London E. C. 3.

s)   L. Rose & Co. Ltd. (Palomino & Vergara).—Grosvenor Road, St. Albans.

s)   Saccone & Speed Ltd.—32 Sackville St. Piccadilly, London W. 1.

s)   Geo. G. Sandeman Sons & Co. Ltd.—20 St. Swithin's Lane, London E. C. 4.

s)   Adam Scott & Co. Ltd. (A. R. Valdespino y Hno.). 11 South William St., Dublín.

s. tw)   Seager, Evans & Co. Ltd.—Depford, London S. E. 8.

s)   Sheen, Chas. H. & Sons Ltd.—222 Brohnwill Road, Catford, London S. E. 6.

s)   Joseph Shore & Son Ltd.—11 Easy Row, Birmingham.

s)   H. Sichel & Sons Ltd. (Agustín Blázquez).—3 Robert Street, Adelphi, London W. C. 2.

s)   Sinclair Birch & Co.—33 St.-Mary-at-Hill, London E. C. 3.

s. sw)   Smith & Hoey Ltd.—Trinity Vaults, Coopers Row, London E. C. 3.

s)   W. E. Smith & Co. Ltd.—13 Maze Pond, London S. E. 1.

s. tw. aw)   Southard & Co. Ltd.—56 Palace Road, East Molesey, Surrey.

s. sw)   Stephenson, Routley & Co. Ltd.—8 Southgate, Manchester 3.

s)   J. Stonehill & Co. Ltd.—14 Bonhill St., London E. C. 2.

s. b. sw)   Walter Symons & Co. Ltd. (Hijos de Jiménez Varela-Vinos Tarragona, S. A.).—Monument Buildings, 11-15 Monument Street, London E. C. 3.

s)   C. H. Tapp & Co. Ltd. (Marqués del Real Tesoro, Sociedad Limitada).—3-4 Lincoln's Inn Fields, London W. C. 2.

s)   David Taylor & Son (R. D. Ferraro).—14 Eastcheap, London E. C. 3.

s)   Peter Thomson.—6 Alexandra St., Perth.

s. aw. tw)   Trans-Continental Agencies Ltd. (Luso-Vinicola Ltda.-Salvador Ramos).—193 Victoria St., London S. W. 1.

s. aw. sw. tw)   L. R. Voight Ltd.—24 & 25 Great Tower St., London E. C. 3.

s)   Wholesale Wine Distributors Ltd.—Aslett St. Garrat Lane, London S. W. 18.

s)   Williams & Humbert Ltd.—Walsingham House, 35 Seething Lane, London E. C. 3.

s)   Wilson & Valdespino Ltd.—110 Cannon St., London E. C. 4.

s)   B. Wood & Son (Wine shippers) Ltd.—4 New London Street, London E. C. 2.

tw. s. sw.)   WoodhaMs & Co. (Marqués de Irún) (La Vinícola Ibérica).—71-3 Leeds St., Liverpool 3.

s. tw)   J. S. Woolley & Co. Ltd. (M. S. de Orovio).—74 Borough High Street, London E. 1.

s)   Yates Brothers Wine Lodges Ltd.—54 Carnarvon St., Manchester 3.

s. tw)   Edward Young & Co. Ltd. (Luis Caballero-Miguel Mendoza y Cía.).—5 Lloyds Avenue, London E. C. 3.

s)   L. Zimmermann & Sons)London) Ltd. (García Díaz).—107 Cannon Street, London E. C. 4.

AMERICAN IMPORTERS OF SPANISH TABLE WINES

Austin Nichols & Co., Inc.—58th St. & 55th Drive. Maspeth, N. Y.

Banfi Products Corp.—148 Ave. of the Americas. New York, N. Y. 10013.

Briones & Company.—57-60 Broadway. Bronx, N. Y. 10463.

Cazanove Opici Import Co.—2020 E. 177th St. Bronx, N. Y. 10473.

Cella Bros., Ins.—468-470 Greenwich. New York, N. Y. 10013.

Classic Imports Co.—79 W. St. Brooklyn, N. Y. 11222.

C. Daniele & Co., Inc. 220-222 E. 125th St. New York, N. Y.

Bay Distributors, Inc.—3225 S. Mac Dill Ave. Tampa, Fla.

N. Polanco, Inc.—2177 N. W. 8th Ave. Miami,. Fla. 33127.

Tampa Wholesalers Liquor Co.—P. O. Box 15397 Tampa, Fla. 33614.

Empire Distributors, Inc.—1700 Marietta Blvd., N. W. Atlanta, Ga. 30318.

State Wholesaler, Inc.—436 Armour Circle, N. E. Atlanta, Ga. 30324.

Armanetti Liquors, Inc.—7324 N. Western Avenue. Chicago, Ill. 60645.

Barton Brands, Inc.—200 S. Michigan Ave. Chicago, Ill. 60604.

The Garofalo Co., Inc.—99 S. Water Market. Chicago, Ill. 60608.

La Preferida Liquors, Inc.—177 S. Water Market. Chicago, Ill. 60608.

Mallars & Co.—5145 N. Milwaukee Ave. Chicago, Ill. 60630.

Morand Bros, Beverage.—2555 S. Leavitt St. Chicago, Ill. 60608.

Slected Brands, Inc.—7215 S. Coles Ave. Chicago, Ill. 60649.

Wertner Smith Co., Inc.—2777 S. Floyd St. Louisville, Ky, 40221.

Distilled Brands, Inc.—26-15 4th St. L. I. C., N. Y. 11107.

Eastern Wine Corp.—Bronx Terminal Market. 151 St. & Cromwell Ave. Bronx, N. Y. 10451.

Empire Liquor Corp.—850 E. 140th St. Bronx, N. Y. 10454.

Excelsior Wine & Spirits Corp.—136 E. 57th St. New York, N. Y. 10022.

Foreing Brands, Inc.—101 W. 31st. St. New York, N. Y.

Foreing Vintages, Inc.—45 Rockefeller Plaza. New York, N. Y. 10020.

The Jos. Garneau Co.—555 Madison Ave. New York, N. Y. 11793.

A. B. Sales, Inc.—435 Eldora St., Wichita, Kansas 67202.

Wines Unlimited.—P. O. Box 5106. New Orleans, La. 70115.

Carlton Co.—11 South Gay St. Baltimore, Md. 21202.

John Gross.—11 South Gay St. Baltimore, Md. 21202.

Key Wine & Liquots.—1221 De Soto Rd. Baltimore, Md. 21223.

Maynard & Child Inc.—4804 Benson Avenue. Baltimore, Md. 21227.

Mullens, Inc.—10 Thompson Sq. Charlestown, Mass.

Pastene Wine & Spirits.—15 Poplar St. Somerville, Mass. 02143.

Leone & Son Wine Co.—5805 Lincoln St. Detroit, Mich. 48008.

Viviano Wine Importers, Inc.—15100 Second Blvd. Detroit, Mich. 48203.

Mid-West Wine Co., Inc.—1376 University Ave. St. Paul, Minn. 55104.

Central States Wine Co.—6611 Clayton Rd. St. Louis, Mo. 63155.

Kansas City Wholesale Liquor Co.—1109 Cherry St. Kansas City, Mo.

General Wines & Spirits Co.—375 Park Avenue. New York, N. Y. 10022.

Frank M. Hartley.—10 Hillside Ave. New York, N. Y. 10040.

Italian & French Wine Co.—1055 E. Delavan Ave. Buffalo, N. Y. 14215.

Kobrand Corp.—134 E. 40th St. New York, N. Y. 10016.

Major Liquor Dist.—345 Underhill Blvd. Syosset, N. Y. 11791.

McKesson Liquor Co.—155 E. 44th St. New York, N. Y. 10017.

Mohr International Ltd.—274 Madison Ave. New York, N. Y. 10016.

Bonanza Beverage Co.—2670 So. Western St. Las Vegas, Nevada 89102.

American Vineyards.—2220 Center St. Cleveland, Ohio.

Excello Wine Co.—1401 E. 17th Ave. Columbus, Ohio. 43211.

Imperial Foods.—505 Woodland Ave. Cleveland, Ohio.

Rimi Wine Co.—1854 Scranton Rd. Clveland, Ohio 44113.

Superior Wine & Spirits Inc.—7212 Keystone St. Philadelphia, Pa. 19135.

Central Beverages Corp.—5357 River St. Central Falls, R. I.

Charles Fradin, Inc.—154 Marraganot Ave. Providence, R. I. 02907.

Tennessee Wine & Spirits Co.—827 5th Ave. N. Nashville, Tenn. 37219.

Terk Distributing Co., Inc.—10008 2nd St. Odessa, Texas 79760.

White Rose Distributing Co.—1601 Ballinger St. Fort Worth, Texas 76102.

The Globe Distributing Co.—3145 V St. N. E. Wáshington, D. C. 20018.

Bay Wholesale Liquor.—238 S. Webster St. Green Bay, Wisc.

Monarch Wine Co., Inc.—4500 Second Avenue. Brooklyn, N. Y. 11232.

Monsieur Henri Wines, Ltd.—131 Morgan Avenue. Brooklyn, N. Y. 11237.

Charles Morgenster & Co.—200 E. Sunrise Highway. Freeport, N. Y. 11520.

Munson Shaw Co.—99 Park Ave. New York, N. Y. 10016.

North America Wines Corp.—57-02 48th St. Maspeth, N. Y. 11378.

Park Benziger & Co., Inc.—647 White Plains Rd. Scarsdale, N. Y. 10583.

Petrocelli & Seagre, Inc.—29-28 41st Ave. Long Island City, N. Y. 11101.

Renfields Importers Ltd.—425 Park Ave. New York, N. Y. 10022.

Robinson Lloyds Ltd.—100 Fairchield Ave. Plainview, N. Y. 11803.

San Martina Wines, Inc.—85 Wrburton Ave. Yonkers, N. Y. 10701.

Schenley Import Co.—1290 Ave. of the Americas. New York, N. Y. 10019.

Schieffelin & Co.—30 Cooper Square. New York, N. Y. 10003.

Frank Schonmaker Selections Ltd.—14 E. 69th St. New York, N. Y. 10021.

Seggerman Slocum, Inc.—35-02 Northern Blvd. L. I. C., N. Y. 11101.

Service Liquor Distributors.—1890 Maxon Rd. Schnectady, N. Y. 12301.

Silver Hill Products, Inc.—310 Northern Blvd. Great Neck, N. Y. 11021.

Somerset Importers Ltd.—100 Park Ave. New York, N. Y. 10017.

Standard Food Products Corp.—45-11 33rd St. L. I. C., N. Y. 11101.

Standard Wine & Liquor, Co., Inc.—26-15 Brklyn. Expressway. Woodside, N. Y. 11377.

W. A. Taylor & Co.—1212 Ave. of the Americas. New York, N. Y. 10036.

«21» Brands, Inc.—23 W. 52nd St. New York, N. Y. 10019.

Josept Victori & Co., Inc.—65-67 Noth Moore St. New York, N. Y. 10013.

M. S. Walker, Inc.—2-4 Evergreen Pl. Deer Park, N. Y. 10010.

Julius Wile & Sons, Inc.—320 Park Ave. New York, N. Y. 10020.

Wine Merchants Ltd.—335 Pulaski, St. Syracuse, N. Y. 13201.

Winegate Imports, Inc.—1940 Flushing Ave. Ridgewood, N. Y. 11237.

Admiral Wine & Liquor Co.—115 Coit St. Irvington, N. J. 07111.

American B. D. Co.—62 Fifth Ave. Hawthorne, N. J. 07506.

Cameron Craig Ltd.—60 Park Place. Newark, N. J. 07102.

Gilhaus Beverage Corp.—559 Lehigh Ave. Union, N. J. 07083.

J. & J. Distributors Co.—16 Bleecker St. Milburn, N. J. 07041.

Merchants Wine & Liquor.—4415 Marlton Pike. Pennsauken, N. J. 08109.

Perrone Wines & Spirits.—560 Bercik St. Elizabeth, N. J. 07201.

Reirman Industries.—300 Frelinghausen Ave. Newark, N. J. 07114.

Renfield Importers.—611 Rahway Ave. Union, N. J.

Vincoe Winery.—675 River St. Paterson, N. J. 07524.

Alliance International.—1246 Folsom St. San Fco., Calif. 94103.

Ansor Corp.—120 Montgomery, St. San Francisco, California.

Bercurt-Vandervoort Co.—1701 Montgomery, St. San Francisco, Calif. 94103.

Bertolli West Goast.—444 Cabot Rd. San Francisco, California 94111.

Browne-Vinters Co.—340 N. Madison Ave. Los Angsles, Calif. 90004.

August L. Casazza.—12 Minna St. San Fco., Calif. 94105.

M. Cooper & Sons.—585 Venice Blvd. Venice, Calif. 90291.

F & M Importing Co., Inc.—3947 Landmack St. Culver City, Calif. 90230.

Kobrand Corp.—3600 Wilshire Blvd. Los Angeles, Calif. 90005.

Los Angeles IMporting Co.—1160 Monterey Pass Rd. Monterey Park, Calif. 91754.

Duke Molner Wholesale Liquor.—1025 Highland Ave. Los Angeles, Calif. 90038.

Monsieur Henri Wines.—California. 3005-07 Bandini Blvd. Vernon, Calif.

National Wine & Liqueur.—Importing Co. 655 Fourth St. San Fco., Calif. 94107.

Renfield Importers, Ltd.—1709 W. 8th St. Los Angeles, Calif.

Seggerman Bonsal & Co.—680 Beach St. San Francisco, Calif. 94109.

Munson Shaw Co.—292 La Cienega Blvd. Beverly Hills, Calif. 90211.

W. A. Taylor & Co.—1645 Rollins Rd. Burlingame, Calif. 94010.

World Beverages, Inc.—149 California St. San Francisco, Calif. 94111.

Johnny Barton, Inc.—P. O. Box 1294. Stamford, Conn.

Fisher Wines, Inc.—P. O. Box 112. West Haven, Conn. 06516.

Allan S. Goodman.—180 Goodwin St. East Hartford, Conn. 06101.

Heublein, Inc.—330 New Park Ave. Hartford, Conn. 06101.

Max S. Lewis Co., Inc.—P. O. Box 1204. Hartford, Conn.

Robert F. Philipp.—P. O. Box 1192. Stamford, Conn. 06904.

AMERICAN IMPORTERS OF SHERRY WINES

* Biones and Company.—57-60 Broadway. Bronx, New York 10463.

* Somerset Importers, Ltd.—100 Park Avenue. New York, N. Y. 10017.

* Julius Wile Sons & Co., Inc.—320 Park Avenue. New York, N. Y. 10022.

* McKesson & Robbins, Inc.—155 East 44th Street. New York, N. Y. 10017.

* Munson G. Shaw Co.—99 Park Avenue. New York, N. Y. 10016.

* Schenley Industries, Inc.—1290 Ave. of the Americas. New York, N. Y. 10019.

* Monsieur Henri Wimes Ltd.—131 Morgan Avenue. Brooklyn, N. Y. 11201.

Barton Distilling Co.—75 East 55th Street. New York, N. Y.

Empire Liquor Corp.—850 East 140 St. Bronx, N. Y. 10454.

North America Wines.—57-02 48th St. Maspeth, L. I., N. Y. 11378.

Eastern Wine Corp.—Bronx Terminal Market. Bronx, N. Y. 10451.

San Martina Wines, Inc.—85 Warburton Ave. Yonkers, N. Y. 10701.

Blue Crest Wine & Spirit Corp.—40-06 35th Ave. Long Island City, N. Y.

21 Brands Inc.—23 West 52nd St. New York, N. Y. 10019.

* Joseph Victori & Co., Inc.—65-67 North Moore St. New York, N. Y. 10013.

W. A. Taylor & Co.—1212 Ave. of the Americas. New York, N. Y. 10036.

Excelsior Wine & Spirits.—136 East 57th St. New York, N. Y. 10022.

Star Industries, Inc.—31-10 48th Avenue. Long Island City, B. Y.

Standard Food Products Corp.—4511 33rd St. Long Island City, N. Y. 11101.

Kobrand Corp.—134 East 40th St. New York, N. Y. 10016.

Standard Wines Liquor Co., Inc.—47-50 30tj St. Long Island City, N. Y.

Austin, Nichols & Co., Inc.—58th St. & 55th Drive. Maspeth, N. Y.

* Members of this Chamber.

Marine Tobacco.—48-43 32nd Pl. Long Island City, N. Y.

Winegate Importers, Inc.—250 West 57th St. New York, N. Y. 10019.

Foreing Vintages, Inc.—45 Rochefeller Plaza. New York, N. Y. 10020.

Distilled Brands, Inc.—26-15 4th St. Long Island City, N. Y. 11107.

Affiliated Destillers Brands Corp.—1290 Ave. of the Americas. New York, N. Y. 10019.

Seggerman & Slocum, Inc.—35-02 Northern Blvd. Long Island City, N. Y.

Browne-Vinters Co.—375 Park Ave. New York, N. Y. 10022.

Reitman Industries.—300 Frelinghuysen Ave. Newark, N. J. 07114.

Camerson Craig Ltd.—60 Park Place. Newark, N. J. 07102.

Stewart-Hill Co., Inc.—45 E. Bigelow St. Newark, N. J.

Hoffman Importers.—Distributing Co. 772 Communipaw Ave. Jersey City, N. J.

International Wine Co.—841 Clinton Ave. Kemilworth, N. J.

American B. D. Co.—62 Fifth Avenue. Hawthorne, N. J. 07506.

Perrone Wine & Spirits.—550 Bercik St. Elizabeth, N. J. 07201.

Leonard Kreusch, Inc.—7814-20 Tonnelle Avenue. North Bergen, N. J. 07047.

Garden State Liquor Warehouse.—1080 Garcen State Road. Union, N. J.

Vincove Winery.—675 River St. Paterson, N. J. 07524.

Bollers Beverages, Inc.—441 E. Jersey St. Elizabeth, N. J. 07206.

S. S. Pierce & Co.—133 Brookline Avenue. Boston, Mass.

Pastene Wine & Spirits Co.—15 Poplar St. Somerville, Mass. 02143.

Charles Gilman & Sons, Inc.—2419 Mass. Ave. Cambridge, Mass.

Johnny Barton, Inc.—P. O. Box 1294. Stamford, Conn.

Max S. Lewis Co., Inc.—P. O. Box 1204. Hartford, Conn.

Fisher Wines, Ltd.—P. O. Box 112. West Haven, Conn. 06516.

Pioneer Liquoer Co.—St. Louis, Mo. 63110.

Central States Wine Co.—6611 Clayton Road. St. Louis, Mo. 63155.

Consolidated Destilled Prods, Inc.—3247 S. Kedzie Avenue. Chicago, Ill. 60623.

Old Gold Distributors.—2241 So. Pulaski Road. Chicago, Ill. 60623.

Harry M. Siegel.—2446 18th St. N. W. Wáshington, D. C.

John Gross & Co.—11 South Gay St. Baltimore, Ma. 21202.

Tampa Ohlse Liquor Co.—Box 15397. Tampa, Fla. 33614.

Young Market Co.—500 South Central Ave. Los Angeles, Cal. 90054.

SPECIAL REGISTER OF SPANISH WINE AND LIQUEUR EXPORTERS

ALAVA

Cooperativa Vinícola Rioja Alavesa.—Postas, 50. Vitoria.
Ardau, S. A.—San Bartolomé, 26. Areta (Llodio).
Vinos de los Herederos del Marqués de Riscal, S. A.—Carretera, 1. Elciego.
Bodegas Palacio, S. A.—Cra. Elciego. Laguardia.
Faustino Martínez Pérez-Albéniz.—Av. Navarra, 41. Oyón.

ALBACETE

Cooperativa Agrícola Almanseña y Caja Rural.—José Antonio,. 157. Almansa.
Concepción Soriano Gandía.—General Orgaz, 1. Almansa.
Sucesores de Alfonso Abellán, S. L.—General Dávila, número 40. Almansa.
Audelino Carrión Poquet.—San Roque, 35. Alpera.

ALICANTE

José de Barrio, Sucesor.—Maisonnave, 32 y 57. Alicante.
Bodegas Levantinas Españolas, S. A.—Pardo Jimeno, número 45. Alicante.
Bodegas Schenk, S. A.—Av. de Alcoy, 107. Alicante.
Grupo Sectorial de Exportadores de Vinos de Alicante, Jumilla y Almansa.—Pintor Lorenzo Casanova, 4. Alicante.
Loidi y Zulaica, S. L.—A. Aguilera, 10 y 12. Alicante.
Federico Madrid Astor.—Carratalá, 46. Alicante.
Ricardo Madrid Arias.—Av. Loring, 14. Alicante.
Bodega Cooperativa de Monóvar.—Cra. Ronda. Monóvar.
Exportadora de Vinos, S. A.—Estación F. C. Monóvar.

Angel Ortigosa.—Arrabal Cuartel, s/n. Monóvar.
Salvador Poveda Luz.—Pintor Benjamín Palencia, 19. Monóvar.
Primitivo Quiles Quiles.—Luis Martí, 18. Monóvar.
Juan García Hurtado e Hijos.—Sancho Medina, 15. Villena.
Bernardo Hernández Hernández.—M. Pelayo, 87. Villena.
Martín Hernández Menor.—Brigada Reyes, 17. Villena.
Hijo de Luis García Poveda, S. A.—Muelle, 4. Villena.
Antonio Tomás Conca.—Gran Capitán, 10. Villena.

BADAJOZ

Zacarías de la Hera e Hijos, S. A.—Cra. Sevilla, 2-8. Almendralejo.

BALEARES

Comercial Industrias Agrícolas de Mallorca, S. A.—Villanueva, 20. Palma de Mallorca.
Jorge Perelló Serra.—Cra. Sóller, km. 2,5. Palma de Mallorca.
J. L. Ferrer.—Conquistador, 75. Benisalem.
Jaime Ripoll Isern.—Calvo Sotelo, 19. Benisalem.

BARCELONA

Francisco Alegre Serra.—Viladomat, 196. Barcelona-15.
Anchisi, Rafecas y Roig, S. A.—Ali-Bey, 5. Barcelona-10.
Antich, S. A.—Rda. San Pablo, 32. Barcelona-15.
Regina Bachero Arnal.—Santa Catalina, 36. Barcelona-14.

Bardinet, S. A.—Av. C. L. Varela, 189. Barcelona-13.

Alberto Bastardas Parera.—Caspe, 141 bis. Barcelona-13.

Bofill & Roig, S. en C.—Balmes, 205. Barcelona-6.

Bosch y Cía., S. A.—Merced, 10. Barcelona-2.

Pedro Campderrós Dinares.—Olzinellas, 5. Barcelona-14.

María Canals Carbó.—Román Macaya, 25. Barcelona.

Francisca Casals Pedrol.—Conde de Asalto, 109. Barcelona.

Castell del Remey, S. A.—Almogávares, 10-16. Barcelona-5.

Cavas del Ampurdán, S. A.—Angeles, 3. Barcelona-1.

Cinzano, S. A.—Paseo de Gracia, 112. Barcelona-8.

Codorníu, S. A.—Av. José Antonio, 644. Barcelona-7.

Cointreau y Cía., S. en C.—Vía Layetana, 110. Barcelona-9.

Destilerías Abril, S. A.—León XIII, 43. Barcelona.

Destilerías Montplet, S. L.—Valencia, 645. Barcelona-13.

E. J. Escat, S. A.—Av. José Antonio, 654. Barcelona-10.

Antonia Fontanet Fernández.—Wad-Ras, 232. Barcelona-5.

Pedro Giró Casanellas.—Párroco Triadó, 52. Barcelona-14.

Grupo de Exportadores de Vinos Panadés y Norte-Cataluña.—Vía Layetana, 16. Barcelona.

Elisa Juan Pastor.—Menéndez Pelayo, 40. Barcelona-12.

Martini & Rossi, S. A.—Rambla de Cataluña, 1. Barcelona-2.

Pedro Masana Rodó.—Wad-Ras, 168. Barcelona-5.

Masía Bach, S. A.—Balmes, 34. Barcelona-7.

Ramón Mestre Serra.—Vía Layetana, 30. Barcelona-3.

Jaime Mussons Llopart.—Avila, 2, 4 y 6. Barcelona.

Juan Antonio Nadal Giró.—San Vicente, 3. Barcelona-1.

José Noguera Comas.—Consejo de Ciento, 581. Barcelona-13.

Pentavin, S. A.—Nuestra Señora de Port, 260. Barcelona.

Antonio Roqué Gabarella.—Tapiolas, 47. Barcelona-4.

S. A. Puigmal.—Pasaje Vieta, 9. Barcelona-5.

Jaime Vila Montaña.—Av. José Antonio, 492. Barcelona-11.

Vinos Espumosos Naturales, S. A.—Av. José Antonio, 644. Barcelona-7.

Alella Vinícola, Bodega Cooperativa.—Av. Generalísimo, 70. Alella.

Jaime Serra Güell.—Escuelas Pías, 1. Alella.

Destilerías Mollfulleda, S. A.—Rambla P. Fita, 31. Arenys de Mar.

Manuel Lladó Parer-Faras.—Olivera, 19. Arenys de Mar.

Modesto Soler, S. A.—Bellsolell, 3. Arenys de Mar.

Hermandad Sindical de Labradores.—José Antonio, sin número. Artés.

Agustín Bofill Borrás, Sucesor.—Prim, 57. Badalona.

Bosch y Cía.—E. Maristany, 115. Badalona.

Pedro Corominas e Hijos, S. A.—Av. José Antonio, 103. Cornellá de Llobregat.

Federico Esteve Volart.—M. Santa Cruzada, 117. Cornellá de Llobregat.

La Agrícola Regional, S. A.—Can Castells. Esparraguera.

Ricardo Mont Mata.—L. Miró, 75. Esplugas de Llobregat.

Amadeo Altimiras Vall.—Av. Generalísimo, 20. Las Franquesas del Vallés.

Destilerías Montaña, S. A.—Pl. Maluquer, 20. Granollers.

José Ventura Valls.—Pl. Maluquer, 27. Granollers.

Asunción Baqués Llopart.—Mayor, s/n. Guardiola Frontubi.

José Casas Borrás.—Vilardosa, 20. Hospitalet de Llobregat.

Anacleto Cerdán González.—Onésimo Redondo, 144. Hospitalet de Llobregat.

Jaime Socias Pina.—Llobregat, 22. Hospitalet de Llobregat.

Francisco Carreras Carrió.—Cra. de Vich, 13. Manresa.

Costa y Montserrat, S. L.—Pl. Infantes, 10. Manresa.

Asunción Grau Plans.—Cra. de Vich, 1. Manresa.

Rosa Rial Playa.—Juan Jorbá, 18. Manresa.

Valentín Roqueta Prat.—Cra. de Vich, 95. Manresa.

José Selga Torras.—Cra. de Vich, 51. Manresa.

Antonio Alemany Pous.—Calvo Sotelo, 26. Martorell.

Luis Santacana Faralt «Rubricatus».—Santacana, 18. Martorell.

José Cid Raimí.—M. Jacinto Verdaguer, 2. Masnou.

José García Sensat.—M. Jacinto Verdaguer, 5 y 6. Masnou.

Delfín Mas Abad.—General Mola, 16. Molíns de Rey.

Canaleta y Cía.—Generalísimo, 19. Mongat.

José Piñol Ortells.—San Jorge, 15. Mongat.

Cavas Hill.—Buenavista, 2. Olérdola-Moja.

Cavas Parés Baltá, S. A.—Afueras. Pachs del Panadés.

Was, S. A.—Afueras, s/n. Plá del Panadés.

Canals & Nubiola, S. A.—Mayor, 6. San Esteban de Sasroviras.

Rafael Bravo Pijoán.—San Pedro de Premiá.

Paciano Carbó Sabaté.—Av. Mártires, 52. San Sadurní de Noya.

Castellblanc, S. A.—San Antonio, 3. San Sadurní de Noya.

Cavas Andrés Viu, S. A.—San Isidro, s/n. San Sadurní de Noya.

Cavas del Conde de Caralt, S. A.—Milá y Fontanals, sin número. San Sadurní de Noya.

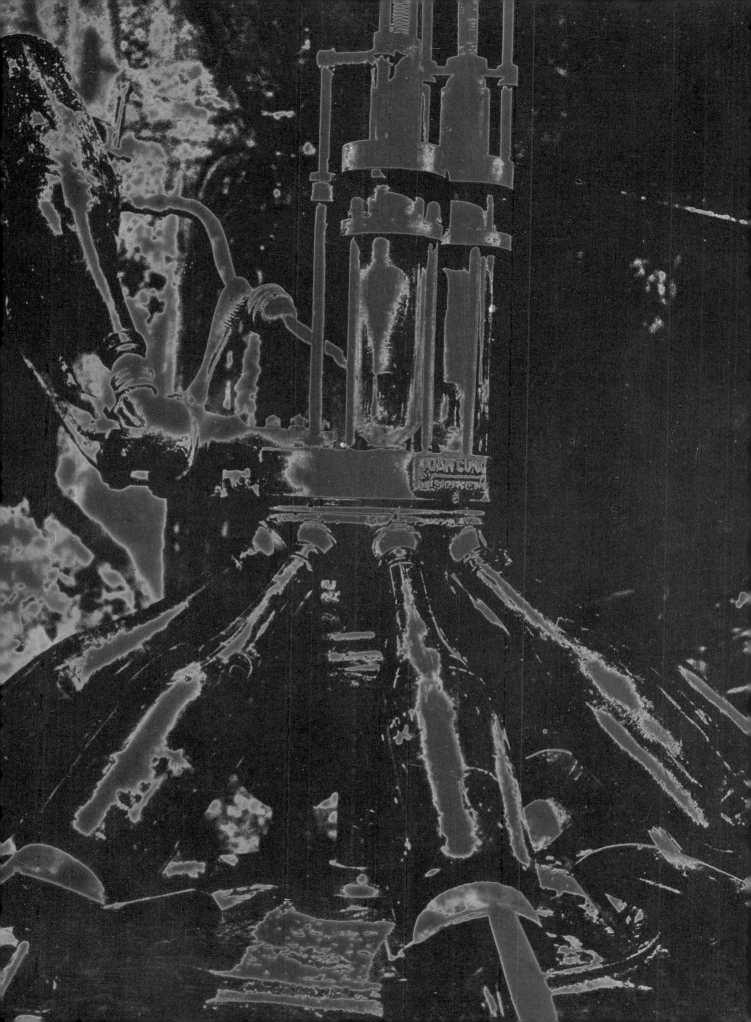

BOTTLING MACHINE AS SEEN BY AN ARTIST

Cavas de la Serra.—Cra. de Gélida, s/n. San Sadurní de Noya.

Luis Escribá de Romaní.—Marqués de Monistrol. San Sadurní de Noya.

José Esteve Vendrell.—Montserrat, 21. San Sadurní de Noya.

Freixenet, S. A.—Estación, 2. San Sadurní de Noya.

La Industrial Champanera, S. A.—Jaime Raventós, 6. San Sadurní de Noya.

José Mata Capellades.—Tamarit, 7. San Sadurní de Noya.

Juan Mata Gabarró.—Marcos Mir, 2. San Sadurní de Noya.

José Mestres Manobéns.—Pl. Generalísimo, 8. San Sadurní de Noya.

Juan Miró Galofré.—Pl. M. Raventós, 1. San Sadurní de Noya.

Manuel Segura Viudas.—Can-Ferrer del Mar. San Sadurní de Noya.

Unión Champanera, S. A. E.—Av. Mártires, 37. San Sadurní de Noya.

Raymat, S. A.—Afueras. Santa María de Cervelló.

José Robert Mestre.—San Pedro, 8. Sitges.

Francisco Solé Mulet.—Beltrán y Mursitu, 16. Viladecans.

José Alegret Sanromá.—So, 22. Villafranca del Panadés.

Aquila Rossa, S. A.—Rda. M. Ráfols, 2-12. Villafranca del Panadés.

J. B. Berger, S. A.—P. Alegret, 92. Villafranca del Panadés.

Bodegas Bosch Güell, S. A.—Comercio, 40. Villafranca del Panadés.

Cavas Raventós Catasús, S. A.—San Pedro, 8. Villafranca del Panadés.

Cointreau y Cía., S. en C.—Comercio, 1. Villafranca del Panadés.

Cooperativa Vinícola del Panadés.—Rbla. Nuestra Señora, 1. Villafranca del Panadés.

Destilerías Virben, S. A.—B. Lostau, 4-10. Villafranca del Panadés.

Juan Font Guasch.—Palma, 29. Villafranca del Panadés.

José Freixedas Bové.—Calvo Sotelo, 89. Villafranca del Panadés.

José Freixedas y Cía., Ltda.—Cid, 21. Villafranca del Panadés.

Pedro Galimany Mas.—Valls, 19. Villafranca del Panadés.

Antonio Gallemi Casanellas.—Duque de la Victoria, 5. Villafranca del Panadés.

Ramón Gusí Bernadó.—Oviedo, 4. Villafranca del Panadés.

Fermín Hill Arrufat.—General Valles, 3 y 5. Villafranca del Panadés.

Luis Marcé y Cía., S. L.—Pasteur, 9. Villafranca del Panadés.

Antonia Marrugat Miret.—Cid, 2. Villafranca del Panadés.

Antonio Mascaró Carbonell.—21 de Enero, 9. Villafranca del Panadés.

Juan Montaner Montané.—Comercio, 40 bis. Villafranca del Panadés.

Domingo Montserrat Caraltó.—Comercio, 30. Villafranca del Panadés.

Juan Mory y Cía., S. A.—Villafranca del Panadés.

Francisco Olivella Ferrari.—Avda. Barcelona, s/n. Villafranca del Panadés.

Domingo Rubió Martí.—Sarriera, 19. Villafranca del Panadés.

José María Sogas Muntané.—Duque de la Victoria, 33. Villafranca del Panadés.

José María Tetas Vendrell.—Pasteur, 5. Villafranca del Panadés.

Miguel Torres Carbó.—Comercio, 34. Villafranca del Panadés.

Manuel Giró Carlos.—Rambla Caudillo, 106. Villanueva y Geltrú.

CADIZ

Miguel M. Gómez, S. A.—A. de Apodaca, 21. Cádiz.

Hijos de A. Blázquez, S. R. C.—Pl. San Antonio, 16. Cádiz.

Lacave y Cía., S. A.—Ahumada, 18. Cádiz.

S. A. N. I. V. O.—Beato Diego de Cádiz, 9. Cádiz.

M. Pérez de Vargas Quirós y Cía., S. R. C.—Fuentenueva, 29. Algeciras.

Francisco Garrido García.—Av. Solano, 7. Chiclana.

Vinícola Chiclanera, S. A.—Alameda de Solano, 5. Chiclana de la Frontera.

Manuel de Argüeso, S. A.—Ing. Antonio Gallego, 8. Jerez.

Francisco Aroca Aroca.—Salas, 6 y 8. Jerez.

Barón de Algar y Cía., S. A.—Pl. Carrizosa, 9. Jerez.

Bartolomé Benítez Mateos.—María Antonia de Jesús. Tirado, 4. Jerez.

Bertola, S. A.—Canto, 5-9. Jerez.

Bodegas Marqués del Mérito, S. A.—Alvar Núñez, 59. Jerez.

Bodegas Quintillo, S. A.—Enrique Rivero, 15. Jerez.

José Bustamante, S. L.—San Francisco Javier, 3. Jerez.

Miguel Cala Ramírez.—Ang. Santiago, 3. Jerez.

Manuel de la Calle Jiménez.—Lechugas, 1 y 3. Jerez.

Julio Coveñas Cotrino.—Jerez.

Croft. Jerez, S. A.—Gravina, 1. Jerez.

Chaves y González, S. A.—Pl. San Andrés, 5. Jerez.

Eduardo Delage, S. L.—Clavel, 3. Jerez.

Jaime F. Diestro, S. A.—San Juan de Dios, 13. Jerez.

Destilerías Valdespoust, S. A.—Pozo del Olivar, 21. Jerez.

Díez Hermanos, S. A.—Ferrocarril, 2. Jerez.

Pedro Domecq, S. A.—San Ildefonso, 3. Jerez.

Manuel Fernández y Cía., S. L.—Cristal, 4. Jerez.

Fernando García Delgado, Sucesor.—San Telmo, 3 y 5. Jerez.

Garvey, S. A.—Guadalete, 14. Jerez.

M. Gil Galán, S. A.—Ferrocarril, 14. Jerez.

M. Gil Luque.—Rodrigo León, 7. Jerez.

González, Byass & Cía., Ltda.—M. M.ª González, 12. Jerez.

Luis G. Gordon.—Puerta Nueva, 3. Jerez.

José María Guerrero Ortega.—Sor Eulalia, 24 y 26. Jerez.

Manuel Guerrero y Cía.—H. Perdida. Jerez.

Herederos de Marqués Real Tesoro, S. A.—Pajarete, 3. Jerez.

José María Jurado, S. A.—Avda. de Fernando Portillo, s/n. Jerez.

Onofre Lorente.—Jerez.

Emilio Lustau, S. A.—Pl. del Cubo, 4. Jerez.

Mackenzie & Cía., Ltda.—Don Juan, 4 al 10. Jerez.

Emilio Martín Hidalgo.—Clavel, 29. Jerez.

M. Misa, S. A.—General Moscardó, 2. Jerez.

Diego Narváez Pozo.—Clavel, 32. Jerez.

Rafael O'Neale.—Cid, 4. Jerez.

Rafael Ortega Palencia.—Frías, 4. Jerez.

Luis Páez Lobato.—Clavel, 6. Jerez.

Palomino y Vergara, S. A.—Colón, 1 al 25. Jerez.

Antonio Parra Guerrero.—Juan D. Lacos, 24. Jerez.

José Pemartín y Cía., S. A.—Pizarro, 17. Jerez.

Cayetano del Pino y Cía., S. L.—Cardenal Herrero, 6. Jerez.

Racimo, S. L.—Pizarro, 17. Jerez.

Manuel Antonio de la Riva, S. A.—Alvar Núñez, 44. Jerez.

Tomás Rivero y Hermanos, S. L.—Molinos de Viento, 4. Jerez.

J. Ruiz y Cía.—San Francisco de Paula, 6 y 8. Jerez.

Zoilo Ruiz Mateos, S. A.—General Queipo de Llano, 34. Jerez.

Félix Ruiz y Ruiz, S. L.—San Juan de Dios, 7. Jerez.

José Sánchez Mesa.—F. de la Cuadra, 6. Jerez.

Sánchez Romate Hermanos, S. A.—Lealas, 26. Jerez.

Sandeman Hermanos y Cía.—Pizarro, 10. Jerez.

José de Soto, S. A.—Matadero, 7. Jerez.

A. R. Valdespino, S. A.—Pozo Olivar, 16. Jerez.

Javier Vergara y Gordon.—Taxdirt, 28. Jerez.

Juan Vicente Vergara, S. A.—Avda. Alcalde Alvaro Domecq, 8. Jerez.

Williams & Humbert, Ltda.—Nuño de Cañas, 1. Jerez.

Wisdom & Warter, Ltda.—Pizarro, 7. Jerez.

Bodegas Sancho, S. A.—Cardenal Almaraz, 3 y 5. Puerto de Santa María.

Luis Caballero, S. A.—Federico Rubio, 93. Puerto de Santa María.

Cuvillo y Cía., S. R. C.—Valdés, 6. Puerto de Santa María.

Destilerías del Guadalete.—Generalísimo Franco, 8. Puerto de Santa María.

Duff Gordon y Cía., S. A.—F. Caballero, 4. Puerto de Santa María.

Hijos de Jiménez Varela, S. L.—Albareda, s/n. Puerto de Santa María.

F. Javier Jiménez.—Rosas, 4 al 8. Puerto de Santa María.

Osborne y Cía., S. A.—F. Caballero, 2. Puerto de Santa María.

Portalto, S. A.—Póstigo, s/n. Puerto de Santa María.

Carlos y Javier de Terry, S. L.—Valdés, 7 y 9. Puerto de Santa María.

Fernando A. de Terry, S. A.—Santísima Trinidad, 4. Puerto de Santa María.

Ximénez y Cía., S. L.—Ribera del Río, 17 y 19. Puerto de Santa María.

Manuel de Argüeso, S. A.—Bolsa, 18. Sanlúcar de Barrameda.

Antonio Barbadillo, S. A.—Luis de Eguilaz, 11. Sanlúcar de Barrameda

Bodegas Infantes de Orleáns-Borbón, S. A. E.—Baños, 1 Sanlúcar de Barrameda.

Criadores, Almacenistas y Distribuidores de Vinos de Jerez, S. A.—Puerto, s/n. Sanlúcar de Barrameda.

Florido Hermanos.—Carmen, 14. Sanlúcar de Barrameda.

Manuel García Monge, S. A.—Pl. Victoria, 2 y 4. Sanlúcar de Barrameda.

Francisco García de Velasco.—Sebastián Elcano, 2. Sanlúcar de Barrameda.

Herederos de Argüeso.—Mar, 8. Sanlúcar de Barrameda.

Hijos de J. Dlegado Zuleta, S. A.—Carmen, 26. Sanlúcar de Barrameda.

Hijos de A. Pérez Megía, S. A.—Fariñas, 56. Sanlúcar de Barrameda.

Hijos de R. Pérez Marín, S. R. C.—Barriada de la Playa. Sanlúcar de Barrameda.

Ramón Insúa Baena.—Virgen de los Milagros, 113. Sanlúcar de Barrameda.

Carlos Otaolaurruchi, S. A.—Huerta Pago del Calvario, s/n. Sanlúcar de Barrameda.

Pedro Romero, S. A.—Trasbolsa, 55. Sanlúcar de Barrameda.

Vinícola Hidalgo y Cía., S. A.—Banda de la Playa. Sanlúcar de Barrameda.

Viuda de Esteban Bozzano.—Comisario, 11. Sanlúcar de Barrameda.

CASTELLON

Pérez Esteve.—Gandía, 22. Castellón.

Miguel Vidal Ferrer.—Teodoro Llorente, 1. Castellón.

M. Agustí Hidalgo, S. A.—General Mola, 181. Almazora.

Licor Carmelitano de los PP. Carmelitas Descalzos.—Afueras, s/n. Benicásim.

CIUDAD REAL

Industrias Celum, S. L.—San Marcos, 14. Alcázar.

Venancio Alcaide Barba.—Calvo Sotelo, 147. Aldea del Rey.

José Honorato Garrigós Senchermes.—Gral. Aguilera, 23. Argamasilla de Alba.

Cooperativa del Campo San Isidro Labrador.—Carretera Torralba, s/n. Bolaños de Calatrava.

Cooperativa del Campo Corza de la Sierra.—Maestro Lara, s/n. Cózar.

Cooperativa del Campo Daimieleña.—P.º Carmen, sin número. Daimiel.

Oleivinícola Centro de España, S. A.—F. Estación ferrocarril, s/n. Daimiel.

Ramón Jiménez-Valladolid Fernández-Pacheco.—Murillo, 8. Manzanares.

Cooperativa Nuestra Señora del Rosario.—Membrilla.

Cooperativa Agrovitivinícola San Isidro.—2 de Mayo, número 21. Pedro Muñoz.

Francisco Gómez Hernández.—Muñoz Grandes, 25. Pozuelo de Calatrava.

Cooperativa del Campo Nuestra Señora de las Virtudes.—Cra. Moral-Calatrava. Santa Cruz de Mudela.

Cooperativa Local del Campo Santísimo Cristo de la Vega.—Pedro Arias, 73. Socuéllamos.

Cooperativa del Campo Santa Catalina.—Camino Cruces, s/n. La Solana.

Adolfo Buendía.—San Mateo, 5. Tomelloso.

Jonás Torres y Cía., S. A.—José Antonio, 91 y 93. Tomelloso.

Andrés Abarca Pascual.—Mari Sánchez, 1. Valdepeñas.

Bodegas Bilbaínas, S. A.—Generalísimo, 89. Valdepeñas.

Bodegas Espinosa, S. A.—Cra. de Madrid-Cádiz, 198, 3. Valdepeñas.

Bodegas Iberia. G. Sánchez Rustarazo.—Av. Generalísimo, 82. Valdepeñas.

Cooperativa La Invencible.—R. Caro Patón, 90. Valdepeñas.

Cruzares, S. A.—Salida de los Llanos, 7. Valdepeñas.

Carmelo Madrid, S. A.—Cristo, 35. Valdepeñas.

Luis Megía, S. A.—Cruces, 29. Valdepeñas.

Angel Pintado Bárcenas.—Francisco Morales, 51. Valdepeñas.

Redruello y Faro, S. R. C.—Sebastián Bermejo, 42. Valdepeñas.

Alfredo Sánchez Gómez.—General Mola, 6. Valdepeñas.

Francisco Sánchez Delgado.—Esperanza, 10. Valdepeñas.

Gerardo Sánchez Gómez.—Madrilas, 6. Valdepeñas.

Abel Tarancón Rodero.—Torrecilla, 85. Valdepeñas.

Milagros Sánchez Rustarazu.—Valdepeñas.

Videva, S. A.—Agrupación de Vinicultores. Travesía del Horno, 16. Valdepeñas.

CORDOBA

Antonio Alarcón Costant.—M. de Santamarina, 14. Córdoba.

Carbonell y Cía., de Córdoba, S. A.—A. de Saavedra, 15. Córdoba.

Rafael Cruz Conde, S. A.—Bodega, 2. Córdoba.

Destilerías Repullo, S. A.—Colombia, 2. Córdoba.

Moreno, S. A.—Fuente de la Salud. Córdoba.

Pérez Barquero, S. A.—12 de Octubre, 8. Córdoba.

Juan del Pozo Baena.—Reloj, 1. Córdoba.

Cristóbal Moreno Navas.—Queipo de Llano, 12. Doña Mencía.

Aragón y Cía., S. A.—Ancha, 31 y 33. Lucena.

Torres Burgos, S. A.—Ronda de Lucena, s/n. Lucena.

Alvear, S. A.—Av. María Auxiliadora, 1. Montilla.

Bodegas Navarro, S. A.—Av. Antonio y Miguel Navarro, 1. Montilla.

Compañía Vinícola del Sur, S. A.—Burgueños, 5. Montilla.

J. Cobos, S. A.—Horno, 47. Montilla.

Antonio Espejo Rubio.—Marqués de la Vega y Armijo, 26. Montilla.

Tomás García, S. A.—Llano de Palacio, 7. Montilla.

José Jaime Ruiz, S. A.—Av. de las Mercedes. Montilla.

Graeia Hermanos, S. A.—J. M.ª Alvear, 54. Montilla.

Montialbero, S. A.—Dámaso Delgado, 29. Montilla.

Montisol, S. A.—Llano de Palacio, 4. Montilla.

Montulia, S. A.—Beato Juan de Avila, s/n. Montilla.

Navarro y del Pino, S. A.—Arcipreste Fernández Casado, s/n. Montilla.

Luis Ortiz-Ruiz y Ortiz.—Llano de Palacio, 4. Montilla.

Carmen Pérez-Barquero Manjón.—Márquez, 1. Montilla.

Miguel Velasco Chacón, S. A.—Burgueño, 1. Montilla.

Vinsol, S. A.—Apartado 66. Montilla.

Moriles, S. A.—Conde de Colomera, 15. Los Moriles.

Antonio Altamirano Martín-Montijano.—Ramón y Cajal, 31. Rute.

Hijo de Juan Antonio Molero.—Alfonso de Castro, 53. Rute.

Diego Molina Reyes.—Colón, 2. Rute.

Francisco Sánchez Ayora.—Duquesa, 38. Rute.

Tejero, Molina y Rabasco, S. R. C.—Cra. Montoro, 54. Rute.

LA CORUÑA

Amalia Suárez Gómez. Destilería La Murciana.—Av. Generalísimo, 241. El Ferrol.

CUENCA

Román Cantanero Serrano.—Hermanos Silva, sin número. Fuente de Pedro Naharro.

GERONA

Juan Esclasáns Milá.—Alfar, 30. Figueras.
Ramón Bonet, S. A.—Rambla Vidal, 14. San Feliu de Guixols.
José Coll Costa.—Cruz, 8. Llansá.
Cooperativa Agrícola Mollet de Perelada.—C.ª Espollá, s/n. Mollet de Perelada.
Miguel Mateu Pla Cavas del Ampurdán.—San Juan, sin número. Perelada.
Ramón Mestre Serra.—Cra. de Rosas. Vilajuiga.

GRANADA

Castañeda, S. A.—Elvira, 21. Granada.
Francisco Montero Martín.—C.º de la Vía, s/n. Motril.

GUIPUZCOA

Loidi y Zulaica, S. L.—Idiáquez, 5. San Sebastián.
S. A. V. I. N., S. A.—P.º Urumea, s/n. San Sebastián.
Marie Brizard & Roger.—Buenavista, 34. Pasajes.
Yllarramendi y Cía.—B.º San Esteban. Usúrbil.

HUELVA

Francisco Andrade Zarza.—Delgado Hernández, 30. Bollullos del Condado.
José Calvo Cadaval.—Pedro Larios, 12. Bollullos del Condado.
José María Clemente Neble.—P.º de José Antonio, 16. Bollullos del Condado.
Rafael Díaz Caparrós.—Ramón de Carranza, s/n. Bollullos del Condado.
Diego Espina Benítez.—Santa Ana, 1. Bollullos del Condado.
José Iglesias Carrellán.—Padre Domínguez García, 10. Bollullos del Condado.

José y Miguel Martín.—Almaraz, 40. Bollullos del Condado.
Juan Oliveros Perea.—Bollullos del Condado.
Francisco Ramos Mantis.—General Mola, 68. Bollullos del Condado.
Antonio Villarán Ramos.—Bollullos del Condado.
Enrique Flores Macías y Cía.—Moguer.
Bodegas Pichardo, S. A.—Carlos M. Morales, 5. La Palma del Condado.
Hijos de Julián Espinosa, S. R. C.—General Franco, 8. La Palma del Condado.
Rafael Salas López.—Huelva, 20. La Palma del Condado.
Manuel Galán Sánchez.—Calvo Sotelo, 60. Villalba del Alcor.

LEON

Hipólito de la Fuente Alvarez.—Av. de Roma, 7. León.
Cándido González y Cía., S. A.—Cra. Trobajo, s/n. León.
Planta de Elaboración y Embotellado de Vinos, S. A.—Vega, s/n. Armunia de la Vega.
Bodega Comarcal Cooperativa Vinos del Bierzo.—Cacabelos.
Sucesores de M. Villarejo y Toledo, S. L.—Salinas, 8. Villafranca del Bierzo.
Pío Villanueva Valcárcel.—Av. Obelar. Villafranca del Bierzo.

LERIDA

María Guarda Novell.—Plaza Noguerola, 7. Lérida.
Miguel Palau Miró.—Av. San Rufino, 24. Lérida.
Emilio Justo Torres.—Pl. Berenguer IV, 3. Lérida.
Antonio Casanovas Nicolau.—Av. Generalísimo, 30. Seo de Urgel.
Samuel Pereña Reixarch.—Generalísimo, 30. Seo de Urgel.
Juan Alavedra Alfonso.—Pl. del Carmen, s/n. Tárrega.
Mora, Vila y Cía., S. en C.—S. Pelegrín, 41. Tárrega.

LOGROÑO

José María Aznar Zueco.—General Franco, 42. Logroño.
Braulio Benes Cañas.—Primo de Rivera, 6. Logroño.
Bodegas Franco Españolas, S. A.—Cabo Noval, 1. Logroño.
Bodegas Marqués de Murrieta.—Norte, 32. Logroño.
Exportadora Vinícola de la Ribera, S. A.—Cabo Noval, 2. Logroño.

FROM THE WINE-CELLAR TO THE TAVERN
(Photo Guillén Franco.)

Unión Territorial de Cooperativas del Campo.— Pío XII, s/n. Logroño.

Francisco Viguera Cabredo.—Rúa Vieja, 29. Logroño.

Bodega Cooperativa San Isidro.—Aldeanueva de Ebro.

Bodegas de la Torre y Lapuerta, S. A.—Trinidad, 1. Alfaro.

Cooperativa del Campo San Antonio.—Cra. Zaragoza, sin número. Alfaro.

Bodega Cooperativa Nuestra Señora de Vico.—General Franco, 15. Arnedo.

Faustino Rivero Ulecia.—Royo, 33. Arnedo.

Bodega Cooperativa San Miguel.—Cra. de Zaragoza, kilómetro 29. Ausejo.

Bodega Cooperativa San Isidro El Labrador.—Autol.

Bodega Cooperativa Santa Daría.—Cra. de Logroño, sin número. Cenicero.

Bodegas Lagunilla, S. A.—Av. Estación, 9. Cenicero.

Bodegas Riojanas, S. A.—Estación, 1. Cenicero.

AGE, Bodegas Unidas, S. A.—Fuenmayor.

Bodegas Montecillo, S. A.—C. del Patio, 34. Fuenmayor.

Francisco Canals Pascual.—General Mola, 1. Fuenmayor.

Bernal, S. Ildefonso y Cía., Ltda.—19 de Julio, 24. Haro.

Bodega Cooperativa Interlocal Virgen de la Vega.— Carretera Casalarreina, s/n. Haro.

Bodegas Bilbaínas, S. A.—B.º Estación. Haro.

Bodegas Gómez Cruzado, S. A.—B.º Estación. Haro.

Bodegas Rioja Santiago, S. A.—B.º Estación. Haro.

Comiañía Vinícola Norte de España, S. A.—B.º Estación. Haro.

La Rioja Alta, S. A.—B.º Estación, s/n. Haro.

R. López Heredia (Viña Tondonia, S. A.).—B.º Estación. Haro.

Martínez Lacuesta Hermanos, Ltda.—General Mola. número 93. Haro.

Federico Paternina, S. A.—Cra. Casalarreina, s/n, Haro.

Milagros Pozo Martínez.—Cuevas, 4. Haro.

Hijo de Carlos Serres.—Cuevas, 14. Haro.

Bodega Interlocal Cooperativa Santa María La Real.— Nájera.

Bodegas Berberana, S. A.—Alta. Ollauri.

Bodega Cooperativa San Isidro El Labrador.—Carretera, s/n. Pradejón.

Bodega Cooperativa San Cosme y San Damián del Valle de Opón.—El Redal.

Bodega Cooperativa Sonsierra.—Cra. Briones-Peña Cerrada. San Vicente de la Sonsierra.

Bodega Cooperativa Nuestra Señora de Valvanera.— Tirgo.

Bodega Cooperativa Nuestra Señora de la Anunciación.—El Parral, s/n. El Villar de Arnedo.

MADRID

AGE, Bodegas Unidas, S. A.—Madrid.

Benedictine, S. A.—Reina, 31. Madrid.

Casli, S. A.—Soto Mayor, 13. Madrid.

Cepesa.—Víctor Pradera, 95. Madrid.

C. O. E. S.—Eduardo Dato, 18. Madrid.

Compañía Ibérica de Alimentación y Distribución, Sociedad Anónima (IBADISA).—A. Maura, 9. Madrid.

Cosecheros y Abastecedores, S. A.)C. A. S. A.).— Santa Leonor, s/n. Madrid.

Teódulo-Ramón Díaz Muñoz-Yerro.—P.º de los Melancólicos, 5. Madrid.

Rogelio González Pindado.—Hileras, 2. Madrid.

Grupo Coop. Vinícola Exportador de la Unión Nacional de Cooperativas del Campo.—Lope de Vega, 42. Madrid.

Hijos de Antonio Barceló, S. A.—Francisco Silvela, 54. Madrid.

Diego López G.ª Gallo.—P. Unaneu, 17. Madrid.

Martini & Rossi, S. A.—Cra. Barcelona, km. 12. Madrid.

Rodríguez & Berger.—Reina, 27. Madrid.

Antonio Secilla Sánchez.—Mesón de Paredes, 85. Madrid.

Guadalupe Zapardiel Serrano.—Paseo Extremadura, número 30. Madrid.

S. A. Alcoholes de Chinchón.—Ronda, 16. Chinchón.

Destilerías La Pajarita.—Cra. Barcelona, km. 14,800. Torrejón de Ardoz.

MALAGA

Luis Barceló, S. A.—San Nicolás, 3. Málaga.

Casa Romero, S. L.—Tizo, 3 y 7. Málaga.

Compañía Mata (UBASA).—Purificación, 1 al 7. Málaga.

Flores Hermanos, S. A.—Plaza de Toros Vieja, 5. Málaga.

José Garijo Ruiz.—Av. Generalísimo Franco, 12. Málaga.

Grupo de Ordenación Comercial Málaga.—Alameda de Colón, s/n. Málaga.

Hijos de Antonio Barceló, S. A.—Malpica, 1. Málaga.

Hijos de José Suárez Villalba, S. L.—Av. Juan Sebastián Elcano, 141. Málaga.

Carlos J. Krauel, S. A.—Molina Lario, 2. Málaga.

Larios, S. A.—Juan Díaz, 2. Málaga.

La Vinícola de Andalucía, S. A.—Calvo, 4. Málaga.

López Hermanos, S. A.—Salamanca, 1. Málaga.

Pérez Texeira, S. A.—Calvo, 15. Málaga.

Guillermo Rein.—Salitre, 34. Málaga.

Scholtz Hermanos.—D. Cristán, 11. Málaga.

MURCIA

José Barceló Alemán, S. A.—Saavedra Fajardo, 12. Algezares.

Francisco Capel Zaragoza.—C.º Estación. Espinardo.

Cayetano Gutiérrez Torres.—Parque, 19. Cartagena.

Diego Zamora Conesa, S. R. C.—Real, 136. Cartagena.

Enrique Martínez Martínez.—Sepulcro, 9. Santa Lucía-Cartagena.

Antonio Bleda García.—Cra. Yecla, 16. Jumilla.

Juan Carcelén Herrero.—Barón del Solar, 3. Jumilla.

Cooperativa Agrícola San Isidro.—Cra. Murcia, s/n. Jumilla.

Jesús García Carrión.—Pl. Caudillo, 17. Jumilla.

Francisco Gil González.—Fueros, 16. Jumilla.

Jaime Gil Tomás.—Cra. Yecla, 23. Jumilla.

Fermín Gilar Guardiola.—Cra. de Murcia, 25. Jumilla.

Francisco González Sánchez.—Cra. Murcia, 28. Jumilla.

Francisco Martínez Herrero.—B.º Iglesias, 57. Jumilla.

Pedro Luis Martínez Guardiola.—B.º Iglesias, 53. Jumilla.

Manuel Sánchez Cano.—José Antonio, 175. Molina del Segura.

Joaquín Belmonte Pellicer.—Cra. Alcantarilla. Nonduermas.

Destilerías Bernal, S. A.—Av. Generalísimo, 90. El Palmar.

NAVARRA

Cooperativa Vinícola Navarra.—Ciudadela, 5. Pamplona.

H. de Carlos Eugui, S. A.—Av. Guipúzcoa, 15. Pamplona.

Grupo Norte de Exportadores de Vinos.—Av. Zaragoza, 12. Pamplona.

Vinícola Navarra, S. A.—Roncesvalles, 2. Pamplona.

Taberna Hermanos, S. R. C.—San Antón, 3. Pamplona.

Carmen Uguet de Resaide.—Postillo, 2. Ablitas.

Bodega Cooperativa San Gregorio.—San Gregorio, 1. Azagra.

Bodega Cooperativa Nuestra Señora del Romero.—Carretera de Tarazona, s/n. Cascante.

Bodega Cooperativa Cirbonera.—Ligués, 27. Cintruénigo.

Julián Chivite Marco.—Barón de la Torre, 2. Cintruénigo.

Bodega Cooperativa San José.—Cra. Madrid, s/n. Corella.

Bodega Herederos de Camilo Castilla, S. A.—Santa Bárbara, 40. Corella.

Bodega Cooperativa Virgen Blanca.—La Cadena, s/n. Lerín.

Bodega Cooperativa San Roque.—Cra. de Tudela, s/n. Murchante.

Cecilio Carricas Pérez.—Cra. Zaragoza. Olite.

H. Beaumont y Cía., S. R. C.—Señorío de Sarriá. Puente La Reina.

Bodegas Muerza, S. A.—Pl. Vera Magallón, 16. San Adrián.

Viuda de Primitivo Gurpegui.—Av. Celso Muerza, 6. San Adrián.

Cooperativa Vinícola de Tafalla.—Cra. de Estella. Tafalla.

Zumos de Navarra, S. A.—Cra. de Estella. Tafalla.

Licorera del Bidasoa, S. A.—Paraje de Ubela. Vera de Bidasoa.

H. de Pablo Esparza.—Av. S. Huici, 1 y 3. Villava.

ORENSE

Cuevas y Cía., S. L.—Av. Pontevedra, 17. Orense.

Bodega Cooperativa Monterrey.—Albarellos de Monterrey.

Bodegas Gallegas, S. L.—Estación, 9. Los Peares.

Cooperativa Vitivinícola del Ribeiro.—Valdepereira-Ribadavia.

PONTEVEDRA

Antonio Bandeira.—Aragón, 27 (Calvario). Vigo.

Lago e Hijos, Ltda.—Felipe Sánchez, 12. Vigo.

López y Sasal, S. L.—Queipo de Llano, 14. Vigo.

Vicente Pérez Villar.—Av. General Mola, s/n. Villagarcía de Arosa.

SANTANDER

Compañía Hispanoamericana de Intercambios, S. A.—San Fernando, 16. Santander.

Van Den Bergh y Cía., S. R.—Hernán Cortés, 17. Santander.

SEGOVIA

Nicomedes García Gómez.—Obispo Quesada, 5. Segovia.

Destilerías y Crianza del Whisky, S. A.—Palazuelos de Eresma.

SEVILLA

Kurt Mansfeld Coen.—Av. Manuel Siurot, 2. Sevilla.

Peinado y Cía.—Velázquez, 4. Sevilla.

Hijo de M. Nocea.—Pl. Doctor Nocea, 10. Cazalla de la Sierra.

Sucesor de Angel Lorenzo.—San Benito, 8. Cazalla de la Sierra.

Sucesor de Gabriel López-Cepero.—Daoíz, 2. Cazalla de la Sierra.

José García Núñez.—Santa Inés. Lebrija.

Eurovinícola, S. A.—Cra. de Sevilla a Cádiz, s/n. Los Palacios.

José Gallego Góngora.—J. A. Primo de Rivera, 59. Villanueva del Ariscal.

TARRAGONA

Bodegas Tapias, S. A.—Mar, 17 y 18. Tarragona.

Cograma, S. A.—Cra. Universidad Laboral, s/n. Tarragona.

Dalmau Hermanos y Cía., Sucesores.—Real, 9. Tarragona.

De Müller, S. A.—Real, 27. Tarragona.

Destilerías Tarraconenses, S. L.—San Miguel, 18. Tarragona.

Dubonnet Española, S. A.—Castaños, 6. Tarragona.

Ferd. Steiner, S. A.—San Miguel, 37. Tarragona.

José López Bertrán y Cía.—Nueva S. Fructuoso, 23. Tarragona.

Juan Mory & Cía., S. A.—León, 44 y 46. Tarragona.

José Oliver, S. A.—Castaños, 6. Tarragona.

José María Pamies Torres.—Smith, 59 bis. Tarragona.

Pernod, S. A.—Apodaca, 28. Tarragona.

René Barbier y Cía., S. V. Ltda.—A. Clavé, 1. Tarragona.

La Tarraco Vinícola, S. L.—Real, 23. Tarragona.

José Tuset Durán.—Smith, 24. Tarragona.

Unión Agraria Cooperativa.—Tívoli, 21. Tarragona.

La Union Agrícola, S. A.—Smith, 55. Tarragona.

La Vinícola Ibérica, S. A.—Torres Jordí, 1 al 15. Tarragona.

Vinos Padró, S. L.—Av. Generalísimo, 56. Brafim.

Vinos Nolla, S. L.—Virgen del Camino, 28. Cambrils.

Juan Solé Bargallo.—Mariscart, 82. La Canonja.

Antonio Doménech Piñol.—Ancha, 1. Ginestar.

Amigó Hermanos y Cía.—Gaudí, 28. Reus.

Bodegas Salvat, S. A.—Av. Mártires. Reus.

Francisco Cavallé.—Tívoli, 18. Reus.

Cochs' S. A.—San Celestino, 15. Reus.

Amadeo Ferraté.—F. Soler, 6. Reus.

José María Martí Roig.—C.ª Morato, 3 y 7. Reus.

Ramón Mestre Serra.—Pl. Morlius, 1. Reus.

S. A. F. Miró Sans.—San Lorenzo, 15. Reus.

Emilio Miró Salvat.—Av. del Generalísimo, 45. Reus.

Juana Pi Fortuny.—Riudoms, 1. Reus.

Francisco Simó y Cía.—Riudoms, 16. Reus.

Vinícola Reusense, S. A.—Espronceda, s/n. Reus.

Vinos Ricart, S. A.—Av. Calvo Sotelo, 41. Reus.

Vinos y Vermuts Rofes, S. A.—San Miguel, 2. Reus.

Viuda de Luis Quer, S. L.—Av. Calvo Sotelo, 12. Reus.

Vinos Conca del Gayá.—C.ª Estación, 3 y 5. Salomó.

Juan Miralles Carulla.—A. Farigola, 34. Valls.

Pablo Rovira Nogués.—Cra. de Valls, 42. Vendrell.

TOLEDO

Unión Territorial de Cooperativas del Campo.—Carlos V, 12. Toledo.

Tomás Muñoz Sánchez.—Turco, 5. Carmena.

Antonio Poveda Merino.—Monjas, 4. Casarrubios del Monte.

Manuel Fernández-Avilés Zamorano.—Miguel de Cervantes, 15. Noblejas.

Manuel Sánchez Salinas.—Plaza del Conde, 4. Noblejas.

María González Lambea.—José Antonio, 39. Quintanar de la Orden.

Hijos de Francisco Serrano.—C. Quintanar, s/n. Quintanar de la Orden.

VALENCIA

Bodegas Levantinas Españolas, S. A.—Serrería, 13. Valencia.

Bodegas Schenk, S. A.—Camino Hondo del Grao, 78. Valencia'

Cherubino Valsangiacomo, S. A.—Vicente Brull, 21. Valencia.

C. Augusto Egli, S. L.—Maderas, 25. Valencia.

Ferd. Steiner, S. A.—Francisco Cubells, 42. Valencia.

Vicente Gandía Pla, S. R.—Maderas, 15 al 23. Valencia.

A. y J. Garrigós, S. L.—Consuelo, 13. Valencia.

Grupo de Ordenación Comercial de Exportadores de Vinos de Valencia.—Arquitecto Alfaro, 27. Valencia.

José Hernández Iranzo.—Méndez Núñez, 27. Valencia.

Hijos de Pons Hermanos.—Av. del Puerto, 199. Valencia.

J. Antonio Mompó, S. A.—Arquitecto Alfaro, 27. Valencia.

Regadíos y Energía de Valencia, S. A.—Av. Navarro Reverter, 2. Valencia.

José Rubio Antón.—Av. Burjasot, 159. Valencia.

Sanivo.—Serrano, 46. Valencia.

Vicente Selma Mendizábal.—Juan Verdaguer, 73. Valencia.

Teschendorff & Cía.—Peaña, 11. Valencia.

Vento Galindo, S. L.—Guillén de Castro, 119. Valencia.

Zumos Internacionales, S. A.—Sorní, 9. Vaencla.

Juan Vicedo Pla.—Letor Romero, 48. Benipeixcar.

Vinos Españoles, S. R.—Autopista de Silla, km. 252. Catarroja.

Resurrección Navarro Carrión.—Colón, 26. Cheste.

Antonio Arráez Garrigós.—Arcediano Ros, 35. Fuente la Higuera.

Eduardo García Pérez.—J. Garrigós Hernández, 8. Real de Montroy.

Cooperativa del Campo de la Castilla Valenciana COVIÑRS.—Av. Gral. Varela, 4. Requena.

Cooperativa Vinícola Requenense.—Av. General Pereira, 3. Requena.

Ramón Mestre Serra.—Requena.

Antonio Pérez Calvo.—Rambla, 43. San Antonio.

Emilio Gil Navarro, S. L.—Cra. Real de Madrid, s/n. Silla.

Zumos y Conservas, S. A.—Tradición, 31. Tabernes Blanques.

VALLADOLID

Alder, S. A.—Plaza de Oriente, 45. Nava del Rey.

Bodegas Vega-Sicilia, S. A.—Valbuena del Duero.

VIZCAYA

Arrién Elorriaga y Cía., S. R. C.—Alhóndiga Municipla. Bilbao.

Barbier, S. A.—Zamácola, 51. Bilbao.

Bodegas Aranguren, S. R. C.—Alhóndiga Municipal, número 135. Bilbao.

Destilerías Zuvillaga, S. A.—Particular del Norte, 13. Bilbao.

Antonio Mendieta Bilbao.—Alhóndiga Municipal, 135. Bilbao.

Fernando Peña Arístegui.—Bilbao.

José Santiago Román.—Alhóndiga Municipal, sótano, número 69. Bilbao.

Rojas y Cía., S. R. C.—Alhóndiga Municipal. Bilbao.

ZAMORA

Bodegas Otero, S. A.—Av. del General Primo de Rivera, 22. Benavente.

ZARAGOZA

Aragonesa de Exportaciones Vinícolas, S. A.—Pedro de Luna, 35. Zaragoza.

Aragonesa Vinícola, S. A.—Enlace de carreteras, s/n. Zaragoza.

Bodegas Monteviejo, S. L.—Paseo María Agustín, 65. Zaragoza.

Francisco García Blasco.—Paseo María Agustín, 89. Zaragoza.

Balbino Lacosta Tello.—Coso, 5. Zaragoza.

Sucesores de Gerónimo Paricio, S. L.—Coso, 186. Zaragoza.

Cooperativa Vitícola San José.—Carretera, s/n. Aguarón.

Bodega Cooperativa Sindical Agraria San Valero.—Avenida del Ejército Español, 22. Cariñena.

Cariñena Vitícola.—Cra' de Valencia, s/n. Cariñena.

evilla siempre eterna

ARENAL DE SEVILLA. TORRE DE ORO
(Water colour by Rodríguez Miranda.)

A GLASS OF CLARET WINE
(Photo Ernest Foye.)

NAMES AND ADDRESSES OF THE OFFICIAL AGRICULTURAL SERVICES IN MADRID

MINISTERIO DE AGRICULTURA (Paseo Infanta Isabel, 1. Tels.: Central, 2277455; Información, 2394709).

SUBSECRETARÍA

Oficialía mayor. Sección asuntos generales.

DIRECCIÓN GENERAL DE AGRICULTURA.

Subdirección General de la Producción Agrícola.

Subdirección General de Protección de los Cultivos y Fomento de la Calidad.

SECRETARÍA GENERAL TÉCNICA.

DIRECCIÓN GENERAL DE CAPACITACIÓN AGRARIA (Bravo Murillo, 101. Tel. 2533300).

INSTITUTO NACIONAL AGRONÓMICO (Ciudad Universitaria, s/n. Tel. 2444807).

INSTITUTO NACIONAL DE INVESTIGACIONES AGRONÓMICAS (Avenida Puerta de Hierro. Teléfono 2440200).

FONDO DE ORDENACIÓN Y REGULACIÓN DE PRODUCCIONES Y PRECIOS AGRARIOS (F. O. R. P. P. A.) (Beneficencia, 8. Teléfono 2216420).

MINISTERIO DE COMERCIO (Paseo Castellana, 13. Tel. 2257980).

SUBSECRETARÍA

Subsecretaría de Comercio.
Dirección General de Comercio interior.
Dirección General de Comercio exterior.

COMISARÍA GENERAL DE ABASTECIMIENTOS Y TRANSPORTES (Almagro, 33. Tel. 4199800).

COMISIÓN DE COMPRA DE EXCEDENTES DE VINO (Almagro, 33).

DELEGACIÓN NACIONAL DE SINDICATOS (Paseo del Prado, 18-20).

SINDICATO NACIONAL DE LA VID, CERVEZAS Y BEBIDAS (Tel. 2397000).

PROVINCIAL AGRICULTURAL DELEGATIONS

ALBACETE: San Antonio, 23. Teléfono 1608.

ALICANTE: Teniente Alvarez Soto, 1. Teléfonos 211729 y 218008.

ALMERÍA: Navarra Rodrigo, 20. Teléfonos 212657 y 2136 75.

ÁVILA: Plaza Nalvillos, 3. Teléfono 211272.

BADAJOZ: M. Torrero, 17. Teléfonos 233246 y 221515.

BARCELONA: Junqueras, 2. Teléfonos 2217689 y 2324113.

BILBAO: Alameda de Mazarredo, 17. Teléfono 215204.

BURGOS: H. Alcázar, 4. Teléfono 201340.

CÁCERES: Avenida de España, 22. Teléfonos 212784 y 211925.

CÁDIZ: A. R. Carranza, 20. Teléfono 212842.

CASTELLÓN: Cardenal Vives, 13. Tel. 220006.

CIUDAD REAL: Ronda Santa María, 21. Teléfono 212539.

CÓRDOBA: Avenida del Generalísimo, 24. Teléfono 225484.

CUENCA: Cervantes, 13. Teléfono 211436.

GERONA: Jaime I, 26. Teléfono 201339.

GRANADA: Gran Vía, 19. Teléfono 222393.

GUADALAZARA: Teniente Figueroa, 12. Teléfonos 211100 y 211954.

HUELVA: Gran Vía, 5. Teléfono 1921.

HUESCA: P. Huesca, 10. Teléfono 21150.

JAÉN: Plaza Alfonso, 8. Teléfono 232180.

LA CORUÑA: P. Cancela, 26. Teléfono 237256.

LAS PALMAS: A. L. Jones, 49. Teléfonos 264700 y 254435.

LEÓN: Paseo Lealtad, 5. Teléfono 222165.

LÉRIDA: José Antonio, 15. Teléfono 211614.

LOGROÑO: General Franco, 2. Teléfono 211061.

LUGO: Plaza de España, 27. Teléfonos 211031 y 214132.

MADRID: Velázquez, 20.

MÁLAGA: Córdoba, 10. Teléfono 222530.

MURCIA: González Adalid, 4. Teléfonos 212709 y 214627.

ORENSE: Capitán Eloy, 17. Teléfono 21019.

OVIEDO: Doctor Casal, 2. Teléfono 212975.

PALENCIA: Plaza San Lázaro, 4. Teléfonos 3250 y 4335.

PALMA DE MALLORCA: Sindicato, 215. Teléfono 217309.

PAMPLONA: Carlos III, 36. Teléfono 230034.

PONTEVEDRA: J. Costa, 8. Teléfono 852190.

SALAMANCA: Gran Vía, 16. Teléfono 7607.

SAN SEBASTIÁN: Avenida de España, 28. Teléfonos 16596 y 14319.

SANTA CRUZ DE TENERIFE: José Naveiras, 36. Teléfono 243190.

SANTANDER: Pje. Puntida, 2. Teléfonos 225085 y 223953.

SEGOVIA: Plaza Franco, 9. Teléfono 3174.

SEVILLA: Plaza de España. Teléfonos 231948 y 231399.

SORIA: Cortes de Soria, 7. Teléfono 211082.

TARRAGONA: Real, 28. Teléfono 204308.

TERUEL: General Varela, 5. Teléfono 1559.

TOLEDO: N. Viejo, 8. Teléfono 213598.

VALENCIA: Plaza del Caudillo, 5. Teléfonos 214682 y 219928.

VALLADOLID: General Franco, 1. Teléfonos 222442 y 227789.

VITORIA: Olaguibel, 2. Teléfono 211615.

ZAMORA: Fray Diego de Deza, 26. Teléfono 1402.

ZARAGOZA: General Mola, 15. Teléfonos 227190 y 225245.

APPENDIX V

NAMES OF THE VITICULTURAL AND ENOLOGICAL ESTABLISHMENTS IN SPAIN

ALCÁZAR DE SAN JUAN (Ciudad Real): Canalejas, 15. Teléfono 540537.

ALMENDRALEJO (Badajoz): Carretera de Sevilla. Teléfono 532.

HARO (Logroño): Paseo Torrero. Teléfono 168.

JEREZ DE LA FRONTERA (Cádiz): Granja. Teléfono 346307.

JUMILLA (Murcia): Paseo de la Asunción, s/n. Teléfono 38.

REQUENA (Valencia): Plaza García Morato, 1. Teléfono 15.

REUS (Tarragona): Paseo Sunyer. Teléfono 303716.

VALDEPEÑAS (Ciudad Real): Buensuceso, 15. Teléfono 311133.

VILLAFRANCA DEL PANADÉS (Barcelona): Amalia, 27. Teléfono 8920050.

REGIONAL DELEGATIONS OF THE MINISTRY OF COMMERCE

ALICANTE: Subdelegación. Avenida Méndez Núñez, 4.

BARCELONA: Vía Layetana, 32.

BILBAO: Viuda de Epalza, 2.

CASTELLÓN: Subdelegación. Trinidad, 1.

CEUTA: Agustina de Aragón, 4.

LAS PALMAS: José María Durán, 4.

MÁLAGA: Atarazanas, 2.

MELILLA: Subdelegación. Cervantes, 4.

MURCIA: Gran Vía José Antonio, 11.

OVIEDO: Quintana, 36.

PALMA DE MALLORCA: San Sebastián, 9.

SAN SEBASTIÁN: Guetaria, 2, triplicado.

SANTA CRUZ DE TENERIFE: Pilar, 1.

SANTANDER: Plaza Porticada, 5.

SEVILLA: Plaza de España, Puerta Navarra.

VALENCIA: Ribera, 3.

VALLADOLID: General Franco, 6.

VIGO: García Barbón, 30.

ZARAGOZA: Coso, 42.

SPANISH CHAMBERS OF COMMERCE ABROAD

GERMANY:

Cámara Española de Comercio, Schaumainkai 83. 6 Frankfurt am Main 70.

ALGERIA:

Cámara Española de Comercio. 8, rue Amperes. Argel.

Cámara Española de Comercio. 14, avenue Cheikh Larbi Tebessi. Orán.

ARGENTINE:

Cámara Española de Comercio. Avenida Belgrado, 863, 8.º pido. Buenos Aires.

Delegación de la Cámara Española de Comercio. Sarmiento, 199. Mendoza.

AUSTRALIA:

Cámara Española de Comercio. Macquarie Chambers. 183 Macquearie Street. Sydney. N. S. W., 2.000.

BELGIUM:

Cámara Española de Comercio. Rue de la Science, 19. Bruselas-4.

BOLIVIA:

Cámara Española de Comercio. Avenida Camacho, 1.484. Casilla de Correos número 1.434. La Paz.

BRAZIL:

Cámara Española de Comercio. Rua Libero Badaró, 471, piso 18. Sao Paulo.

COLOMBIA:

Cámara Española de Comercio Hispano-Colombiana. Calle 22, número 6-27, piso 10, oficina 1.001. Apartado aéreo 12.040. Bogotá.

COSTA RICA:

Cámara Española de Comercio. Calle Alfredo Volio, entre Avenidas 8 y 5, número 340. Apartado 1.327. San José.

CUBA:

Cámara Española para el Comercio con Cuba. Calle Cárcel, 51. La Habana.

JEREZ. SHERRY
(Photo Guillén Franco.)

CHILE:

Cámara Española de Comercio. Ahumada, número 370, 8.º piso. Santiago de Chile.

DENMARK:

Cámara de Comercio Hispano-Danesa. H. C. Oerstedsvej, 7 B. Copenhague V.

ECUADOR:

Cámara Española de Comercio. Pedro Carbó, 416. Apartado 1.304. Guayaquil.

THE UNITED STATES:

Cámara Española de Comercio del Medio Oeste de Estados Unidos. 55 East Washington Street Dep. 1.818. Chicago, Illinois 60.602.
Cámara de Comercio. 500 Fifth Avenue Room 833. Nueva York. N. Y. 10.036.
Cámara Española de Comercio de la Costa del Pacífico. Mobil Oil Building 612. South Flower Street. Suite 668. Los Angeles, 90.017 (California).

PHILIPINES:

Cámara Española de Comercio. 510 Romero Salas. Apartado de Correos 2.941. Manila.

FRANCE:

Cámara Española de Comercio. 32, avenue de L'Opera, 75. París-2 E.
Cámara Española de Comercio. 9, rue Thiers. Bayona.
Cámara de Comercio Hispano-Francesa. 3, rue Aldebert. Marsella-6 E.

GUATEMALA:

Cámara Española de Comercio. Plazuela de España, 11-59. Zona 9. Edificio «Galerías España», 6.ª planta. Apartamento 64. Guatemala, C. A.

HONDURAS:

Cámara Española de Comercio e Industria. Edificio Bolívar, 2.º piso. Apartamento 186. San Pedro Sula.

BRITAIN:

Cámara Española de Comercio. 3 Hans Crescent. Londres, S. W. 1.

ITALY:

Cámara Española de Comercio. Vía Rugabella, 1. Milán.

MOROCCO:

Cámara Española de Comercio. 6, rue de l'Eglise. Teléfonos 756-02/631-65. Casablanca.
Cámara Española de Comercio. Avenida de España, 42. Tánger.
Cámara Española de Comercio. Mohamed Torres, 10, 1.º Tetuán.

MÉXICO:

Cámara Española de Comercio e Industria. Balderas, 143. Esquina Arcos de Belén. Apartado postal 1.678. México I. D. F.

Cámara Española de Comercio. Avenida de la Reforma, 703-2.º. Apartado postal 75. Puebla Pue.

Cámara Española de Comercio e Industria. Zamora, 300. Apartado postal 313. Veracruz. Ver.

NORWAY:

Cámara de Comercio Hispano-Noruega. Spansk-Norks. Handelskammed Tollbught 2. Oslo.

PANAMÁ:

Cámara Española de Comercio. Edificio de la Embajada de España. Calle 83 (frente al parque Porras). Apartado 1.857. Panamá.

PERÚ:

Cámara de Comercio Hispano-Peruana. Avenida I'acna, 338. Oficina número 33. Casilla postal 3.838. Lima.

PUERTO RICO:

Cámara Española de Comercio. Calle Recinto Sur, 301. San Juan de Puerto Rico-00901. Apartado de Correos 894. San Juan de Puerto Rico-00902.

DOMINICAN REPUBLIC:

Cámara Española de Comercio. Calle Padre Bellini, 12. Apartado 967. Santo Domingo.

EL SALVADOR:

Cámara Española de Comercio e Industria. Cuarta Avenida Sur, 322, pido 6.º, despachos 614 y 615. San Salvador.

SWITZERLAND:

Cámara Española de Comercio. Bleicherweg, número 20. 8.002. Zurich.

URUGUAY:

Cámara Española de Comercio. Calle 83, número 1.315. Montevideo.

VENEZUELA:

Cámara de Comercio y Producción Venezolano-Española. Edificio «Cámara de Industriales», piso 4.º, esquina de Puente Aanauco. Apartado de Correos 3.086. Caracas.

APPENDIX VII

SPANISH COMMERCIAL OFFICES ABROAD

GERMANY: Schloss-Strasse 4. Bonn/Rhein.

ALGERIA: 7, rue Hamani (ex Charras). Argel.

ARGENTINE: Avenida Corrientes, 330. Buenos Aires.

AUSTRALIA: Macquarie Chambers, 183. Macquarie Street Sidney N. S. W. Box 4461. G. P. O. Sidney N. S. W. 2001.

AUSTRIA: Stern wartestrasse 61-62. Viena XVIII.

BELGIUM: 29, boulevard du Régent. Bruselas.

BRAZIL: Praia de Botafogo, 142. Río de Janeiro.

CANADÁ: Bonaventure Building. Rue de la Gauchetiere. Montreal 3 P. Q.

COLOMBIA: Apartado aéreo 8644. Calle 42, número 13/65. Bogotá.

CUBA: Oficios y Acosta, 420. La Habana.

CHILE: Calle Monjitas, 386. Santiago.

DENMARK: H. C. Orstedsvej, 7 B. Copenhague-V.

UNITED STATES: 2558 Massachusetts Ave. N. W. Washington 8.
Chrysler Building, 405 Lexington Avenue, room 54-10. Nueva York, N. Y. 10.017.
55 East Washington Street. Chicago 2.
870 Market St., Flood Bldg., room 542. San Francisco 2.
1840 International Trade Mart. Nueva Orleans.

FRANCE: 27, avenue George V. París (8.1).

GREAT BRITAIN: 3 Hans Crescent. Londres 8. S. W. 1.

GREECE: Valaoritou, 1. Atenas, T. T. 134.

GUATEMALA: 7.ª Avenida, 11-59. Zona 9.ª (edificio «Galerías España»).

HOLLAND: Burg. Patijnlaan, 67. La Haya.

ITALY: Lungotevere Mellini, 7. I. 00193. Roma.

JAPAN: Mori Bldg., 4th, 8-11. I chome. Nishi Azabu. Minato-ku. Togio.

LEBANON: Rue Hamra. Immeuble Strand. 3me étage Beirut.

MOROCCO: 30, rue de la Somme. Rabat.

MAURITANIA: Boite postale 356. Nouakchott.

PERÚ: Avenida Wildon, 1802. Lima

PORTUGAL: Avenida Sidonio Pais, 28, 3.º D. Lisboa.

R. A. U.: 32, Sharia Mohammed Sabri Abou Allam (ex Gamed Sharkass). El Cairo.

REPUBLIC OF SOUTH AFRICA: O'Seculo Building, 1st. Floor, 286, Bosman St. Pretoria (P. O. Box 1633).
P. O. Box 5.5363. Johannesburgo.

RUMANIA: Strada Episcopiet, 5. Bucarest.

SYRIA: P. O. Box 2738. Damasco.

SWEDEN: Sveavagen, 29. Estocolmo.

SWITZERLAND: Effingerstrasse 4. Berna.

URUGUAY: Plaza Cagancha, 1342. Montevideo.

VENEZUELA: Avenida Principal el Bosuqe (Chacaito). Edificio Pichoncha, pido 1.J. Apartamento 11. Caracas (Venezuela). Apartado postal número 61.394.

PERMANENT DELEGATIONS FOR COMMERCIAL AFFAIRS

C. E. E.: 23 y 27, rue de la Loi. Bruselas-4 (Bélgica).

G. A. T. T.: 15, rue du Jeu de l'Arc. Ginebra (Suiza).

O. C. D. E.: 44, avenue d'Iena. París, 16 (Francia). (Dirección telegráfica de las oficinas: OFCOMES).

BULGARIA: Delegación Comercial de Bulgaria en España. Tutor, 11. Teléfonos 2475553 y 2474135. Madrid-8.

CHECOSLOVAQUIA: Delegación de las Empresas Checoslovacas de Comercio Exterior. Padre Damián, 21, 5.º. Teléfono 2501755. Madrid-16.

HUNGARY: Delegación del Comercio Exterior de Hungría en España. Avenida General Perón, número 33, 6.º. Teléfono 2540870. Madrid-20.

POLAND: Cámara Polaca de Comercio Exterior en España. Rafael Salgado, 7, 6.º derecha. Teléfono 2500457. Madrid-16.

RUMANIA: Representación Conuslar y Comer- de Rumania en España. Avenida Alfonso XIII, 157. Teléfonos 2590820 y 2501174 Madrid-7.

YUGOSLAVIA: Señor Peter Rainl. Plaza del número 4, 11.º Madrid-13 (Representante de un conjunto de firmas exportadoras yugoslavas).

RUSTIC CORNER
(Photo Guillén Franco.)

SURFACE AREA OF VINEYARD IN THE REGIONS PROTECTED BY THEIR RESPECTIVE «DENOMINACION DE ORIGEN» IN THE YEAR 1969-70

Denominación	Hectares
Jerez	11,529
Málaga	5,000
Montilla-Moriles	15,989
Manzanilla-Sanlúcar de Barrameda	300
Rioja	35,972
Tarragona	33,500
Alella	1,300
Priorato	3,500
Alicante	39,670
Valencia	45,720
Utiel-Requena	38,390
Cheste	7,230
Cariñena	22,300
Ribero	5,600
Valdeorras	4,500
Panadés	17,020
Huelva	18,400
Navarra	6,008
Jumilla	27,590
Mancha	197,193
Valdepeñas	245,335
Manchuela	62,320
Méntrida	23,400
Almansa	—
TOTAL	867,766

GRAPE PRODUCTION

Year	Direct consumption	Vinification	Raisins	Total
1960-61	2,274,494	31,405,267	318,500	33,998,261
1961-62	2,665,241	32,980,840	239,850	35,885,931
1962-63	2,738,707	35,95,8610	206,030	38,903,817
1963-64	2,926,945	38,151,041	233,400	41,311,386
1964-65	3,458,263	50,083,333	407,059	54,548,655
1965-66	2,8029,44	39,903,315	251,350	42,957,609
1966-67	2,926,776	45,991,715	201,590	49,120,081
1967-68	2,620,000	34,382,000	198,000	37,200,000
1968-69	3,211,163	34,068,710	175,330	37,455,203
1969-70	2,724,028	35,927,360	108,140	38,759,528

ESTIMATED PROVINCIAL PERCENTAGE IN RELATION TO THE TOTAL SURFACE AREA OF VINES CULTIVATED AND PRODUCED IN THE 1969-70

PROVINCES	Cultivated Surface Area		Vinicular production %
	Table grapes %	Wine grapes %	
Alava	—	0.42	0.77
Albacete.	0.59	6.64	7.19
Alicante.	11.61	3.39	1.22
Almería	9.66	0.10	0.17
Asturias.	—	0.05	0.06
Avila	1.85	0.76	0.36
Badajoz	15.89	3.87	4.62
Baleares	0.16	0.29	0.25
Barcelona	2.27	2.97	5.70
Burgos.	—	1.39	1.30
Cáceres	0.85	0.69	0.18
Cádiz	0.63	0.82	4.87
Castellón.	5.02	1.10	0.81
Ciudad Real	0.82	16.10	14.79
Córdoba.	0.69	1.15	2.46
La Coruña.	0.04	0.08	0.18
Cuenca	—	5.88	3.59
Gerona	0.19	0.59	0.70
Granada	1.21	0.49	0.23
Guadalajara	0.31	0.32	0.15
Guipúzcoa	—	—	0.01
Huelva	0.78	1.34	2.59
Huesca	—	1.13	0.14
Jaén.	2.25	0.10	0.16

PROVINCES	Cultivated Surface Area		Vinicular production %
	Table grapes %	Wine grapes %	
Las Palmas	1.43	0.04	0.01
León	0.08	0.23	3.65
Lérida.	0.63	0.68	0.68
Logroño.	0.50	0.90	8.64
Lugo	—	0.00	0.00
Madrid	1.78	1.66	1.62
Málaga	5.40	1.19	0.25
Murcia.	3.63	3.24	1.65
Navarra.	0.65	2.53	2.74
Orense.	—	1.21	2.47
Palencia	—	0.57	0.84
Pontevedra.	—	0.61	0.21
Salamanca	1.19	0.93	0.83
Santa Cruz de Tenerife . .	0.57	0.26	0.16
Santander	—	—	0.02
Segovia	—	0.43	0.53
Sevilla.	1.58	0.28	0.72
Soria	0.01	0.19	0.12
Tarragona	0.35	5.12	4.85
Teruel.	0.17	1.33	0.87
Toledo.	0.60	8.33	6.33
Valencia	20.92	5.94	6.93
Valladolid	1.06	1.75	1.17
Vizcaya	—	—	0.01
Zamora	3.20	2.16	1.54
Zaragoza.	1.27	5.99	3.20

PRODUCTION OF ORDINARY WINES EXPRESSED IN HECTOLITRES

Years	Blancos	Tintos	Clarets
1959-60	8,822,072	5,607,484	2,175,717
1960-61	8,854,588	8,805,795	2,831,969
1961-62	9,017,077	6,668,660	2,723,972
1962-63	9,545,893	9,117,619	3,660,571
1963-64	9,924,623	9,774,320	3,829,289
1964-65	10,210,124	11.013,018	4,993,035
1965-66	8,608,341	8,909,091	4,02,6192
1966-67	9,858,013	8,111,733	4,795,238
1967-68	8,935,710	6,567,449	4,011,287
1968-69	7,480,429	7,206,768	3,786,950
1969-70	8,884,258	6,930,245	3,771,920

PRODUCTION OF SPARKLING WINES EXPRESSED
IN HECTOLITRES

Year	Pévillant ~~Sharp~~	Procuced in ~~wine-cellars.~~ bottles	Produced in large vats	Carbonated ~~Gasified~~	Total
1964-65.	150,250	104,238	122,190	96,762	473,440
1965-66.	305,700	104,318	122,210	95,303	627,531
1966-67.	276,700	104,610	102,565	114,072	597,947
1967-68.	150,200	104,550	93,990	113,020	461,760
1968-69.	180,200	104,690	95,910	112,332	493,132
1968-69.	180,200	104,690	95,910	112,332	493,132
1969-70.	147,800	103,390	96,020	94,701	441,911

PRODUCTION OF WINES PROTECTED BY THE «DENOMINACION
DE ORIGEN» IN THE YEAR 1969-70

	Hectolitres		Hectolitres
Jerez	1,176,555	Navarra.	115,680
Montilla-Moriles	605,292	Málaga	51,016
Manzanilla-Sanlúcar de		Rioja	838,154
Barrameda.	31,500	Alicante.	288,800
Tarragona	609,700	Valencia.	827,022
Alella	344,00	Utiel-Requena	716,184
Priorato.	46,550	Cheste	161,994
Cariñena.	392,350	Jumilla.	284,000
Ribero	254,800	Mancha.	2,420,085
Valdeorras.	175,500	Manchuela.	941,432
Panadés.	648,150	Méntrida	258,300
Huelva	575,000	Valdepeñas	3,450,470
Almansa.	—		

MAIN IMPORTERS OF SPANISH WINES AND LIQUEURS

COUNTRY	Quantity in hectolitres	Value in pts.
West Germany	243,360	349,659
East Germany	230	105
Andorra.	40,520	81,801
Austria	139,150	96,771
Bulgaria.	70,290	37,125
Denmark	59,970	145,912
Finland	35,200	47,543
France.	451,730	248,805
Hungary.	197,770	121,700
Ireland	14,250	50,023
Italy	50,980	182,502
Norway	494,20	61,806
Low Countries	348,280	859,012
United Kingdom	713,900	1,863,989
Sweden	206,340	182,968
Switzerland	521,780	368,593
Checoslovakia	7,660	6,891
Belgium	51,740	88,568
Cameroon.	103,590	67,081
Congo	4,950	4,229
Guinea Ecuatorial	25,840	94,326
Nigeria	240	1,287
Unión Aduanera Ecuatorial	225,580	136,206
Senegal	220	625
Togo	13,600	13,470
Canada	42,010	131,050
Colombia.	9,200	32,366
Dominican Republic	3,560	13,404
United States	211,140	702,041
Guatemala.	340	1,265
Mexico.	3,340	32,081
Panamá	2,980	15,316
Venezuela	51,580	194,872
Australia.	1,340	6,740
New Zealand.	1,460	5,896
Japan	8,030	21,918

Statistics given by the State Customs.

GROWTH OF WINE AND LIQUEUR IMPORTS 1965-1971

Year	Hectolitres wines	Hectolitres liqueurs	Total imports	Value in pts.
1965	2,510	39,825	42,335	370,354,483
1966	2,996	50,881	53,847	490,457,089
1967	4,026	56,084	60,110	535,189,107
1968	4,367	73,064	76,351	727,202,156
1969	5,540	109,690	115,230	1,074,362,000
1970	5,378	47,844	53,222	503,616,091
1971	5,000	119,350	124,350	1,162,336,000

SPANISH EXPORTS OF WINES AND LIQUEURS

Kind Year 1967	Quantity in litres	Value in pts.
Sparkling. . . .	457,944	21,573,288
Generosos. . . .	70,603,199	2,117,947,886
Table wine . . .	97,854,764	597,096,858
Comunes	95,427,301	453,481,315
Vermouths . . .	566,881	15,831,878
Mostos y mistelas.	10,111,145	106,111,113
Brandies	3,039,803	164,318,431
Liqueurs	548,290	27,912,716
TOTAL . .	278,609,327	3,504,273,485

Kind Year 1969	Quantity in litres	Value in pts.
Sparkling. . . .	713,000	35,753,000
Generosos. . . .	83,990,000	2,508,790,000
Table wine . . .	83,709,000	770,572,000
Comunes	85,704,000	553,430,000
Vermouths . . .	302,000	10,857,000
Mostos y mistelas.	12,221,000	123,524,000
Brandies	5,260,000	298,107,000
Liqueurs	1,484,000	55,415,000
TOTAL . .	273,383,000	4,356,448,000

Kind Year 1968	Quantity in litres	Value in pts.
Sparkling. . . .	579,423	29,037,067
Generosos. . . .	80,295,864	2,517,921,585
Table wine . . .	80,536,147	670,711,237
Comunes	76,411,468	478,384,696
Vermouths . . .	544,206	17,110,459
Mostos y mistelas.	10,035,896	98,440,103
Brandies	3,906,991	254,724,276
Liqueurs	481,076	25,825,692
TOTAL . .	252,791,071	4,097,855,115

Kind Year 1970	Quantity in litres	Value in pts.
Sparkling. . . .	681,000	38,866,000
Generosos. . . .	92,133,000	2,904,752,000
Table wine . . .	109,466,000	969,075,000
Comunes	123,028,000	721,339,000
Vermouths . . .	878,000	37,039,000
Mostos y mistelas.	17,608,000	143,218,000
Brandies	6,138,000	386,536,000
Liqueurs	1,775,000	75,322,000
TOTAL . .	351,687,000	5,276,147,000

Kind Year 1971	Quantity in litres	Value in pts.
Sparkling. . . .	783	43,102,000
Generosos. . . .	104,665	3,309,587,000
Table wine . . .	98,564	1,027,269,000
Comunes	150,194	966,663,000
Vermouths . . .	5,965	221,401,000
Mostos y mistelas.	43,270	395,468,000
Brandies	8,151	513,210,000
Liqueurs	1,742	89,638,000
TOTAL . .	420,806	6,587,609,000

SHERRY, THE ARISTOCRAT OF WINES
(Photo Guillén Franco.)

CONTENTS

PART ONE

THE WINES OF SPAIN

PART TWO

WINE AND THE VINEYARD

PART THREE

GASTRONOMY AND WINES

Page